THE DEAD STRAIGHT GUIDE TO

LED ZEPPELIN

NIGEL WILLIAMSON

The Dead Straight Guide to Led Zeppelin

This edition © Red Planet Publishing Ltd 2014
Text © Nigel Williamson 2007–2014

This first edition published November 2014 by
Red Planet Publishing Ltd
www.redplanetzone.com

Email: info@redplanetzone.com
Previously published as The Rough Guide to Led Zeppelin

Distributed by Combined Book Services in the UK:
and Consortium in the USA

Printed in the UK by CPI

Design: Mark Young
Production: bounford.com
Proof Reading: Matt White
Publisher: Mark Neeter

Picture Credits
Redferns, Corbis and Private collections (see web for details)
Cover image: Globe Photos Inc/REX

A catalogue record for this book is available from the British Library

ISBN: 978-1-905959525

www.redplanetzone.com

THE ESSENTIAL LED ZEPPELIN COMPANION

DEAD STRAIGHT MUSIC GUIDES

THE DEAD STRAIGHT GUIDE TO

LED ZEPPELIN

NIGEL WILLIAMSON

CONTENTS

LED ZEPPELIN

ACKNOWLEDGEMENTS

The bulk of this book's text originally appeared in 2007 under the title *The Rough Guide to Led Zeppelin*. Grateful acknowledgements to all the books, films, interviews and websites quoted herein. This book also draws on interviews by the author with Jimmy Page and with Robert Plant, who was kind enough to give the project his personal blessing.

ABOUT THE AUTHOR

Nigel Williamson is a former news editor of *The Times* and a respected rock writer and journalist, whose work has appeared in many papers and journals, including *Uncut*. His books include *Journey Through the Past: The Stories Behind the Classic Songs of Neil Young* (2002), *The Rough Guide to Bob Dylan* (2004), now republished as *The Dead Straight Guide to Bob Dylan*, *The Rough Guide to The Blues* (2006), *The Rough Guide to Led Zeppelin* (2007) and *The Rough Guide to The Best Music You've Never Heard* (2008).

INTRODUCTION

The rock world in 1968 was an amazing place. The Beatles had just released the White Album and The Rolling Stones had come storming back with *Beggars Banquet*. Jimi Hendrix was at his explosive peak, The Who were soon to release Tommy, and Cream were the heaviest group around.

It was unsurprising, then, that few took much notice of a new group called Led Zeppelin, fronted by a session guitarist who had played on records by Lulu and Tom Jones and a singer nobody had heard of from an obscure band called Hobstweedle.

In fact, although they couldn't have known it at the time, Led Zeppelin's timing was perfect. Within two years, The Beatles had split, the Stones had retreated into tax exile, Hendrix was dead, Cream were no more and Pete Townshend was agonising over how to follow The Who's groundbreaking rock opera. Zeppelin stepped into the breach and remained the mightiest band in the world until 1980, when they called it a day following the death of John Bonham.

I confess that as a teenage rock fan I was one of those who initially ignored them. In 1969, I was 15 and fighting daily battles with the authorities at my local grammar school over my shoulder-length hair. Every Saturday afternoon a bunch of us would meet in Bromley High Street, Kent, to sit in the sound-proofed booths of WH Smith, listening to new LPs that we didn't have the money to buy. The staff were indulgent and would usually allow you to hear both sides of an album and, if it wasn't too busy, maybe one side of a second album, too. When we'd pushed our luck too far and been thrown out, we'd drink coffee and share a packet of ten Senior Service at Lyon's Tea Shop in the market square or, if one of us had enough cash to score a quid deal that week, we'd retire to the municipal Library Gardens for a badly-rolled joint.

One Saturday in late March 1969, I was scuffling around Bromley High Street as usual with a bunch of school friends when a student from the local Technical College handed us a flyer advertising a show that evening featuring Led Zeppelin. I was already an enthusiastic attender of gigs at the college and had seen various bands there, including Jethro Tull. But I had no interest in seeing Zeppelin: I'd read about them in *Melody Maker* and concluded – stupidly, as it turned out – that they were simply a hyped-up new version of the old Yardbirds, whom I regarded with studied adolescent disdain as little more than a pop group who didn't qualify as a serious part of the "underground rock" scene. My best friend Pete Badham, however, took a more enlightened view and reckoned they were well worth his pocket money. Several decades later he was able to write in *Led Zeppelin: The Concert File* that he had "felt privileged to be in at the start of something special". I didn't get to see them until almost two years later at the Royal Albert Hall after I'd recognised the folly of my youthful snobbery and I've been kicking myself ever since over that missed opportunity to see one of the earliest gigs by one of the greatest bands of all time in a venue that probably held no more than 300 people.

In the years since, I've interviewed Jimmy Page several times and Robert Plant on numerous occasions. It's always dangerous for rock journalists to claim they've become 'friends' with the stars they write about but I like to think that Plant has become just that. The first time I met him more than a decade ago, he arrived two hours late and apologised profusely. He then added, with a twinkle in his eye, that when Zep were in their pomp, I'd have been kept waiting not for two hours

but two weeks. I took to him immediately and we further bonded over a mutual love of African and Arabic music and a passion for gardening that, on one famously non-rock 'n' roll occasion, found us swapping tips on the propagation of strawberry plants, much to the bemusement of those around us. Several years later, I was highly flattered when a taped interview I'd done with him was released as a bonus disc with some copies of his most recent album, *Mighty Rearranger*.

In making some of the most visceral rock music ever heard, both live and on record, Led Zeppelin acquired mythological status – in the truest sense of the word. At a distance of 30 years and more, it has become almost impossible to tell which of the outrageous stories about them are true, which have grown in the telling and which are total fiction. This book attempts to unravel the myths from the truth, as well as analysing the band's music and providing a guide to the solo careers of its individual surviving members. It's a story that – like Zeppelin's unforgettable music – has it all. We shall never see their like again.

Nigel Williamson
Hever, Kent

PRE-FLIGHT
1944–1968

1

"The four musicians that eventually came together as Led Zeppelin were a gift from on high..."

JIMMY PAGE, 2005

PRE-FLIGHT

1944–1968

In rock 'n' roll mythology, many of the great groups have a fateful moment when the principal players meet by chance or accident, recognise in a moment glowing with poetic resonance that they share a common destiny, and resolve to unite forces to take on the world. The famous encounter between John Lennon and Paul McCartney at a church fête in Woolton, Liverpool in 1957, or Mick Jagger and Keith Richards bumping into each other on a platform at Dartford railway station four years later come to mind. But the genesis of Led Zeppelin wasn't quite like that.

Indeed, the first meeting between Jimmy Page and Robert Plant was almost comical – according to Plant, his future colleague and the band's larger-than-life manager, Peter Grant, mistook the singer for a roadie. What's more, unlike The Beatles or The Rolling Stones whose members broadly shared a common social, cultural and geographical background, the two men came from very different sides of the street. Page hailed from the metropolitan suburbs of Surrey within easy reach of swinging London. At 24 he was already a pop star, an urbane, seasoned session man who had played on dozens of top ten hits and secured legendary status as the guitarist with The Yardbirds. Plant was from the stolid, unfashionable part of the West Midlands known as the Black Country. At 19 he was still a gauche ingénue, with only a couple of failed solo singles to his name and a few unsuccessful bands and was contemplating the unwelcome prospect of having to quit music for a job in an accountant's office to support his pregnant wife and their imminently due child.

The same disparities of background and experience existed between bassist John Paul Jones and drummer John Bonham, soon to unite as the band's crunching rhythm section. Jones was a sophisticated, in-demand session player and arranger whose credits included working with The Rolling Stones and who moved in the same hip London music industry circles as Page. Bonham was a mate of Plant's from the Black Country with a rough and ready style who balanced playing in a string of failed groups with working on a building site as a hod carrier and whose philosophy of drumming was simply to hammer away until the skins broke and his hands bled. As Plant recalled in 2005: "It was very obvious that Jimmy and Jonesy had a far more lateral collection of thoughts and ambitions and knowledge of what was going on than me and Bonzo. We were just wide boys from the sticks." It was out of these polar opposites that the loudest, heaviest and many would say greatest rock 'n' roll band the world has ever known was forged.

In fact, Plant was far from first choice as the lead singer for the new group that The

LED ZEPPELIN

1

Yardbirds' guitarist and manager Peter Grant were putting together. "I don't think he'd played much down in the south of England so consequently I hadn't heard of him," Page candidly admitted some years later. Top of his wish list had been the likes of Stevie Winwood, Steve Marriott and then Terry Reid. The latter turned the gig down but suggested instead his West Midlands mate, Plant. Hence on July 20, 1968, Page, Grant and Yardbirds bassist Chris Dreja found themselves travelling to Birmingham to see Plant singing at the local teacher training college with the unpromisingly named Hobbstweedle.

The gig, by everyone's account, was not very good and Page reckons there were only about a dozen people in the audience. Nor did the band's covers of songs by Love, Buffalo Springfield and Moby Grape, and Hobbsweedle's own fey, *Lord of the Rings*-influenced fairy-ringed fancies, fit the vision Page had in mind for the new group at all.

Yet he heard something in Plant's voice that thrilled him and invited him to spend a few days at the plushly renovated Victorian boathouse that was his home on the River Thames at Pangbourne in Berkshire, 30 miles upstream from central London, with the intention of exploring if there was sufficient common ground for them to work together. The would-be singer arrived at the guitarist's pop star home clutching a bunch of his favourite LPs and just enough money for his train fare back home if it all went horribly wrong. Fortunately, as they played each other their favourite albums and bounced around ideas, they discovered a musical bond. It was in that record-playing session that Led Zeppelin were, in effect, born.

Yet we are getting ahead of our story. Because each of the four members of Led Zeppelin came from very different backgrounds and brought such contrasting experiences

to the group, some serious pre-history is necessary.

JIMMY PAGE

James Patrick Page was born on January 8, 1944 in Heston, Middlesex, into a respectable, middle-class family, his father a clerk in a wartime aircraft works and his mother a doctor's secretary. An only child, many of his earliest memories are of long holidays spent at a great-uncle's farm near Northampton, where Page went fishing and chased butterflies. When the weather kept him inside, his stamp collection occupied much of his time and there was no early indication of any musical talent. There wasn't even a family piano.

In 1952, his father took a step up in the world to became an industrial personnel officer and the family moved to a comfortable house in Miles Road, Epsom, a prosperous and leafy country town in Surrey. Music didn't enter his life in a serious way until four years later when he heard Elvis Presley's 'Baby Let's Play House'. Yet while most of his contemporaries (including a young Robert Plant) were attracted by the voice and Presley's image, Page was far more interested in the musical accompaniment. In particular, he was drawn to the sound of the guitarist Scotty Moore.

A few months later, on his 13th birthday, his parents bought him a Spanish acoustic guitar with steel strings. His mother recalls sending him to a guitar teacher in Kingston for half-a-dozen lessons, but the tuition was rudimentary and essentially Page set about teaching himself. A school friend showed him how to tune his guitar and he bought himself a copy of Bert Weedon's manual, *Play in a Day*.

Weedon had made his name as the featured soloist in Mantovani's band and went on to become the improbable progenitor of British rock'n'roll guitar, for around the same time as Page was poring over *Play In A Day* and forcing his fingers to form the unfamiliar chord positions, George Harrison, Eric Clapton, Jeff Beck, Brian May, Pete Townshend and a number of others who were to become household names were teaching themselves by following the same instruction book. "I always thought the good thing about guitar was that they didn't teach it at school," Page later observed. "Teaching myself to play was the first and most important part of my education."

Unlike Robert Plant's parents, who were appalled by their son's attraction to rock 'n' roll and told him it was 'the devil's music', Page's mother and father were supportive of his ambitions and his father acted as guarantor when he bought his first electric guitar on a hire purchase agreement – a cheap copy of a Fender Stratocaster called a Grazioso.

At school, Page was a good hurdler, a decent artist and bright enough to pass all his exams, but once the guitar took over, he swiftly lost interest in everything else and left school in 1961 against his parents' wishes. However, although he was by now seriously proficient on the guitar and playing in local bands around Epsom, a professional music career still seemed a distant and unrealisable dream and he applied for a job as a laboratory assistant.

Before he had a chance to take up the job, he was spotted at Epsom's Ebisham Hall playing with a local rock 'n' roll outfit called Red-E-Lewis and the Redcats by a singer and would-be manager called Chris Tidmarsh. Better known as Neil Christian, he was impressed enough with Page's ability to offer him a job in his backing group, The Crusaders, and called upon Page's parents to reassure them that pop music wasn't as risky a venture as they might fear and offered plenty of exciting opportunities for a young musician as highly

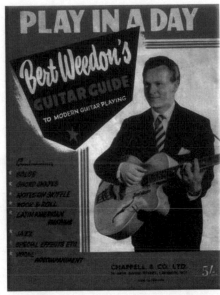

British guitar hero Bert Weedon's enormously influential basic playing manual remains in print today

talented as their son. Christian was polite and persuasive, the flattery helped no end and parental approval was duly given. At the age of 17, Page became a professional guitar player.

The Crusaders played rudimentary versions of Chuck Berry and Bo Diddley songs, but in their lead guitarist, who took the stage name Nelson Storm, it was clear they had a potential star in the making. Soon Page was making £20 a week – at the time probably double the average working wage – and he bought himself an orange Gretsch Country Gentleman guitar and a foot pedal, making him one of the first guitarists in London with such a gadget. Both his expertise and his equipment contributed to a fast-growing reputation and among those who came to check him out were Jeff Beck and future Led Zeppelin bass player, John Paul

LED ZEPPELIN

1

Korner (right) and Cyril Davies at The Crawdaddy, Richmond, with a young Charlie Watts on drums

Jones. "I can remember people saying, 'You've got to go hear Neil Christian and The Crusaders, they've got this unbelievable young guitarist'," Jones recalls. "I'd heard of Pagey before I'd heard of Clapton or Beck."

His time in The Crusaders was cut short when one night in late 1961 at a gig in Sheffield the tyro guitarist collapsed. Always slightly built (Beck describes him as resembling "a shrimp" at this time), it seemed he lacked the constitution for life on the road and its accompanying regime of bad food and lack of sleep. Glandular fever was diagnosed and the guitarist reluctantly returned to his parents' home in Epsom. When he had recovered, they persuaded him to enrol at art college in Sutton, Surrey.

Page was a talented artist and insists that he was serious about his studies and for a time wanted to become a painter. But a brush and easel were never going to take the place of a guitar and amp and art school, as for so many British musicians of his generation, provided the convenient means to a quite different end.

First, it kept his parents happy. Secondly, he received a government grant. And third and most importantly of all, the student life gave him plenty of free time to practise the guitar.

His parents could hardly have been more supportive, turning over the downstairs front room of the family home to their only son as a music den. Among the visitors who played with him there was Jeff Beck, introduced by his sister Annetta, who knew Page as a fellow art student. "It was a lot of fun," Page's mother later recalled. "The jam sessions forced Jim's father and myself to develop an opinion about so-called heavy rock music. I found that I have a thing for it."

Page stayed 18 months or so at college before he began to feel the urge again to play somewhere bigger than his parents' front room. During his time at art school, he had been turning up at London's Marquee Club to watch Blues Incorporated. Led by Alexis Korner and Cyril Davies, they were the first serious British blues band and a major influence on a generation of young musicians, including Mick Jagger, Brian Jones, Charlie Watts, Jack Bruce and Ginger Baker, all of whom played with them at one time or another. Page had also been asked to join when he was in The Crusaders, an invitation he declined, although he occasionally joined them in jam sessions. It was on one such evening that he met Eric Clapton for the first time. "He came up to me and said, 'You play like Matt Murphy, Memphis Slim's guitarist," Page recalled. He was impressed by Clapton's sharp ear for he admitted that he had, indeed, "been following Murphy quite heavily".

When Blues Incorporated fell apart, Korner soon transferred his allegiance to the rival Flamingo Club. But as Page re-emerged onto the London gigging scene, he continued to turn up at the Marquee's blues nights to jam during the interval spot and also played at those other

1

Éminence grise: Page (cravatted, centre) with (left to right) pop babe Lulu, Yardbird Keith Relf, producer Mickie Most, Herman's Hermit Derek Leckenby and the famously dentally challenged Peter Noone

shrines of the early London R&B scene, The Crawdaddy Club in Richmond and Eel Pie Island. Suddenly, it seemed there were legions of like-minded musicians – young white British guys raised in the lace-curtained gentility of the home counties and obsessed with the music of black sharecroppers from the Mississippi Delta. "Most of us had the same upbringing," Page recollects. "We'd been locked away with our blues records and then we came out with something really new to offer Britain. It just exploded from there."

That explosion was taking place simultaneously all over the country. In London it produced Tthe Rolling Stones and The Yardbirds. In Newcastle, it gave birth to The Animals. The Spencer Davis Group would soon emerge in Birmingham, and the ripples crossed the Irish Sea to Belfast, where Van Morrison was putting together a band called Them.

Yet although Page would eventually join The Yardbirds, he was not to be part of the first wave of British R&B groups, who would go on to conquer America in the wake of The Beatles. Instead, a potentially far more lucrative offer came along when he was invited to join the elite crew of top London session musicians. The initial invitation came from tape operator Glyn Johns and one of Page's first sessions found him playing on

LED ZEPPELIN

1

'Diamonds' by Jet Harris and Tony Meehan, who had just left The Shadows. The single went to number one and his art school days were over. "I was missing lectures, taking days off and I finally had to make a choice," he later remembered. "I was really enjoying the work. Many of the sessions were really good and I was allowed to do the solos, which I found to be really constructive work. So it was down to painting or playing. It wasn't too difficult a decision."

'Diamonds' was followed by a session with Carter-Lewis and The Southerners and Page was briefly persuaded to join them, before he realised that studio work was far more lucrative. As he seemed able to play in any style and imitate almost any other guitarist, demand for his skills was high, particularly as at the time the supply was severely limited. Indeed, just about the only other serious guitarist on the London session scene was Big Jim Sullivan, and as the British beat boom got into full swing, it became de rigeur that if you needed a guitarist you booked Big Jim or 'Little Jimmy', as Page inevitably became known.

Soon he was playing on early recordings by the likes of Them, The Kinks and The Who (see page 10) as top producers such as Shel Talmy and Mickie Most preferred Page's known virtuosity to gambling on the unknown talent of the groups' resident guitar players. Sometimes, they were up to the task, which is why Page was only required to play rhythm guitar behind Pete Townshend's lead on The Who's 'I Can't Explain'. On other occasions, such as Them's first session, not only the guitarist but the entire band were replaced by session players. "The group went in thinking they were going to record and all of a sudden they find these other people playing on their records," Page recalled of the first Them sessions. "It's a miracle they didn't replace Van Morrison as well."

One American authority has asserted that Page played on "anywhere between 50 to 90 per cent of the records released in Britain in the 1963–65 era". It's a ridiculous exaggeration – but perhaps not that ridiculous. Page was in huge demand, playing up to a dozen sessions per week. For a while, he didn't seem to care what he played on as long as he was paid well enough and alongside his hipper clients, he provided the guitar parts for the likes of Burt Bacharach, PJ Proby, Herman's Hermits and Cliff Richard. His guitar can be heard on a number of TV jingles from the time and he admits to having been paid to record cheap muzak for supermarkets.

Eventually he grew tired of prostituting his talents and later referred to his sessioning period with some embarrassment as "grovelling around". Stepping from the anonymous shadows of uncredited accompanist to take the spotlight, in 1965 he recorded his first – and only – solo single, 'She Just Satisfies'. Released on Fontana, it found the guitarist singing and playing every instrument except the drums, while the B-side included backing vocals from his girlfriend of the time, the American singer-songwriter Jackie De Shannon. The record failed to bother the chart compilers and Page swiftly decided that singing and a solo career were not for him.

Producing, however, was a different story. Sometime early in 1965, Andrew Loog Oldham, who in addition to managing The Rolling Stones had by now set up his own label, Immediate, contacted him and asked him to produce Eric Clapton for a British blues series he was planning. Together they cut four tracks, 'Telephone Blues', 'I'm Your Witchdoctor', 'Sittin' on Top of the World' (later to become a Cream favourite) and 'Double Crossing Time'. Around the same time he was also sounded out about replacing Clapton in The Yardbirds. But the money he

THE STORY: **PRE-FLIGHT**

was making playing sessions (at the time he could be heard on no less than three records in the British top ten) was too good to give up for an uncertain life in a beat group and he was still wary following his collapse on the road with Neil Christian and The Crusaders. He recommended instead his friend Jeff Beck, who was probably second on the group's shopping list in any case.

Page also recorded several more tracks with Clapton. Little more than blues jams taped in the front room of Page's parents' home, they were never intended for release but appeared on two compilations called *Blues Anytime*, released by Immediate in 1968, much to Clapton's chagrin. Although Page denied all blame for their release, it led to a rupture in their friendship that was never really healed.

The relationship between Page and Beck, however, continued to flourish. Page was present in the studio when The Yardbirds recorded 'Heart Full of Soul', the follow-up single to their breakthrough hit 'For Your Love', and lent him his fuzz box to play on the track. A group of Indian musicians had also been booked for the session and Page ended up buying a sitar from them, making him probably the first British rock guitarist to experiment with the instrument, ahead of George Harrison. In May 1966, the two guitarists recorded an instrumental called 'Beck's Bolero' in London's IBC Studios, on which they were backed by The Who's drummer Keith Moon, bass player John Paul Jones and keyboardist Nicky Hopkins. Despite the title and the fact that it subsequently appeared as the B-side of Beck's first solo single, 'Hi Ho Silver Lining', the track was largely written and produced by Page, who enjoyed the experience so much that there was talk of the two guitarists forming a group. Names that were thrown around as possible members included John Entwistle on bass (rather than Jones at this stage) and either

The Small Faces' Steve Marriott or The Spencer Davis Group's Stevie Winwood on vocals.

In the event the plans came to nothing but it was clear that Page was growing increasingly frustrated and felt his own creativity was being stifled as a guitar-for-hire session man. At the second time of asking, in June 1966, he agreed to join The Yardbirds.

Initially, he deputised on bass for Paul Samwell-Smith, who had quit suddenly and went on to become an acclaimed producer. But the understanding was always that once the band's other guitarist Chris Dreja had learnt the bass parts, Page would switch to guitar, giving The Yardbirds a dream-like double lead attack.

Sadly, the Beck-Page incarnation of The Yardbirds never delivered on its huge promise and was to last a mere four months. In October 1966, just two dates into an American tour, the increasingly erratic Beck walked out. The band decided not to replace him and continued as a quartet. Page did his best to steer The Yardbirds in a musically credible direction, developing at least some of the elements that he would subsequently explore further in Led Zeppelin. But his efforts were derailed by producer Mickie Most, whose relentless pursuit of hit singles and contempt for the album format led to such miserable covers as 'Ha! Ha! Said the Clown' (on which Keith Relf was actually the only Yardbird to appear) and meant that the interesting ideas Page had for The Yardbirds' 1967 LP *Little Games* were left sadly under-developed.

By early 1968, it was clear the group was staggering towards a messy end and their final gig came in July that year at an end-of-term dance at Luton Technical College. Together with Dreja, Page began putting together a new line-up and attempted to recruit singer Terry Reid and drummer BJ Wilson. Both declined and Dreja also left the scene to take up a career

LED ZEPPELIN

1

JIMMY PAGE'S 1960s SESSION TOP TWENTY

From the tens (if not hundreds) of recordings in the 1960s to which Page contributed as a hired sessionman, these are among the more famous hits that 'Little Jimmy' played on...

DIAMONDS
Jet Harris and Tony Meehan 1963

TWIST AND SHOUT
Brian Poole & The Tremeloes 1963

THE CRYING GAME
Dave Berry 1964 (Page played acoustic while Big Jim Sullivan played the fuss guitar parts)

YOU REALLY GOT ME
The Kinks 1964

TERRY
Twinkle 1964

WALK TALL
Val Doonican 1964

AS TEARS GO BY
Marianne Faithfull 1964

SHOUT
Lulu & The Luvvers 1964

TOBACCO ROAD
The Nashville Teens 1964

Here Comes The Night
Them 1965

IT'S NOT UNUSUAL
Tom Jones 1965

I CAN'T EXPLAIN
The Who 1965

DIGGIN' MY POTATOES
Heinz 1965 (some discographies also claim Page played on Heinz's 1965 hit 'Just Like Eddie')

I'M NOT SAYIN'
Nico 1965

THE PIED PIPER
Crispin St Peters 1966

TIME DRAGS BY
Cliff Richard 1966

SUNSHINE SUPERMAN
Donovan 1966

OUT OF TIME
Chris Farlowe 1966

WITH A LITTLE HELP FROM MY FRIENDS
Joe Cocker 1968

LITTLE ARROWS
Leapy Lee 1968

Page also played on an early version of the Rolling St ones' 'Heart of Stone', but only on a demo tape, not the final release. Other less-known bands he sessioned with include Carter-Lewis and the Southerners, the Lancastrians, the Primitives, the Factotums, Les Fleurs De Lys and The Fifth Avenue.

A pensive-looking Band of Joy hugging the trees, with Plant second from left and Bonham over his shoulder

in photography. Enter fellow session man John Paul Jones, a wild and untamed Midlands drummer named John Bonham and a young, little-known singer from West Bromwich called Robert Plant....

ROBERT PLANT

Robert Anthony Plant – later 'Percy' to his friends – was born on August 20, 1948 in West Bromwich, Staffordshire. His father was a civil engineer and the family soon moved to an affluent new home in the upscale Hayley Green area of the quiet Worcestershire town of Kidderminster, famous mostly for its manufacture of high quality carpets. Plant was by all accounts a bright child who devoured books and at 11 he earned a place at the King Edward VI grammar school in nearby Stourbridge, although by then he had already fallen in love with rock 'n' roll and decided he wanted to be Elvis. By the age of 13 he was spending hours in front of his bedroom mirror perfecting Presley's hip wiggle and pelvic gyrations as he sung 'Hound Dog' in an uncertain, quavering voice that was just beginning to break.

LED ZEPPELIN

1

His passion for rock 'n' roll horrified his strait-laced middle-class parents who, he claims, denounced the new sounds coming out of Memphis, New Orleans and other American cities as 'the devil's music'. One of his favourite stories has them cutting the plug off his record player after he had spun Chris Kenner's 'I Like It Like That' 17 times in one hour (see interview). As his school studies fell by the wayside, Plant put his enquiring mind to work researching the roots of early rock

'n' roll and soon discovered the Delta blues and the electrified sounds emanating from Chicago on labels such as Chess and Vee-Jay.

By 14 or 15, he was hanging out not with his fellow grammar school pupils but with a more bohemian crowd from Stourbridge Art School and using his pay packet from a Saturday job in Woolworths to buy the first LP release of Robert Johnson's legendary sessions, recorded a quarter of a century earlier. He also began singing with a school group called Andy Long

NIGEL WILLIAMSON INTERVIEWS ROBERT PLANT ABOUT

Parts of this interview were published in *Uncut* in May 2005 but the full transcript appears here for the first time...

What was the first music you heard and appreciated when you were growing up?
For me it was always about the voice. There were novelty songs that were a backdrop to a child's life, like 'The Laughing Policeman'. But then I heard the blue note – that mournful dip in the scale that you didn't hear in English music and which had nothing to do with childhood at all.

So who was that?
It was Elvis and that emotional delivery he borrowed from Arthur Crudup and Johnnie Ray. I didn't know anything about the technical ability. It was purely a subliminal thing. I just heard this sound and suddenly it was there – quite prematurely I think, because I must have only been eight or nine. We'd go over and visit my father's brother and he was playing stuff like Jackie Wilson and Marv Johnson and I somehow recognised the conviction of it. I didn't even know it was called conviction. I didn't know anything about sexuality or the innuendo of the lyrics or that it was part

of a movement. I just knew the call and the pleading in the voice. When I first heard Elvis singing 'Love Me' I couldn't believe the sound. His confidence and his assertion were stupendous.

And what was the first record you remember buying?
I had a red-and-cream Dansette Conquest Auto record player for Christmas 1960 and I went out and bought 'Shop Around' by Smokey Robinson and The Miracles. It was a pop record and nice and chummy but again it was because of the voice and there was a song on the B-side called 'Who's Loving You', which was unbelievably beautiful. It just destroyed me because it was all there – the Sunday morning prayer meeting in church, Detroit on fire, Parchman Farm and every experience that generation of black musicians encapsulated. The stature of those songs and voices had to lead you back to the blues, as did Elvis. The wilder rock 'n' roll was borrowing all the time from black music.

So when did you first hear the pure blues?
I got a compilation called *Preachin' the Blues* with Memphis Slim, Jimmy Reed and

and his Original Jaymen and despite stern parental disapproval, by 1963, Plant's father was driving his 15-year-old son every week to the Seven Stars Blues Club in Stourbridge, on the grounds that this at least allowed him to keep an eye on the bad company their son was keeping. At the club, Plant happily jammed – on washboard and kazoo – with the Delta Blues Band, murdering songs by the likes of Johnson, Muddy Waters and Howlin' Wolf. Grammar school could no longer hold him and that

summer he left, although he couldn't quite shed the shackles of parental expectation at such a young age and began training as a chartered accountant. Almost immediately he knew he had made a terrible mistake and that autumn enrolled at a local technical college to get some 'A' levels.

Yet whatever way he looked at it, school, accountancy and college were all distractions from his desired path, as he rebounded from one failed West Midlands band to another – many of

HIS PRE-ZEPPELIN ROOTS

John Lee Hooker. There wasn't much of it about. It was hard to find a Howlin' Wolf record. But there was an art college in Stourbridge that spawned a bohemian sub-culture and we were all finding out about this stuff around the same time and trying to mimic it.

Why do you think all of these white, middle-class boys from the English suburbs were so captivated by the music of a bunch of Mississippi sharecroppers?
Because everything else we were being peddled at the time was such insipid dross. Up until 1963 it's very hard to find any relevant British music at all. There were little islands like Alexis Korner and Lonnie Donegan. But what English boy aged 13 or 14 could get excited about Craig Douglas or Mark Wynter? So you had to go and find something with a bit more power and the blues had that in abundance.

And it must have seemed very bold at the time...
I remember playing 'I Like It Like That' by Chris Kenner over and over again, and to hear him wailing out of New Orleans like that horrified my parents. They cut the

plug off the record player and said it was the devil's music. They honestly said that — but that's when you know you've found the real stuff. Years later when I was sitting in my mum's garden having a cup of tea and a piece of cake on the hammock, I asked her what it was all about. I said, 'Mum, why was it such a terrible deal that you had to get the headmaster round to the house to discuss what had happened to me?' She said I was beyond parental control. What a great phrase! That was the sort of language probation officers used back then. So I said to her, 'But I really wasn't doing anybody any harm. I was just learning about this music, I wanted to hear more of it and I wanted to be with the beatniks.'

When did you know that you wanted to be a singer?
Immediately. Although I played washboard in my first group. I just wanted to make the notes I'd heard. And in the bathtub I found I could sing down the overflow pipe and get a great reverb. Toilets were always good as well. There was a particularly good public convenience in Stourbridge, where I found I could sound like Elvis.

LED ZEPPELIN

them named after his favourite blues songs, such as the Crawling King Snakes (with a certain John Bonham on drums) and Black Snake Moan. He also tried various sartorial fashions, becoming a full-on Mod after seeing The Small Faces and The Who play a concert in Birmingham.

When in late 1966 one of his unsuccessful bands The Tennessee Teens transmuted into Listen and were signed by CBS, he made his recorded debut as a singer on their first and only single, a cover of the Young Rascals'

'You Better Run'. When it flopped the band were swiftly dropped and despatched back to West Midlands oblivion, but CBS persevered with Plant for two solo singles, 'Our Song' (backed with 'Laughing Crying Laughing') and 'Long Time Coming' (coupled with 'I've Got a Secret'), both released in 1967. Listen to these teenage efforts today and while the material is obviously unsuitable, it is just possible to make out the first rumblings of the potent singer he was to become. To

ROBERT PLANT INTERVIEW (Continued)

The first band was called the Delta Blues Band. There was a purism popular at the time that ignored the electric blues so what we played was somewhere between skiffle and Sonny Terry and Brownie McGhee stuff, so it was quite light. We didn't know about heavy then. We hadn't heard Son House and Charley Patton.

There's a story about you seeing Sonny Boy Williamson and going backstage and nicking one of his harmonicas...
That was at Birmingham Town Hall and I'm proud to say it's true. To hear so many of those great artists when I was 15 was amazing – Sleepy John Estes, Big Joe Williams, Bukka White. I was covered in goose bumps. I saw Rosetta Tharpe and what a beautiful woman she was. I wangled my way backstage and she said, 'Boy you're too pretty to stay here in Birmingham. You can come and be my slave'. And I said, 'But I've got to go home and do my homework...'

When did it first occur to you that you could make a living out of singing?
To be honest I don't really know. I was just so busy absorbing so many influences.

I was learning and creating shapes by copying people. I was never really at home with my voice until I was about 23. I'd heard all these great blues singers and I knew I couldn't measure up. I wasn't a blues singer, I was just another white guy trying to make it work and there were guys around doing it much better than I was, like Steve Winwood. He'd make you want to throw the towel in and walk away he was so good. But I knew I could do something with it and I wasn't going to stay at the chartered accountants as an articled clerk. I knew there was another life. I was shaping up for it and my nostrils were starting to flare.

What was the first serious band you were in?
The Crawling King Snakes with Bonzo was where we first started to trip out. It was sloppy, but suitably so and was edging towards The Seeds and the 13th Floor Elevators, albeit accidentally. There were long extended sections where I ad libbed the vocals. It was the same stuff you hear me willowing on about on the first Zep album, really.

Plant's embarrassment, CBS marketed him as a middle-of-the-road balladeer, like a blonde surrogate of Tom Jones or another Long John Baldry, a one-time respected blues singer who had just had a number one hit with the schmaltzy 'Let the Heartaches Begin'.

Away from stilted poses of record company promo shots, other photos of Plant at the time – including one taken at a 'legalise pot' protest – reveal a dope-smoking hippie in velvet kaftan and love beads. Desperate as he

was to succeed, ultimately it was to his relief that both singles flopped hopelessly.

By this time, he had left home amid considerable family rancour: his parents simply couldn't understand how he could throw away a comfortable future as a chartered accountant for the dubious life of an unsuccessful pop singer, and told him so in no uncertain terms. After a period sleeping on friends' sofas (including John Bonham's), he moved into a multi-occupancy

1

Tell us about Bonzo...
I thought he was a bit too pleased with himself. And expensive – he wanted the same money out of an eight-pound gig that I was getting. I wasn't having that! But we formed a partnership and enjoyed a love-hate relationship and formed Band of Joy.

But before that you did a couple of solo singles..,
That was on CBS and I had to sing what they told me. I wanted to do 'Incense' by The Anglos. But they gave me ballads.

They were trying to market me as a blue-eyed soul singer like Long John Baldry or Rod Stewart. I was embarrassed about it.

Was Band of Joy where you started developing the vocal mannerisms we eventually heard on the first Zeppelin album?
I was very arrogant in that band, because I thought we were going to bring the walls down. It was very spirited and powerful and there are definitely elements of what we did on *Led Zeppelin I*. But I think in retrospect as a singer I was slightly

hysterical. I took it way too far with that open-throated falsetto. I wish I could get an eraser and go round everybody's copy of Led Zep I and take out all that 'mmm, mmm, baby, baby' stuff. Get rid of that! Take a ray gun to it...

How can you say that? We love it...
You can love it as much as you like. I don't like it. It wasn't until Zep III that I was able to calm it down and have the confidence to sing in a different style. It was probably Bonzo's fault. In Band of Joy I had to stand by the side of him while he did 45-minute drum solos and I had to develop all those exaggerated mannerisms to counter him!

What did Band of Joy sound like at their best?
We used to play the Speakeasy, because there weren't many places you could do a psychedelic version of 'White Rabbit' which then merged into 'March of the Siamese Children' (from the musical *The King and I*) and went on for 20 minutes. I got banned for life from the Speak one time, with Roy Harper. But that's another story.

1

house in Walsall, full of first-generation immigrants, accompanied by his Anglo-Indian girlfriend Maureen, whom he had met at a Georgie Fame concert in 1966. The couple were to marry in 1968, less than three months after Plant's 20th birthday.

After his failed solo career, Plant was forced to support the pregnant Maureen by taking a day job as a navvy on a road-laying gang (he later claimed that he had been personally responsible for spreading "half the asphalt on West Bromwich High Street"). But when he took off his work clothes of an evening and donned his velvet flares and flower-patterned lace shirt, he spent his nights singing with Band of Joy. The group's first line-up was little more than a soul covers band but when Plant was unceremoniously sacked by a manager who told him he couldn't sing, his response was to form a rival band with the same name and take them in a more psychedelic direction, indulging his new passion for the West Coast

ROBERT PLANT INTERVIEW (Continued)

You were very influenced by the West Coast psychedelic scene of the time. What was the attraction?
There was a romance about it that was so far away from British pop-rock. A lot of the West Coast music had a social conscience and a sense of responsibility for the culture and our time. That had come from Dylan, obviously. He'd ignited that and kicked bubblegum pop into touch. Listen to early Jefferson Airplane or an album like Kaleidoscope's *Beacon from Mars*. Listen to the production, the sound of the guitar. It was saying something different is going on here. They were demanding social change and mixing it with musical exotica. I was captivated by bands like Love and Moby Grape and HP Lovecraft and I was so excited when I met Jimmy because he'd toured with them with The Yardbirds in America in 1967. But he didn't think much of them. He thought they didn't have any power. Or perhaps they were just out of it.

So what went wrong with Band of Joy?
I look back at it now with a bit of a quizzical frown. But you can't knock it and say it was naïve. I'd gone off on this romance and when you're that age what are you going to

do? I was learning and jumping out to play without a parachute. In the end Bonzo said: 'We can't do this. We're broke and starving.' He got an offer to join Tim Rose and I went off with Alexis Korner for a while.

Then you got a telegram from Peter Grant...
Something about joining The Yardbirds. I thought someone was taking the mick so I ignored it.

Fortunately, Peter Grant was not a man to be ignored...
Indeed not. He sent another telegram, which I've kept and got in a frame. I realised it was serious and Peter and Jimmy Page came up to Birmingham to see me. I think Peter asked me where they could find Robert Plant. I said 'Right here' and he said, 'Oh sorry, I thought you were a roadie.' He could have kept his mouth shut but he didn't. That was Peter for you.

Were you aware that you'd been recommended to them by Terry Reid, who had turned the gig down?
Terry and me were good friends because we always seemed to be on the same

sound of bands such as Buffalo Springfield, Moby Grape, Jefferson Airplane and Love. With Bonham on drums, Kevyn Gammond on guitar, Chris Brown on keyboards and Paul Lockey on bass, the second Band of Joy very nearly made it, too, expanding their circle of gigs beyond the West Midlands to London clubs such as UFO and the Speakeasy, supporting Fairport Convention and Ten Years After and joining American singer-songwriter Tim Rose on a tour bill that also included Terry Reid.

circuit. There was Terry, Aynsley Dunbar's Retaliation and the Band of Joy and we always seemed to be playing on the same bill together. He was one of those stellar vocalists, along with Steve Winwood, Jess Roden and Steve Marriott, and he got the offer from his connection with Mickie Most, who shared an office with Peter Grant. But he had an album out and felt he was on his way. The Yardbirds' star was no longer in the ascendant. They were doing OK. But they weren't raising sand, so Terry said to Peter and Jimmy, 'No, I've got this thing going. But you should see my mate. Go and have a look at 'the wild man from the Black Country'.

This was when you were singing with Hobbstweedle...
I hoped you'd forget that! We were doing Buffalo Springfield stuff like 'Rock'n'Roll Woman' and 'Mr Soul' and Moby Grape and Lover songs and it really wasn't very good. I'm astonished they didn't leave straight away because the band overplayed and there was a lot of hubbub and flash but no real content....

Full of optimism, the band recorded some demos at Regent Studios in London in early 1968 but a recording contract remained elusive. One of the tracks, 'Adriatic Sea View', would eventually surface in 1989 when Plant donated it to a fund-raising cassette compilation for a community project at Kidderminster College, run by former Band of Joy guitarist Gammond, who would also reunite with Plant in the late 1990s in his low-key pub band, the Priory of Brion. Covers of 'Hey Joe' and Buffalo Springfield's 'For What It's Worth' from the same session finally emerged on Plant's 2003 two-disc career retrospective, *Sixty Six to Timbuktu*.

Yet by the spring of 1968 it was clear that Band of Joy were going nowhere. The final straw came when the engine dropped out of their van onto the road while on the way to a gig in York. The father of bass player Paul Lockey was summoned out to rescue them and ,faced with a bill of several hundred pounds for a tow-away and a new engine, the band threw in the towel.

Musical history might have been very different if Plant had joined a band from Wolverhampton called Slade, led by his friend Noddy Holder, who had once roadied for one of Plant's bands. But his recruitment was vetoed at the last minute – depending on which story you believe either because Holder didn't want to share the microphone or because the rest of the group thought the golden-maned future golden god of cock-rock was an arrogant hippie poseur. Conceivably, both accounts are true, and it's hard to imagine Plant as a shaven-headed skinhead in boots and red braces chanting 'Cum on Feel the Noize'.

For a while he worked on an *ad hoc* basis as a duo with British blues veteran Alexis Korner, who had been impressed with him at a Band Of Joy gig at the Speakeasy. They even recorded a few tracks for a never released

1

album, including, Operator,which later turning up on a Korner LP and Plant's own *Sixty Six to Timbuktu.*

The sense of drift was deepened when he failed an audition for Denny Cordell's Regal Zonophone label, after a strong recommendation from Tony Secunda, who managed another Midlands band, The Move, with whom Plant was on friendly terms. Cordell, who at the time was preoccupied with masterminding Joe Cocker's career, apparently had "reservations" about Plant's sense of timing as a singer. After this disappointment, he seriously considered going back to a desk and taking his chartered accountancy exams, having promised himself (and Maureen, who was by now pregnant) that if he hadn't made it by the time he was 20, he would settle down in a 'proper job'. In all probability he didn't really mean it, but things were looking desperate when in the summer of 1968, he abandoned the Mississippi Delta for Middle Earth and joined the appallingly monickered Hobbstweedle, named in honour of Tolkien's *The Lord of the Rings*.

Then a telegram from Peter Grant arrived, suggesting that he might care to audition for The Yardbirds. Suspecting a practical joke, Plant ripped it up. Fortunately, the persistent Grant sent a second message in which he invited himself, Jimmy Page and Chris Dreja up to Birmingham to see Hobbstweedle – or rather, to see the band's lead singer. The job in the chartered accountant's office could wait and Plant still has that second telegram framed on his wall.

JOHN PAUL JONES

Born John Baldwin on January 3, 1946 in Sidcup, Kent, the future Led Zeppelin bass player came from a musical family. His parents worked as a musical comedy and variety duo,

but his father Joe Baldwin also had a more serious side as a pianist and arranger for a number of big bands in the 1940s and 1950s, including perennial favourites of the BBC's Light Programme, Ambrose and his Orchestra.

By the time young John had been packed off to Christ's College boarding school, he was already an accomplished piano player and could read music expertly. He was soon playing the pipe organ in the school chapel as if he had been born to it, and at the age of 14 he became choirmaster at his local church. At the same time, his teenage musical curiosity soon led to a passion for the jazz keyboards of the likes of Fats Waller and Jimmy Smith. Keen to play a second instrument, he toyed briefly with the saxophone, at the suggestion of his father, but after hearing the instrumental 'You Can't Sit Down' by the Chicago-based Phil Upchurch Combo, he resolved to become a bassist, his trained musical brain having decided that it was the bass part that gave a song its shape and direction.

After experimenting by restringing the family's ancient ukulele to resemble a bass, he cajoled his father into acting as guarantor on the hire purchase of a solid-body electric bass guitar, which he then amplified via a suitably adapted television set. By late 1960, as he approached his 15th birthday, he was leading an intriguing musical double life, playing organ at Sunday evensong and bass guitar with a beat combo at the church youth club straight afterwards. His first paid engagement came in a band that included his father on piano. Further bookings followed at fetes, weddings, army bases, hunt balls and even Masonic lodges around north-west Kent and London's south-eastern suburbs. One summer, there was even a residency at a yacht club in Cowes on the Isle of Wight. Meanwhile, away from playing with his father, Jones pursued his rock 'n' roll ambitions with a band called

The Deltas, and in early 1963 he gate-crashed an audition in the upstairs room of a Soho pub for a new band being assembled to back two former members of The Shadows, Jet Harris and Tony Meehan – on whose number one hit single, 'Diamonds', a certain session guitarist called Jimmy Page had already played.

Jones got the job, and armed with a new Fender Jazz bass and Vox amplifier, spent the next year touring with Harris and Meehan, adopting the stage name John Paul Jones, inspired by a 1959 film about the American War of Independence naval hero on suggestion of the duo's manager – not, as is widely reported in several of the many books about Led Zeppelin, at the behest of Rolling Stones manager Andrew Loog Oldham, who attempted to launch him on a solo career.

Oldham produced Jones' only solo single, 'Baja', released on Pye in early 1964, a bouncy, beat group instrumental typical of the period which found him playing six-string bass with overdubbed orchestration. The B-side was called 'A Foggy Day in Vietnam' and didn't feature Jones at all but 'The Andrew Loog Oldham Orchestra', and it seems likely that members of The Rolling Stones played on the track. Yet like Jimmy Page's lone solo single, 'Baja''s only useful purpose was to make it evident that the talented but undemonstrative Jones was not cut out to be a solo star.

Instead, he drifted into studio session work, first for Tony Meehan, who by 1964 had become a staff producer at Decca, and then for the likes of Oldham and Mickie Most. "Organ was originally my favourite instrument," he has said of the period. "But for session playing I found it much easier to carry a bass guitar to work than a Hammond."

Paradoxically, the man who was to become Led Zeppelin's 'straight one' was reputedly a bit of a raver in his early years. David Bowie claims that it was an 18-year-old Jones who persuaded him to smoke marijuana for the first time. "Pop music was all pills in those days," Jones later admitted. He also reportedly gate-crashed a coming-of-age party at 11 Downing Street thrown for Caroline Maudling, the daughter of Conservative chancellor of the exchequer, Reginald Mauldling.

Heavily influenced by the thick, fat bass lines he was hearing on Tamla Motown records, Jones went on to play bass (and often keyboards, too) on records by The Rolling Stones, Herman's Hermits, Donovan, Jeff Beck, Cat Stevens, Rod Stewart, Shirley Bassey, Dusty Springfield, Lulu, The Walker Brothers and countless others – many of them far too embarrassing to mention in polite musical company. "You would do The Rolling Stones, The Everly Brothers, French rock 'n' roll sessions, German ones, Engelbert Humperdinck and Tom Jones – and all in the same day quite often," he recalled many years later.

His breakthrough into arranging came on Donovan's 1966 hit 'Sunshine Superman', although it came about by accident. "I happened to be on the session as a bass player but the arranger they'd picked really didn't know anything," he later recalled. "I got the rhythm section together and we went from there. Arranging and general studio direction were much better than just sitting there and being told what to do." His next assignment was arranging for Herman's Hermits (and helping them to sell more records in America during the course of 1966 than The Beatles). Before long he'd landed an even more prestigious gig when he was asked to help out The Rolling Stones on 'She's a Rainbow', creating the elaborately baroque arrangement that is one of the highlights of their 1967 album *Their Satanic Majesties Request*.

On many of his sessions for producers such as Most and Oldham, he would bump into

LED ZEPPELIN

1

Jimmy Page. The two were hardly close friends but there was already developing a strong mutual respect, reinforced when Jones came up with the orchestral arrangement and played the cello on the title track of The Yardbirds' 1967 album *Little Games* and contributed to the band's misconceived single, 'Ten Little Indians'.

Jones was also invited by Page to play on 'Beck's Bolero', a 1966 track that also featured The Who's drummer Keith Moon. He was only wheeled in after first choice John Entwistle failed to show up, but the track worked so well that it became an early template for the sound of the new band that Page would eventually form two years later – and which, of course, would feature Jones on bass and keyboards.

It was after working in the studio with Page on Donovan's 1968 hit single 'Hurdy

Gurdy Man', that Jones rang the guitarist to enquire about a new band he was putting together out of the ashes of The Yardbirds. His wife had pointed out to him a news item in *Disc & Music Echo* which reported that Page was recruiting musicians and he wondered whether he might need a bass player. Session work was beginning to pall for him, just as it had for Page.

"John Paul Jones was an incredible arranger and musician and he didn't need me for a job," Page subsequently recalled. "It was just that he felt the need to express himself and he thought that we might be able to do it together. He had a proper music training and he had quite brilliant ideas." Jones confirms his disenchantment with his lucrative life as a session player. "I was becoming a vegetable and I wasn't saying anything musically," he

JOHN PAUL JONES SESSIONS

As a bass player, keyboardist and arranger, John Paul Jones was involved in literally hundreds of sessions in the mid-1960s. These ten are the tip of the iceberg but display the sheer diversity of his talents. How many of them he ever put on the stereo when he got home for his personal listening pleasure is another matter...

'SUNSHINE SUPERMAN'
Donovan 1966

'NO MILK TODAY'
Herman's Hermits 1966

'A GROOVY KIND OF LOVE'
Wayne Fontana and The Mindbenders 1966

'THE THIRD DEGREE'
Marc Bolan 1966

'HI-HO SILVER LINING'
Jeff Beck 1967

'TEN LITTLE INDIANS'
The Yardbirds 1967

'SHE'S A RAINBOW'
The Rolling Stones 1967

'THE BOAT THAT I ROW'
Lulu 1967

'MATTHEW AND SON'
Cat Stevens
1967

'DELILAH'
Tom Jones 1968

explained many years later. "I was churning this stuff out, and making a ton of money, doing 20–30 arrangements a month for everybody – and going crazy." Page told Jones he was going to see an unknown singer Terry Reid had told him about, and promised to call him when he'd checked them both out.

JOHN BONHAM

John Henry Bonham was born on May 31, 1948 in Redditch, about 10 miles south of Birmingham in the green and pleasant rolling pastures of Worcestershire. The son of a carpenter and the oldest of three children, his future calling was evident from an early age as he bashed pots and pans and any other household object from which he could coax a rhythm. "I'd wanted to be a drummer since I was about five years old," he later recalled. "Later I played a bit of acoustic guitar but it was always drums, first and foremost. I felt nothing for any other instrument."

At the age of 10, his mother bought him a snare drum (he'd already attempted to make his own with a coffee tin and a piece of loose wire), and by the age of 15 his father had bought him his first full kit, a second-hand job on which most of the metal had rusted. His drive was evident to all; it was simply that nobody knew where it was going to take him. "He will either end up as a dustman or a millionaire," one of his school reports concluded.

Bonham himself had no doubts about his direction. "As soon as I left school, I decided I was definitely going to be a drummer. I was very determined," he told a percussion magazine in the 1970s. By 1964 he was drumming with his first band, Terry Webb and The Spiders, dressed in a uniform of purple jackets with velveteen lapels and a boot-lace tie, topped off with Elvis Presely-style greased-back hair. A highlight of their repertoire was a version of

Little Richard's 'Good Golly Miss Molly', the drum pattern from which later was reborn as 'Rock and Roll' on *Led Zeppelin IV*.

A brief sojourn in another group, the Nicky James Movement, came to an abrupt end when the combo's hire-purchased equipment was repossessed at a gig. Next he replaced future Move drummer Bev Bevan in The Senators, with whom Bonham reputedly recorded a 1964 single called 'She's a Mod' – presumably with the grease now washed out of his hair. A spell with Pat Wayne and The Beachcombers followed before he joined a group called A Way of Life and then Locomotive, who were not named after Bonham's relentless rhythmic style, although they might well have been. Then, at 18, his promiscuous drumming career almost came to a premature end when he married Pat Phillips, a girl he had met at a dance near his family's home in Kidderminster and with whom he would soon have a son, Jason. "I swore to Pat that I'd give up drumming when we got married," he later said. "But every night I'd come home and sit down at the drums and just play. I'd be miserable if I didn't."

Home by this stage was a 15-foot caravan trailer and the Bonhams were so broke that he had to give up smoking to meet the rent on even this humble residence. On the grounds that he could hardly earn any less money making music than he was casual labouring as a hod-carrier on a building site, he eventually decided to give drumming one last go. If it didn't work out, he again promised Pat he would find another career.

Bonham contacted Robert Plant, who he knew from the small-town scene around Kidderminster and asked if his band, the Crawling King Snakes, could use a drummer. As it happened, they had just lost their regular sticksman but Plant and his colleagues were at first far from certain. 'Bonzo', as he was almost universally known, already had a reputation

LED ZEPPELIN

as the loudest drummer around. His muscles bulging from carrying hod-loads of bricks and with his bass drum reportedly lined with aluminium to make it sound like a cannon, he'd been evicted from The Beachcombers for drowning out the rest of the band and some of the more timid club owners around Birmingham had made it clear that they wouldn't book any band in which Bonham hammered. He hit his kit with such force that he could wreck more sticks and skins in a single night than a less aggressive drummer might break in a lifetime. "I was always breaking drumheads when I first started playing," he admitted. "Later on I learned how to play louder but without hitting the drums so hard. It has all to do with the swing of the stick." When his sticks broke, he would play with his bare hands – a technique he continued to use for the rest of his life. "You get an absolutely true drum sound because there's no wood involved," he enthused. "It hurts your hands at first but then the skin hardens. I think I can hit a drum harder with my hands than sticks."

The cash-strapped, struggling King Snakes were also concerned that he didn't have a car. "It was a long way to go and pick him up for a gig and we never knew whether we'd have the petrol money to get over there," Plant admitted. In the end Bonham was invited to join but within months the petrol money was proving too much of an issue and he went back to playing with one of his former bands, A Way of Life. Nevertheless, the Plant-Bonham axis had been established and it was soon back in action in late 1967 in Band of Joy, whose live sets became notable not only for Plant's gyrating but for Bonham's crashingly belligerent solos, much inspired by Ginger Baker's extended solo on 'Toad' on Cream's 1996 debut album, *Fresh Cream*. However, Plant's claim that he had to stand alongside the drummer one night at London's Speakeasy while he treated punters

to a 45-minute drum solo is probably a slight exaggeration.

For a moment, it looked as if Band of Joy were on the verge of making it. But when a record deal failed to materialise and the group found themselves splitting nightly fees of £60 to £70 five ways, Bonham accepted an invitation to join the touring band of American singer-songwriter Tim Rose. By now, it seems Baker had created a vogue for loud drummer and suddenly in the summer of 1968, for the first time in his life, Bonham found himself in demand. He was earning the best money of his career to date with Rose and there were offers on the table to join established hit-maker Chris Farlowe and to back Joe Cocker, who was on the verge of a major breakthrough with his extraordinary cover of The Beatles' With a Little Help from My Friends.

But the Midlands mafia has always stuck together and Robert Plant hadn't forgotten his old mate. When Jimmy Page invited him to join The Yardbirds in late July 1968 and suggested Procol Harum's BJ Wilson might make a suitable drummer, an emboldened Plant told his new colleague that he had a much better idea and asked him not to take any decision until he had seen his best friend play. "We needed a drummer who was a good timekeeper and who really laid it down," he later recalled. "And the only suitable candidate I knew was my old mate Bonzo."

THE YARDBIRDS

Despite a line-up that at different times boasted the holy trinity of British rock guitarists in Eric Clapton, Jeff Beck and Jimmy Page, The Yardbirds' career was characterised by under-achievement and disappointment. Even the handful of pop hits they enjoyed never really reflected their true potential. In the end, the group itself seemed uncertain whether it

1

Mickie Most's new, improved Yardbirds all set for an appearance on BBC's Top of the Pops in 1965

wanted to be a blues combo, a pop group or a rock band, and although their use of fuzz tone, feedback and distortion was genuinely innovative, the musical virtuosity of the band's various guitarists failed to compensate for their lack of a strong in-house songwriter. With the benefit of hindsight, it was the links the group forged between British R&B, pop experimentalism, early psychedelia and prototype heavy metal that made The Yardbirds significant in rock history. Yet at the time, it simply gave the impression that the band lacked direction and focus and ultimately left their audience dazed and confused.

Formed at Kingston Art School in 1963 as the Metropolitan Blues Quartet by singer Keith Relf, lead guitarist "Top" Topham, rhythm guitarist Chris Dreja, bass player Paul Samwell-Smith and drummer Jim McCarty, the band first achieved notice on the British blues scene when they took over from The Rolling Stones as the house band at the Crawdaddy Club in Richmond, by which time they had become known as The

Yardbirds. Like the Stones, their repertoire mixed the Chicago blues of Howlin' Wolf, Muddy Waters, Sonny Boy Williamson and Jimmy Reed with the more commercial rock 'n' roll sounds of Chuck Berry and Bo Diddley.

In October 1963, shortly after they had taken over the Crawdaddy residency, Topham was replaced by Eric Clapton, who substantially raised the group's musical prowess. They were still raw, however, when at the end of 1963 they backed Sonny Boy Williamson on a tour of Britain and Germany. "Those English kids want to play the blues so bad – and they play the blues so bad," the great bluesman was reported as saying.

Under the management of Crawdaddy impresario Giorgio Gomelsky, the following year the group signed to EMI's Columbia label and made its album debut in late 1964 with *Five Live Yardbirds*, recorded at London's Marquee Club. The group might have seen itself as an authentic R&B combo, but from the outset the group came under pressure from EMI to record

LED ZEPPELIN

1

a hit single. It eventually came via 'For Your Love', written by Graham Gouldman. Clapton, a true blues purist, was appalled and by the time of the single's release in early 1965, had departed in disgust, to be replaced by Jeff Beck.

'For Your Love' made number three in Britain and six in America and was followed by a further big hit with another Gouldman composition, 'Heart Full of Soul'. By the end of the year, the double A-sided 'Evil Hearted You'/'Still I'm Sad' had made it a trio of top ten hits.

Even better was to come with the psychedelic-tinged 'Shapes of Things', which reached number three in Britain and number ll in America early in 1966 and was followed by the album, 1966's *Yardbirds*, widely known as *Roger the Engineer* and released in America in slightly different form as *Over Under Sideways Down*. It was the only album the band ever recorded of all original material and bounced somewhat erratically between blues-rock, guitar rave-ups and proto-psychedelic experimentalism. By the time it was released in July 1966, however, the band had a new line-up, with Page having replaced departing bassist Paul Samwell-Smith. For a few gigs Page played bass, while Chris Dreja learned the instrument. Page, the consummate session player, apparently needed no instruction. "They were stuck so of course I said 'Well, I'll play.' I offered to play bass for them even though I'd never played a bass guitar before in my life," he recalls. "Then they suggested that I stay on in the group and I did. Session work had become so predictable and boring."

Beck remembers it slightly differently. "We had to talk to him and bribe him with lots of money to come into the group," he says. Whatever the exact circumstances, once Dreja had learned the bass parts, Page switched back to his natural instrument, giving The Yardbirds a twin guitar line-up to die for.

Mickie Most's ambitious Yardbirds album Little Games failed to hit the spot, despite the great psychedelia-meets-super-hero-comic design

Yet for various reasons, the Beck-Page teaming only ever offered tantalising glimpses of its potential, most notably on the single 'Happenings Ten Years Time Ago'. It proved too experimental to chart but was one of the finest recordings The Yardbirds ever made. It also featured Page's future Led Zeppelin colleague John Paul Jones on bass.

The one other recorded monument to the Beck-Page era Yardbirds was 'Stroll On', a variation on 'Train Kept A-Rollin'', recorded for Michelangelo Antonioni's 1967 film *Blow-Up*. The group's appearance in the film was not planned but came about when they filled in at short notice for The In Crowd, who had initially been contracted but were unable to attend on the scheduled filming date. Their performance in the movie was chiefly memorable for Beck smashing his guitar, but by the time the film came out in 1967 and the group appeared at the Cannes Film Festival to promote it, Beck was long gone.

The synergy between Beck and Page was explosive in every way. The two guitarists may have been close friends but there was also a distinct rivalry between them and – according to Dreja – when Page joined, "Jeff felt, justifiably, that his space was being invaded." In August 1966 during a tour of America, Beck suffered some sort of breakdown (or a "freak-out" in the parlance of the time) and The Yardbirds completed the trek with Page as sole lead guitarist. Beck was back the following month for a dozen UK dates supporting The Rolling Stones, on which they reportedly played up a storm, but on a further American tour in October, Beck was sacked after just two dates. His bandmates felt his unreliability and volatility had left them no option. "One time in the dressing room Beck had his guitar up over his head, about to bring it down on Keith Relf, but instead smashed it to the floor," Page recalled of one particularly fraught night backstage. "Keith looked at him with total astonishment and Jeff said, 'What did you make me do that for?'"

When Beck was told that he was being fired, he expected his friend to quit with him in sympathy, turning to Page and asking if he was leaving with him. "No, I'm going to stay behind," his colleague answered uneasily, knowing full well that Beck would regard this as an act of betrayal. "Jeff and I were very close but this strange professional jealousy came between us and I don't understand why," Page confessed years later. The official announcement of his departure cited "persistent ill-health". Some 26 years later, Beck was reunited with his old colleagues when the Yardbirds were inducted into the Rock and Roll Hall of Fame in 1992. At the ceremony he quipped: "I suppose I should say thank you, but they fired me, so fuck 'em!" It was a joke – but with enough of a barb to suggest that the incident still rankled.

Beck was not replaced and The Yardbirds remained as a quartet for the remainder of their career. After a tour of Australia and Singapore, Page took time off to go back-packing in India.

On his return, it was increasingly evident that the weight of the band rested on his shoulders and left to his own devices his growing experimentalism as a guitarist and pioneering use of fuzz tone, wah-wah pedal and even such unusual techniques as scraping a violin bow across his guitar strings would surely have taken The Yardbirds in a new and interesting direction. But with the failure to chart of their last single, 'Happenings Ten Years Time Ago', EMI was agitating for a return to their former hit-making ways.

Their answer was to draft in producer Mickie Most, a ludicrous notion that was a disaster waiting to happen. Page knew Most well and had worked as a session guitarist on many of his hits for the likes of Herman's Hermits and Lulu. But recruiting the master of three-minute throwaway pop songs to produce a serious rock band just as psychedelia was dawning and the world was preparing to enter 1967's "Summer of Love" was hopelessly misconceived. With their musical pedigree, The Yardbirds should have been up there in the vanguard of the new wave of progressive rock groups alongside the likes of Cream, The Jimi Hendrix Experience and Traffic. Instead, while George Martin was helping The Beatles' craft the masterful *Sgt Pepper's Lonely Hearts Club Band*, Most's instincts were to treat The Yardbirds as a lightweight pop group. His decision to have them cover Manfred Mann's 'Ha! Ha! Said the Clown' was particularly crass and inept. Worse, his brazen attempts at commercialism didn't even work. 'Ha! Ha! Said The Clown' flopped and an equally weak cover of Harry Nilsson's 'Ten Little Indians' (described by Page as "an extremely silly song with a truly awful brass arrangement") deservedly suffered the same fate.

The Most-produced 1967 album *Little Games* fared no better and after staggering to number 80 in the *Billlboard* chart in America, it was not even released in the UK. "On half the

LED ZEPPELIN

1

tracks we didn't even hear the playbacks," Page complains today. "Some of them were first takes. We'd spend time on the singles but Mickie Most thought that albums were nothing, just something to stick out after a hit single." Jim McCarty complained the album was "recorded just like a Herman's Hermits LP". Yet despite Most's inappropriate and lightweight production, the album has its moments and contains several pointers to the style Page would develop more fully with Led Zeppelin, not only in his electric guitar work but also on the acoustic 'White Mountain', which reveals the influence of such folk stylists as Bert Jansch and Davy Graham and was originally titled 'Arabic Number'. Some later reissues of the album are bolstered by the inclusion of a live BBC session that includes the original template of the Zeppelin classic 'Dazed And Confused' and 'Think About It', the B-side to the group's final single 'Goodnight Sweet Josephine', which contains some of Page's most explosive pre-Zeppelin playing.

The group spent most of 1967 on the road, often in a blizzard of drink and drug abuse, with singer Keith Relf regularly out of it on stage and frequently singing in the wrong places. They were at last making some decent money – largely because an aggressive human dynamo called Peter Grant (see box page ?) had in January 1967 taken over their management from Simon Napier-Bell – but by the start of 1968 it was becoming increasingly plain that The Yardbirds were no longer serious contenders. A planned live album recorded in New York City in March 1968 was shelved at the band's request, only to be released as *Live Yardbirds! Featuring Jimmy Page* by their US label Epic three years later when Led Zeppelin hit big. The album was swiftly withdrawn after Page's lawyers slapped an injunction on it. "A total embarrassment, recorded on jet lag and by a guy who had never recorded a rock band in his life," was the guitarist's merciless judgement.

The Yardbirds played their final gig in Luton in July 1968, but Relf and McCarty had decided to quit long before that during the preceding tour of America. Indeed, the news leaked back to *Melody Maker* in Britain, who in early June ran an item which reported: "Break-up of the Yardbirds is expected on their return from America... lead guitarist Jimmy Page is to reform the group with a new lead singer and drummer." The group had divided into factions. Relf and McCarty were keen to move in a more folk-rock direction and started the short-lived Together, before enjoying greater success with Renaissance. Page and Dreja favoured a louder, more dynamic and heavier approach, albeit with acoustic elements.

Grant negotiated with the departing duo for Page and Dreja to retain the rights to the Yardbirds name and on July 8, 1968, EMI Records issued a press release stating: "The band will be reformed under the same name by Page and Dreja, who seek two new members."

In the event, their first choices were unavailable and they were turned down by singer Terry Reid and Procol Harum drummer BJ Wilson. A still enthusiastic Dreja stayed around long enough to be part of the scouting mission with Page and Grant to Birmingham to check out Robert Plant, but after a change of heart baled out soon after. "I wasn't interested in becoming a jobbing musician with strangers and made a conscious decision to go into freelance photography," he later explained.

While Page recruited a new line-up that would fit his own musical vision, he kept his hand in playing a few sessions, including one by a Sheffield gas fitter called Joe Cocker on a cover of The Beatles' 'With a Little Help from My Friends'. By the time the track reached number one in the British chart in November 1968, his band was in place – but they were no longer known as The Yardbirds.

THE BALLOON GOES UP
1968–1969

2

"I had it in my mind exactly what I wanted to try and get together. Then it was just a matter of searching around for the right personnel to pull it off."

JIMMY PAGE

"I don't think there was a vision at all, initially."

ROBERT PLANT

THE BALLOON GOES UP

2

1968–1969

As The Yardbirds moved inexorably towards their use-by date in mid-July 1968, Jimmy Page was busy reviving a plan he had originally hatched back in 1966. The cast of The New Yardbirds existed, somewhere, and Page had done his research. In addition, he had some clear ideas about what he wanted to achieve: not so much a phoenix rising from the ashes, more a brand new band with a brand new sound. But there was a lot of work to do to get the venture off the ground.

After The Yardbirds played their final gig in July 1968, Jimmy Page was depressed and disillusioned. As Ritchie Yorke put it in his 1974 book, *Led Zeppelin: The Definitive Biography*, the guitarist was at a crossroads: "He could return to session work. He could go back to art. Or he could lunge ahead and create a new band from the still-engrossing embers of the Yardbirds' fiery career." His indecision did not last long. Although he did a few sessions to keep his hand in and maintain the cash flow, there was never any real doubt that forming a new band was the only real thing on his mind.

Page's first intention was to reform The Yardbirds and with Chris Dreja still at the time part of the set-up, a reconstituted band would at least have had one member of the original line-up to justify the continued use of the name. Asked about the new band by *Go* magazine he reasoned that he was going to keep the old name because "people have associated a type of sound with the name. It's

a heavy beat sound and I want to keep that."

But his mind also went back to a session that he had organised in May 1966 at London's IBC Studios involving John Paul Jones on bass, Nicky Hopkins on piano, The Who's Keith Moon on drums and Page and Jeff Beck on guitars. The session produced a track called 'Beck's Bolero' and Page enjoyed it so much that there was talk of forming a group built around a dual guitar attack with Beck and The Who's rhythm section of Moon and John Entwistle (Jones at this stage was not prepared to give up his lucrative position as a session player and arranger).

Talk turned swiftly to a singer. "The first choice was Steve Winwood, but he was too committed to Traffic," Page later recalled. "Next we thought of Steve Marriott of The Small Faces. He was approached and seemed full of glee about it. A message came back from the business side of Marriott, though, which said 'How would you like to play the guitar with ten broken fingers? You will be if

2

Seminal British R&B band The Small Faces: (from left) Ronnie Lane, Steve Marriott, Ian McLagan and Kenney Jones. Lead singer and guitarist Marriott was a contender for the Zeppelin singing role. 1965's 'You Need Loving' indicates why

you don't stay away from Steve.'" The Small Faces at the time were managed by Don Arden, who had once famously dangled rival manager Robert Stigwood over a second-floor balcony and threatened to throw him head-first onto the pavement below, so Page knew the threat was no joke.

Although the group was to remain stillborn, a name was coined, although there is some dispute as to who first came up with Lead(sic) Zeppelin. Entwistle, to his dying day, insisted that he was the one who had come up with the name when he commented that such a line-up was "so

heavy it will go down like a Led Zeppelin". Moon claimed it was his coinage, a claim supported by both Page and Jones who say that two years later when The New Yardbirds decided a change of name was required, the permission of The Who's drummer was sought. A third explanation is that the name was a joint effort and emerged out of some witty banter and repartee between the two members of The Who.

Whatever the exact origins of the Led Zeppelin name, the putative Page-Beck-Hopkins-Moon-Entwistle line-up was never realised. Moon, it seems, was not serious

BACK TO MINE

2

When Robert Plant made his way down to Jimmy Page's house boat at Pangbourne on the River Thames in late July 1968, it was still far from certain that he was going to be invited to become the lead singer with The New Yardbirds, as the group was initially to be known. The deal was struck when they played each other their favourite records and discovered shared musical tastes. As far as we can reconstruct it at almost 40 years distance, based on Page and Plant's own recollections this is the soundtrack they bonded over. Several of the items were to have a considerable influence on the first Led Zeppelin album...

Joan Baez 'Babe I'm Gonna Leave You'
Howlin' Wolf Howlin' Wolf (aka The Rockin' Chair album)
Incredible String Band. The 5000 Spirits or the Layers of the Onion

Robert Johnson King of the Delta Blues Singers
Larry Williams 'She Said Yeah'
Don and Dewey 'Justine'
Garnet Mimms As Long As I Have You
Buddy Guy A Man & the Blues
Elvis Presley 'Love Me'
Muddy Waters 'You Shook Me'
Iron Butterfly In-a-Gadda-da-Vida
Chuck Berry No Money Down
Little Walter Little Walter

about changing bands and more concerned about making a point to his colleagues in The Who. Without a singer or a drummer, Page gave up and joined Beck in The Yardbirds instead. "The idea just sort of fell apart," he later said. "Instead of being more positive about it and looking for another singer, we just let it slip by. The Who began a tour and The Yardbirds began a tour and that was it."

Yet Page did not forget the idea or the experience and when in the summer of 1968 he began to think about his dream line-up for the new group he still planned to call The Yardbirds, he resolved this time to find his singer before recruiting any other musicians. Winwood and Marriott were unavailable for pretty much the same reasons as before, and so the first choice soon became Terry Reid, whose soulful voice Page knew from his days singing with Peter Jay and The Jaywalkers. Reid had recently gone solo and, encouragingly, was signed to RAK, run by Mickie Most and Yardbirds manager Peter Grant. But Reid felt

his solo career was about to take off and was also doubtful that The Yardbirds could be re-established as a commercially viable entity and declined.

Sadly, his solo career never quite ignited, although almost 40 years on, he remains remarkably good-humoured about turning down the opportunity to join what was to become the biggest rock band in the world and gamely insists that he has no regrets. Instead, he suggested Page should check out his friend Robert Plant.

Page was unfamiliar with the name and it's a cruel but justifiable judgement that Reid's recommendation was probably his greatest contribution to rock history. It's perfectly possible that Plant's cause was also pleaded by others, including noted musical match-maker Alexis Korner, with whom Plant had formed an *ad hoc* duo, and by Tony Secunda, the manager of Procol Harum and The Move, who had tried to get him a solo deal after Band of Joy had split-up and claims that he mentioned him as a likely lad to Peter Grant.

LED ZEPPELIN

2

But even if there were other supporters, there's little doubt that it was Reid's endorsement which, on July 20, 1968, sent Page, Grant and the still-keen Dreja heading up the M1 to see Plant's band Hobbstweedle play at a god-forsaken teacher training college in Birmingham in front of a crowd which Richard Cole – wickedly but by all accounts accurately – described as "barely big enough to fill a Volkswagen van".

The handful who were in the audience that night had no idea that they were witnessing history in the making and, frankly, neither did Jimmy Page. First, he hated the material, which he'd heard before when The Yardbirds had shared shows in America with the likes of Moby Grape and Love. He was unimpressed enough with the American originals and he didn't need to hear a West Midlands band covering them. "It was stuff that I personally didn't like very much," he later admitted. Secondly, although he was impressed by the voice ("Robert was all right... he was singing really well"), he then began to fret over why, if Plant was that good, he hadn't already been snapped up by someone else. "Why isn't this guy a star?" Page wondered to himself, according to Zeppelin roadie-turned-author Richard Cole. "Something's got to be wrong with him. Maybe he has one of those obnoxious personalities and no one can get along with him." There was also opposition from Chris Dreja, who told Page that he didn't think much of Plant's voice at all.

Yet despite such misgivings, Page recognised that Plant's voice "had an exceptional and very distinctive quality", a view reinforced when he listened to a demo Plant had given him from his Band of Joy days. He invited the singer down to his home in Pangbourne for a few days so that they could get to know each other better.

Plant was acutely aware that he was

on trial. "It certainly wasn't a foregone conclusion that I was going to be the singer," he admitted to this writer in an interview in 2005. "But we had a glorious first meeting and an exchanging of ideas. You can smell when people have travelled and had their doors opened a little wider than most and you could feel that was the deal with Jimmy. His ability to absorb things and the way he carried the whole plan was far more cerebral than anything I'd come across before and so I was very impressed. And when it came to the music, we realised we were dealing from the same pack of cards."

Page, however, had a far clearer idea of the musical card game they were playing than Plant. During that same 2005 interview, I asked the singer if at this stage there was a musical vision behind their planning. "I don't think we had a clue," he replied. "We'd never played together before and so you fall back on your roots to see how it works and that's what we did." Asked the same question, Page gave a rather different answer. "I certainly had a good idea of the sort of direction I wanted us to go in," he answered. "It went back to the band I was going to form with Jeff Beck, in which we wanted a Steve Marriott or Steve Winwood type vocalist. That was the call. And the person we accessed at that point for Zeppelin was Terry Reid. If you're familiar with his vocal style on an album like *River*, that's the way I was thinking. And having a really dynamic drummer was always going to be very important within the framework of it, because it was going to be a trio instrumentally with the fourth member being the singer and using the voice as an instrument. I knew the material I wanted us to do, as well. I had a game plan for it. Most definitely."

Sometime in the week following the Hobbstweedle gig, Plant made his way down to Page's house in Berkshire with a

Despite writing 'Hey Joe', Tim Rose was one of a number of successful 1960s performers who got swept away by the tsunami of heavy rockers in the 1970s

pile of his favourite albums and the musical bonding began. His tastes were eclectic and the influences on his singing style unusual, ranging from raw and earthy Delta blues to British folk music, via West Coast 1960s rock. Page didn't think much of the latter, but his own tastes also ran from Howlin' Wolf and Robert Johnson to English folk guitarists such as Bert Jansch and Davy Graham.

One day during his stay, Plant started leafing through Page's record collection. "I pulled out a pile to play and somehow or other they happened to be the same ones that Jimmy had put aside to play to me when he returned, just to see whether I liked them," Plant recalled. "When he saw that I'd picked them out too we just giggled at each other for a bit. We found we had exactly the same tastes in music."

The listening session would have a profound effect on the shape of the first Led Zeppelin, most notably in the decision to cover the traditional 'Babe I'm Gonna Leave You'. Both were enamoured with Joan Baez's version of the song and their retooling of it became an early model of Zeppelin's ability to combine acoustic and electric moods as Page explained to Plant his notion of a new kind of 'heavy music' with quieter touches and dynamic contrasts of light and shade and a band in which the singer and guitarist worked in unison and played off each other. "Jimmy wasn't dominating or anything as I might have expected," Page recalled. "I could suggest things and the two of us rearranged 'Babe I'm Gonna Leave You'. It was good to hit it off like that."

Plant got the gig and before he left he put in a word for his old friend, John Bonham. At this stage, several other names were under consideration for what was still going to be called The Yardbirds. Page and Chris Dreja, who was still very much involved, had drawn up a shortlist and Grant set about contacting the suggested names to see who was available and interested. Dreja was so

LED ZEPPELIN

sure that the drummer was going to be Paul Francis, whom both he and Page knew from their session work, that he even gave an interview in which he stated that the new line-up consisted of Page, Plant, himself and Francis. Somewhat jumping the gun, he went on to claim: "Now we're starting to get things together with the new group, we're very keen to get on the road. Our first set of new shows will be starting in September in Scandinavia, where we have a tour arranged. After this it'll be down to work in England. We've done a fair amount of rehearsing, with some new songs and also plenty of old Yardbirds hits." The announcement of dates in Scandinavia was true enough, but at this stage no rehearsals of any kind had taken place – with or without Francis.

Page's own first choice as a drummer was BJ Wilson of Procol Harum, and in addition to Francis, others on the list included Clem Cattini, who had played sessions for The Yardbirds, and Aynsley Dunbar, at the time leading his own band Aynsley Dunbar's Retaliation, the name of which was perhaps an ironic reference to his having lost out to Mitch Mitchell as the drummer with The Jimi Hendrix Experience on the toss of a coin.

The manner in which Mitchell was chosen is indicative of how little importance was paid to drummers at the time: the prevailing thinking was that they were there to keep the beat and little else. Page thought differently and was looking for a drummer whose chemistry could contribute to the overall sound. "You know, you can get four really good musicians but it doesn't mean they're going to play as a band," he told this writer in 2005. "The thing about Zeppelin was that we always played as a band."

Page was intrigued by what Plant told him about Bonham, who at the time was touring with Tim Rose. The notion of the loudest

drummer in the West Midlands backing a folk singer seemed to fit Page's own vision of a new style of rock music, heavy but with dynamic contrasts between electric and acoustic elements. A hyped-up and over-excited Plant, meanwhile, on his way back home from Pangbourne and now fully enrolled as a Yardbird, hitched to Oxford, where Rose was playing a gig that night, to tell Bonham his news and urge him to audition for the group.

The drummer, however, was unimpressed. "Bonzo said, 'Well I'm all right here, aren't I?' Plant recalls. He'd never earned before the sort of bread he was getting from Tim Rose so I had to try and persuade him. I had nothing to convince him, really, except a name that got lost in American pop history – The Yardbirds."

When Rose's tour arrived in London a few days later on July 31, 1968, Page, Dreja and Grant went to see his band at the Country Club in Hampstead. The guitarist was immediately convinced that Plant had been right. "Although I had in mind the need for a very powerful drummer, I must say I wasn't ready for John Bonham. When I saw what a thrasher Bonzo was, I knew he'd be incredible," Page subsequently recalled. "He was playing 'Hey Joe' as an acoustic number and I could see the whole thing fitting together. He was into exactly the same sort of stuff that I was and he was beyond the realms of anything I could have possibly imagined."

Bonham became the second former member of Band of Joy invited to Page's Pangbourne home to be offered an invitation the guitarist hoped could not be refused. But the drummer was still reluctant. After years of struggle, he now suddenly found himself in the previously unimagined position of being able to play the field. "Joe Cocker was interested and so was Chris Farlowe, along with Robert and Jimmy," he later recalled. "It was baffling. I had so much to consider. It wasn't just a question of who had the best prospects, but also which music was going to be the right kind of stuff. Farlowe was fairly well established and I knew that Cocker was going to make it. When I first got offered the gig, I thought that The Yardbirds were finished. In Britain they had been forgotten."

Uncontactable by phone, Page and Grant pursued Bonham with a series of increasingly frantic telegrams, several of them delivered to his favourite pub, the Three Men in a Boat in Walsall. Eventually Bonham relented. "I knew that Jimmy was a good guitarist and Robert was a good singer so even if we didn't have any success, at least it would be a pleasure to play in a good group," Bonham said later. I already knew what music Robert liked and Jimmy told me what he was into and I decided I liked their music ideas better than Cocker or Farlowe." However, his insistence that musical considerations swayed him did not prevent him seeking further reassurance about his income, given that he had a young family to support. "There were all sorts of negotiations about retainers and Bonzo was very keen to get an extra £25 a week to drive the Transit van," Plant recalls. "His wife Pat wasn't happy at all with us going down there and hanging out with those guys. It was like going to the far side of the Moon."

Peter Grant also confirmed the attempted van-driving scam, adding that "It was remarkable how naïve Robert and Bonzo were." Plant does not disagree. "Me and Bonzo were 20 years old and we were definitely the boys from the black stuff," he cheerfully admitted in 2005. "I don't think we were in awe. We were just really pleased to be offered some kind of security. We

thought we were on to something. But we'd never seen a manager before – let alone Peter Grant."

By the time Bonham finally signed on, other changes that would profoundly affect the line-up were underway. Some time between Page's invitation to Bonham and his acceptance, Chris Dreja retired (or was eased out of the picture). In theory, as an original Yardbird Dreja was the senior member of the new band. In practice, of course, it was very much Page who was calling the shots. With Plant on board, he came to see setbacks to Dreja's continued presence. Apart from a bit of harmonica, Plant did not play an instrument, meaning that the group would in effect be a power trio fronted by a singer. Although Dreja was versatile enough as a bassist and guitarist, Page began to think he needed someone who could also play keyboards. Given the conflict that had dogged The Yardbirds, he further wondered whether a clean break with the past might be beneficial. Inevitably, his thoughts turned to his conversation with John Paul Jones, who came with no such baggage and in addition to his bass playing was an arranger and an excellent keyboardist. Page contacted him and Jones came on board in place of Dreja.

Whether Page and Grant were legally in a position to sack Dreja is debatable. The ex-Yardbird has always insisted that he backed-out of his own accord but it is equally clear that Page actively encouraged him to do so. Whether he jumped or was given a helping nudge overboard, as Keith Shadwick in his excellent *Led Zeppelin: The Story of a Band and Their Music* 1968–1980 put it, Dreja's involvement was "allowed to wither". He turned to a new career in photography and remained on good terms with the band, taking the photograph that appeared on the back jacket of their debut album.

2

LED ZEPPELIN

2

Page also toyed briefly with the idea of a second rhythm guitarist, and according to some sources sounded out "Top" Topham, who had been The Yardbirds' original axeman in 1963 before Eric Clapton's arrival. If so, it was another idea that was allowed to wither. By early August, Page was convinced that he was close to finalising his ideal line-up and a press statement on August 5, 1968 announced that Plant and Jones were now members of the group. Bonham's signature followed a few days later. The New Yardbirds were in place – although the world would soon know them by a rather different name.

FROM THE YARDBIRDS TO LED ZEPPELIN

"The name wasn't as important as whether or not the music was going to be accepted. We could have called ourselves the Vegetables or the Potatoes." *Jimmy Page*

With a tour of Scandinavia due to start in the first week of September, the new band had to get up to speed in double-quick time. Fortunately, when The New Yardbirds, as they were still called, assembled in mid-August in a tiny basement rehearsal room in Gerrard Street in London's Chinatown, according to all four participants it was evident almost from the first note that it was going to work.

Jones had met Bonham and jammed with him when he had visited Page's home prior to agreeing to join, but for the bassist and Plant it was their first encounter. "We all met in this little room to see if we could stand each other," Jones recounts. "Robert had heard I was a session man and he was wondering who was going to turn up. I think he was half-expecting some old bloke with a pipe.

Then Jimmy said, 'Well, we're all here, what are we going to play?'"

After a few blank looks, Page asked his new colleagues if they knew the Yardbirds staple 'Train Kept A-Rollin''. They didn't, but he told them it was "a 12 bar with a riff on G" and with that most rudimentary of instruction, they were away. "He counted it out and the room just exploded," according to Jones. "There were lots of silly grins and 'Oh yeah man, this is it.' It was pretty bloody obvious from the first number that it was going to work."

'As Long As I Have You', a Garnet Mimms song which Plant had sung in Band of Joy, was next up. 'I Can't Quit You Baby', rearranged by Page and Plant from the Joan Baez version followed, and then Howlin' Wolf's 'Smokestack Lightnin'' (another old Yardbirds warhorse) and 'Dazed and Confused'.

An effusive Plant later claimed: "I've never been so turned on in all my life. Although we were all steeped in blues and R&B, we found in that first hour-and-a-half that we had our own identity. I could feel that something was happening within myself and to everyone else in the room. It felt like we'd found something that we had to really be careful of because we might lose it. The power of it was remarkable." Almost 40 years later he was still enthusing: "The rehearsals were really good. Bonzo opened up more and more and Jimmy had the swagger and the musicality. It was very exciting for me to be in the middle of that. I'd never experienced that in my life before."

Page concluded: "At the end of it, we knew that it was really happening, really electrifying." Even the fact that Plant and Bonham were penniless and when they left the rehearsal had to ask the guitarist for money for food and drink could not take the shine off the elation they were all feeling.

THE FIRST LIVE DATES AND RECORDING THE FIRST ALBUM: SEP–DEC 1968

"The ambition was intense and the delivery was intense, and where we were going was intense. Nobody knew where the fuck it was but we all knew that this power was ridiculous from the beginning." *Robert Plant*

The combination of two established musicians and two of raw and untried potential had proved so explosive at the first exploratory rehearsal that they could hardly wait to reconvene, this time over several days at Page's home in Pangbourne. A further and unexpected opportunity to get to know each other better musically presented itself at the end of August in the improbable form of a PJ Proby session, which Jones was committed to arranging. Responsible for booking a band,

he invited both Page and Bonham and even Plant turned up to bang a tambourine.

By the time they departed for the brief Scandinavian tour which was the last contractual obligation of the old Yardbirds, they had worked up a repertoire not too different from the set Page had played with that band in America earlier in the year, with a number of key additions that already looked forward to the material that would appear on the first Led Zeppelin album.

The band's first gig at the Gladsaxe Teen Club in Copenhagen, Denmark, took place on the afternoon of Saturday September 7,

Plant earns his chops in teen clubland in Copenhagen, while Jimmy merely plays them. The fact that topless go-go dancers were sometimes on the same bill means that both had to work very hard to make an impression

LED ZEPPELIN

2

SO WHERE DID THE ZEP NAME COME FROM?

"The name was coined by Keith Moon and it was originally going to be for the band that recorded 'Beck's Bolero' in 1966. But the thought of it all going on the road seemed horrific – they were quite a bunch of characters as you can probably imagine. The band never came about but we remembered the name and we asked Keith if we could use it."
John Paul Jones

Graf von Zeppelin, the airship man, whose descendant would later object to the use of his name by the band

"Led Zeppelin was a reference to a joke that falls flat. It could only have been chosen by Keith Moon, who was a complete lunatic. Since then it has gained something of a satirical flavour."
Robert Plant

"We'd considered Mad Dogs but I was quite keen about Led Zeppelin. It seemed to fit the bill. It had something to do with the expression about a bad joke going down like a lead balloon. It's a variation on that and there's a little of the Iron Butterfly light-and-heavy connotation. Richard Cole asked Keith Moon for his permission when we decided to use the name."
Jimmy Page

"Moon's joke was about going down like a lead zeppelin. In the circumstances the name seemed perfect, but I got rid of the 'a'. I was doodling in the office and it just looked better and I didn't want any confusion over the pronunciation in America."
Peter Grant

"There were several occasions during The Who's career when both Keith Moon and myself were going to leave the band. Once when we were in New York, I sat down with Keith and our chauffeur Richard Cole and tried to come up with possible names for the new band we planned to form. That's when I flashed on Led Zeppelin. I also came up with the idea for a first album jacket with a Zeppelin going down in flames. The reasons behind it are quite simple. In those days it was a favourite line among British rock bands. 'How did you go?' one band would ask another. 'Cor, we went down like a led zeppelin', they'd reply. Not long after Richard Cole went to work for Jimmy Page and Peter Grant and he must have told them the idea. But I was definitely the one who first thought of it. Later on Keith Moon claimed he came up with it, which made me very angry. When I heard that Jimmy Page was going to use it, I was a bit pissed off about it. Later on I didn't care that much. After all, they became an institution."
John Entwistle

1968, and was followed that evening by a second gig at the Brondby Pop Club in the same city. Still billed as The Yardbirds (or rather, The Yard Birds, as the Danish promoter apparently believed they were called), the following day they played two more gigs, supported by a troupe of topless go-go-dancers called The Ladybirds, before they travelled to Norway and Sweden for further gigs.

The set throughout the tour opened with 'Train Kept A-Rollin'' and also included 'Dazed and Confused', on which Page used a violin bow on his guitar, blues standards 'You Shook Me' and 'I Can't Quit You Baby', 'Communication Breakdown', 'How Many More Times' (built around a Howlin' Wolf number), the Page-Plant rearrangement of 'Babe I'm Gonna Leave You' and a number of covers, including Plant's long time favourite 'As Long As I Have You' by Garnet Mimms, Ben E. King's 'We're Gonna Groove', which featured a long organ introduction by Jones, and, somewhat surprisingly, 'Flames' by Elmer Gantry's Velvet Opera, an obscure British psychedelic band who had emerged in the summer of 1967 briefly to become John Peel favourites and achieve a certain notoriety when their second single 'Mary Jane' was banned by the BBC when it was pointed out that it was a slang term for marijuana.

The band knew that they could – and would – play better but the tour had gone well enough and Page and Plant had found a real chemistry as the singer's primeval wail fed off the guitarist's lead lines. "I wasn't trying to scat sing but I found the voice was imitating the guitar," Plant recalls. However, he also confesses, "In Scandinavia we were pretty green. It was very early days and we were tiptoeing with each other. We didn't have half the recklessness that for me became the whole joy of Led Zeppelin. It was a tentative start."

Page felt that Bonham was overplaying and gently reprimanded him, telling the drummer: "You've got to keep it a bit more simple than that." When his words had little effect, Peter Grant stepped in with a characteristically more blunt approach. "Behave yourself Bonham or you'll disappear," the burly manager told him.

Nevertheless, when they returned to Britain on September 18, they felt confidently ready to get straight into the studio and begin recording their debut album. They also had to deal with the issue of the band's name. The Scandinavian shows had been contracted to The Yardbirds before the split and so there had been some logic to using the old name. On their return, Page admitted to *Melody Maker's* Chris Welch, the band's first significant press champion, that he was "not sure whether to call them the Yardbirds or not" and also considered such variations as the 'New Yardbirds' and 'The Yardbirds featuring Jimmy Page'. In the course of the same interview, he noted: "The new chaps are only about 19 and full of enthusiasm. It was getting a bit of a trial in the old group", going on to describe the music as "blues, basically" and "more or less" similar in style to what The Yardbrids had been playing on their final American tour.

But if Page was happy to continue using the Yardbirds name, "the new chaps" were less keen and argued that they needed to differentiate themselves once and for all from the former band. There was also a potential legal problem. Although Relf and McCarty had signed over rights to the Yardbirds name to Page and Dreja back in early July, once the latter had withdrawn, ownership of the name became debatable again. Dreja owned a piece of the name via his stake in the company Yardbirds Ltd, which had been formed in 1965 well before Page's arrival.

LED ZEPPELIN

2

Without his approval, the new line-up would probably have lost any court action if it had called itself The Yardbirds, for unlike Relf and McCarty, the bass player had not signed over his rights. Indeed, he took the exact opposite course of action and instructed his solicitors to write to Peter Grant asking the new line-up to desist from using the old name.

Whether it was Dreja's legal threat or the persuasion of his colleagues, Page took the point. "We dropped the name because we felt it was working under false pretences," the guitarist told *Melody Maker* a couple of years later. "The thing had gone beyond where The Yardbirds had left-off," Plant added. "There was no point in calling it The Yardbirds." After rejecting such names as Mad Dogs and Whoopee Cushion (how history might have been so very different...), they settled upon Le(a)d Zeppelin – the name Keith Moon and/or John Entwistle had come up with two years earlier for the putative Beck-Page super-group – with a suitable amendment to the spelling by Peter Grant (see box on page 38).

On September 27, a week after their return from Scandinavia, the band went in to Olympic Studios in Barnes, west London, to begin recording their debut album, still booked in under the name The Yardbirds. Sessions continued throughout the first week of October, and with Glyn Johns engineering the entire album was completed in just 30 hours studio time. "We had begun developing the arrangements on the Scandinavian tour and I knew what sound I was looking for," said Page, who produced the album. "It just came together incredibly quickly." He added that he knew it was only 30 hours because he had paid the studio bill – a princely sum of just £1,782. The album was "pretty much a recording of the first show, which was why it had so many covers on it. That's all we had ready to play at

the time," according to Jones. In fact, despite the fact that the entire record was done and dusted in 30 hours, in addition to the nine tracks that made the album, the band recorded at least five further numbers, including 'Tribute to Bert Burns (Baby Come On Home)', dedicated to the songwriter and producer who had worked with The Drifters, Ben E. King and The Isley Brothers and had died in 1967; 'Flames', originally by Elmer Gantry's Velvet Opera (perhaps they were dissuaded from releasing this by the fact the Joe Loss Orchestra had also recorded a version); the Garnet Mimms/Band of Joy staple 'As Long As I Have You'; 'Fresh Garbage', a cover of a song by Spirit, one of the West Coast bands Plant so revered but about whom Page was distinctly unenthusiastic; and a version of The Yardbirds' 'Train Kept A-Rollin'', the very first song they had played at the inaugural rehearsal.

Of the additional tracks, only 'Tribute to Bert Burns' has ever been officially released, appearing under the title 'Baby Come On Home' on both the 1993 *Led Zeppelin* box and the 10-CD *Complete Studio Recordings* set issued the same year.

As soon as they had the album in the can, the new band played its first British dates amid continued confusion over what they were actually called. The exact date and venue of their debut UK performance also remains disputed and unverified. This lack of basic information is less surprising than at first might seem: with no album out and the old Yardbirds regarded as a spent force, the new band was seen as no big deal and on some of their initial dates they were paid as little as £75 a night. Hence the untried Page/Plant/Jones/Bonham line-up was pretty much allowed to road test their new show away from the glare of the media – and almost everyone else, come to that. "We couldn't get work in Britain," Grant later complained.

2

WITH a swing towards heavy music in recent months, Led Zeppelin, formerly the Yardbirds, have the potential to become important in this field. Guitarist Jimmy Page, John Paul Jones (bass) and John Bonham (drs) provide a powerful and often imaginative backing for Robert Plant's vocals. Plant and Page particularly appear to have a good rapport going and this could emerge as a prominent feature of Led Zeppelin. They may well be successful in the U.S.—TONY WILSON.

The Melody Maker *announcement of the new band's formation was the first in a number of brilliant PR releases masterminded by Peter Grant. He moved the whole idea of promoting a band way beyond the traditional chart- or singles-based paradigm*

"It seemed to be a laugh to people that we were getting the group together and working the way we were."

According to Dave Lewis and Simon Pallett's book, *Led Zeppelin: The Concert File*, the first UK appearance of the new band may have come at the Mayfair Ballroom, Newcastle, on October 4. Certainly, the concert was listed in the local paper as "The Yardbirds featuring Jimmy Page", but no review appeared and whether the gig ever took place, nobody seems to know or remember. Another contender is Guildford University, at least if you believe the plaque which Jimmy Page unveiled there in 2003 which reads: "THIS PLAQUE IS TO COMMEMORATE THE DEBUT PERFORMANCE OF LED ZEPPELIN, UNIVERSITY HALL, OCTOBER 15, 1968." In fact, it seems certain that their appearance came 10 days later on October 25 and was therefore made somewhat less historic by the fact that by then the band had appeared at London's legendary Marquee Club on October 18 (billed perversely as "The British debut of the Yardbirds") and the following

night at Liverpool University (where the gig was billed as "the last-ever appearance of the Yardbirds"). The first gig at which they were officially billed as Led Zeppelin took place a week later on October 26 in the improbable surroundings of Bristol Boxing Club.

The new group received a significant snub when Led Zeppelin were touted for a slot in the *Rolling Stones Rock'and Roll Circus* television spectacular in December 1968, but were personally vetoed by Mick Jagger, who took one listen to the band's tape and opted for Jethro Tull instead. It was just another example of the prejudice towards the new band, of which both Page and Peter Grant bitterly complained. Perhaps this early slight also contributed to what would become an ongoing rivalry throughout the 1970s when Zeppelin and the Stones vied with each other for the title 'the biggest rock 'n' roll band in the world' (see box page ?).

More memorable, at least for Robert Plant, was a gig at London's Roundhouse on November 9, at which "The Yardbirds now known as Led Zeppelin" (as they were this time billed) were supported by one of his

LED ZEPPELIN

2

heroes, John Lee Hooker. It was the perfect wedding present for a 20-year-old self-confessed blues nut: earlier that same day he had married his eight months pregnant girlfriend, Maureen, although his joy nearly turned to despair when his car broke down *en route* between registry office and venue and he almost missed the gig. Yet further evidence of Led Zeppelin's early inability to land prestige gigs in Britain came with an appearance at the utterly unsuitable Bridge Place Country Club near Canterbury, Kent, on December 13, although the band might have been amused by a concert flyer which tweely announced: "Ladies may come unescorted if they wish." At this early stage, Led Zeppelin's lock-up-your-daughters reputation had clearly still to reach the county they call 'the garden of England'.

While Led Zeppelin honed their live chops around Britain's university campuses and country clubs, Peter Grant was even busier on their behalf behind the scenes, setting up a record deal and organising their first American tour. After first establishing Superhype Inc. to oversee the band's publishing, at the end of October he flew to America to finalise a deal with Atlantic Records – not for The Yardbirds, as he had originally planned and anticipated, but for a new and fabulous beast now called Led Zeppelin.

Grant had already struck a handshake deal with Atlantic for the band under its old name in early August. But this time he had not only a new name to sell, but a copy of Led Zeppelin's already-completed debut album to play to Atlantic founder Ahmet Ertegun and his right-hand man, Jerry Wexler. To make an album without first signing a record deal was an unusual way of working, particularly at the time. But Page had been adamant that he wanted to

finance the making of the LP himself and to present it to the record company on a take-it-or-leave-it basis. The more usual practice of accepting a record company advance to fund making the record would have conceded to the label's A&R department a say in the material, the sound and the production – and, as the guitarist put it, he wanted "artistic control in a vice-like grip". In particular, Page was determined that the new band was to be purely album-led and was adamant that there was to be no repeat of the ludicrous, and at times farcical, search for hit singles that had tarnished The Yardbirds 'reputation at the hands of Mickie Most.

Zeppelin's case was no doubt helped by the fact that Atlantic had just lost its biggest British signing in Cream, who had disbanded and were playing their farewell concerts even as the negotiations were taking place. But one listen to the tapes was more than enough to convince the astute Ertegun that, as Keith Shadwick rather cleverly puts it, here was a band that had that "elusive combination of musical quality and sheer raw excitement that would translate to consumer reaction".

According to Grant, there was still some jockeying when Atlantic said they wanted Tom Dowd to remix the record, but after Page had met Dowd and persuaded him that technically he knew what he was doing, the point was not pushed and Led Zeppelin were allowed to establish the unusual if not unique precedent for the time that they would enjoy total control of their own recordings without label interference. By the time the negotiations had finished, the forceful Grant had turned his original handshake deal into a written five-year contract, a £200,000 advance and a royalty rate said at the time to be the highest ever paid.

JIMMY PAGE'S BOW

The notion that Jimmy Page was the first to play the guitar with a violin bow has always been challenged by fans of The Creation, a London-based mod band of the 1960s who then joined the psychedelic revolution. The band's guitarist Eddie Phillips, who once famously described their music as "red with purple flashes" and allegedly turned down an invitation from Pete Townshend to join The Who, used a violin bow on his guitar on the band's 1966 single 'Making Time' to create a venomous wall of sound.

Page refutes any suggestion that he copied the technique from Phillips and claims that it was suggested to him by a session violinist around the same time. He used it on stage with The Yardbirds on 'I'm a Man' and 'I'm Confused' (later retitled 'Dazed and Confused') and in the studio on the 1967 album *Little Games*, on the tracks 'Glimpses' and 'Tinker, Tailor, Soldier, Sailor.'

He developed it with Led Zeppelin, using it in conjunction with an Echoplex to throw out a wall of reverberating sound, used to particularly devastating effect on 'Dazed and Confused', a showpiece of the band's set from their first gigs through until 1975. The bow was also used in early shows on

'How Many More Times'. After 'Dazed and Confused' was dropped, Page continued to use the violin bow on stage during guitar solos on 'Achilles Last Stand' and 'In the Evening'.

In an odd coda to the Page-versus-Phillips saga, The Creation's second guitarist Kenny Pickett became Zeppelin's roadie on their first tour of America in early 1969.

THE FIRST LIVE REVIEW: TURN DOWN THE VOLUME

"Led Zepplin (sic), the regrouped Yardbirds, made their Marquee debut last week. They are now very much a heavy group, with singer Robert Plant holding his own against a powerful backing trio. Amp troubles didn't help them on this particular occasion but there seemed to be a tendency for too much volume, which inevitably defeats musical definition.

One of the best numbers of the set was 'Days Of Confusion' (sic) featuring interesting interplay of Plant's voice and Page's guitar, on which he used a violin bow, creating an unusual effect. Drummer Bonham is forceful, perhaps too much so, and generally there appears to be a need for Led Zeppelin to cut down on volume a bit."

Tony Wilson,
Melody Maker,
December 14, 1968

LED ZEPPELIN

2

Chateau Marmont, high above Sunset Boulevard, West Hollywood, beloved resort of fading Hollywood stars, and by the 1970s of aspiring rockers

ZEP TAKE AMERICA
1968–1969

"It was just a joke in England. We really had a bad time. They just wouldn't accept anything new. We were given a chance in America."
Jimmy Page

It must have come as something of a relief to Led Zeppelin when they flew out of grey, drab Britain two days before Christmas 1968, bound for the sunshine of California in preparation for their first American tour. They knew they were on to something but their poorly paid, sparsely attended, low-grade smattering of British concerts had been met with only polite applause

and little media interest. Mick Jagger had snubbed them and nobody seemed interested. If the music press paid them any attention at all, it tended to be of the sneering 'they're just a hype' kind.

What a contrast to America, where their record company had already put out a press release about their new signing, predicting Led Zeppelin would be "the next group to reach the heights achieved by Cream and Jimi Hendrix". A grand claim, for sure, but the size of the band's advance said that it wasn't just hype: Atlantic believed it, even if Britain remained sceptical.

Crucially, the band were coming to believe it, too. Jones, Plant and Bonham were all married yet they batted not an eyelid

Vanilla Fudge, looking good, and not looking notorious, but now largely forgotten

when Peter Grant told them they would be spending Christmas away from home. "It's a sacrifice. But there's going to be a pay-off," Page reportedly told them.

Despite his disappointment at not spending Christmas with his month-old baby daughter Carmen Jane, for Plant with his passion for Californian music and his romantic, wide-eyed attachment to the West Coast hippie ideal, it seemed as if he was being offered a free ticket to the promised land. "It was the first time I'd even had a passport, let alone the first time I'd been to America," he recalled in 2005. "To get off the plane in Los Angeles and to go with Bonzo to stay at the Chateau Marmont on Sunset Strip was amazing."

He relished the opportunity to taste at first hand a wild and bohemian lifestyle he had only read about. "We hooked up with Terry Reid and we ended up in the suite Burl Ives had just vacated. Down the corridor were the GTOs, Wild Man Fischer and all those Sunset Strip characters of the time. Rodney Bigenheimer was making coffee. There was all this stuff going on all day and night and me and Bonzo walked in with a TV dinner in a tin-foil tray to put in the oven while we watched *Hawaii Five-O*. It was a complete gas and all that dour Englishness had just disappeared into this powder-blue, post-Summer-of-

LED ZEPPELIN

2

Love Californian sunshine. There were even showers in the hotel rooms! Within 48 hours of arriving, I was just teleported."

But there was work to do. According to Plant, Jones and Page bankrolled that first US tour out of their own pockets (despite the 'Led Wallet' nickname Page came to acquire) and its pared-down nature was in stark contrast to later tours when they flew around America in their own privately-hired jet. "We went around just the four of us with one roadie, who was Kenny Pickett from The Creation, and the tour manager Richard Cole. It was really very basic," Plant recalled.

The band's first gig took place on Boxing Day in Denver, Colorado, supporting Vanilla Fudge and Spirit (whose song 'Fresh Garbage' was a prominent feature of Zeppelin's set). The band's name did not appear on the concert posters but they were warmly enough received. A colder reception awaited five days later in Portland, as the band spent New Year's Eve driving through

blizzards of snow as they attempted to reach Seattle airport to catch a flight to L.A. The weather was so bad that the roads were officially closed and at one point tour manager Cole, who was at the wheel, was forced to pull over by state police and told to discontinue their journey. Once the police had gone, Cole drove on regardless over treacherous mountain passes and wildly swaying suspension bridges and Plant and Bonham were convinced on at least two occasions during the journey that they were going to die. When they eventually arrived in Seattle the weather had shut down the airport and, to add insult to injury, Bonham and Plant, still 20-years old, were refused drinks at the bar because they were under age.

When they got to L.A. for a four-night stint at the Whiskey a Go Go with Alice Cooper, the rigours of the journey had

out there, and heavy, nevertheless failed to rise to the challenge of the Zeppelin laid Page low with a fever. Scheduled to play two sets a night, the guitarist gamely struggled through the first set each evening with a temperature of 104 but the second proved too much and the band's pay was docked accordingly.

The turning point in their fortunes came when the band moved up the coast to San Francisco for four shows at Bill Graham's legendary Fillmore West with Country Joe and The Fish and Taj Mahal. Page was feeling better and Plant was in seventh heaven playing in a city which he had spent 1967's "Summer of Love" dreaming about from the distant greyness of the West Midlands, and for the first time they were allowed longer sets, which provided ample room for the experimentation and improvisation that became the band's forte.

On bootlegs of the San Francisco gigs you can almost hear their confidence growing with each song. "We were playing all right before, but from that point it was really gelling," Page later recalled. "The rest of the boys had gotten more accustomed to the American audiences; they had never been to America before and they were able to gauge things a little better. They felt they could relax more on stage, so right there is when it started happening. From then on we could see that there was some sort of reaction to us. We got standing ovations for each set for the four nights at Fillmore West." Indeed, so well did they go down that by the third night an ecstatic Plant was telling the audience: "We've decided we're going to come and live here, because you're so nice!"

The Fillmore shows also saw some radical innovations to the set, including the introduction of 'Killin' Floor', which swiftly developed into 'The Lemon Song', and it was now evident that some serious momentum was gathering behind Led Zeppelin. "It felt

like a vacuum and we'd come to fill it. You could feel something was happening," Page noted. "First this row, then that row, it was like a tornado and it went rolling across the country."

By the time they hit the East Coast in the last week of January 1969? for gigs in Boston, Philadelphia and New York, the balloon had gone up. Zeppelin were playing like champions and over two nights at New York's Fillmore East, where they were supporting Iron Butterfly, they just blew the headline act away. At the Boston Tea Party on January 26, the band played their usual hour-long set, including everything from their debut album – and the crowd just kept on demanding more. They ended up playing for another three hours, reprising their own material alongside just about every other song they knew, from Beatles covers and Elvis favourites to Chuck Berry and Little Richard songs. According to Jones, when they finally came off, Peter Grant was crying and hugging them. "It was then that we realised just what Led Zeppelin was going to become," the bassist told *NME*'s Nick Kent in 1973.

By the time the tour ended in Miami in mid-February, the band's debut album was out. It entered the *Billboard* chart at 99, jumped to 40 and then to 28, before finally entering the top ten in May. In total, it stayed on the chart for 73 consecutive weeks. No single was released from the album, mainstream radio play was minimal and many of the album reviews struck a distinctly sour note, led by *Rolling Stone*, whose John Mendelsohn sneered that if Led Zeppelin wanted to succeed "they will have to find a producer, editor and some material worthy of their collective talents".

The live reviews from those who had actually seen them play were far better. On the evidence of their shows in Boston, the

LED ZEPPELIN

PETER GRANT: THE MAN WHO LED ZEPPELIN

At a party in Los Angeles in 1973, Peter Grant introduced himself to Bob Dylan as the manager of Led Zeppelin. "I don't come to you with my problems, do I? " was Dylan's only reply. His terse response was a reference to the band's already legendary commitment to industrial-scale on-the-road debauchery, but rather than tearing his hair out over his band's behaviour, Grant not only indulged Zeppelin's excesses but gave the impression that he rather enjoyed the mayhem and was not averse to joining in on occasion. It would then fall to him as manager to apologise for the carnage, placate the hotel management, square the local police and pay for the damage by peeling off prodigious quantities of crisp, new, 100 dollar bills.

Born on April 5, 1935 in South Norwood, Surrey, Grant was a tough wheeler-dealer who you messed with at your peril and whose fame as a manager has probably only been exceeded by Colonel Tom Parker and Brian Epstein. His early life was poverty-stricken and after being evacuated in World War Two, he left school at the age of 13 to work in a sheet metal

factory. His first steps into showbusiness came as a stagehand at the now long-demolished Empire Theatre in Croydon and by the mid-1950s he was a doorman and bouncer at the 2 I's coffee bar in Soho, famous as the cradle that spawned such early British rockers as Cliff Richard, Adam Faith and Tommy Steele.

A spell as a professional wrestler under the name Prince Mario Alassio led to a new career as a bit-part actor and film stuntman, and in the late 1950s and early 1960s he appeared in minor roles in such films as A Night to Remember, The Guns of Navarone and Cleopatra. His size led to a regular gig as Robert Morley's double in a number of films and he also appeared in such popular television series as The Saint

The Yardbirds reinvented, post-Mickie Most, with the energetic Grant (second from left) sporting an interesting moustache. Apparently unembarrassed by this, the band (left to right Jim McCarty, Chris Dreja, Keith Relf and Jimmy Page) sort out cravats for the next show

and Dixon of Dock Green. To supplement his income, he ploughed the money from his acting career into his own transport business, ferrying such groups as The Shadows on package tours of the British Isles. In 1963, he was hired by promoter Don Arden as a tour manager, working for such visiting US artists as Bo Diddley, The Everly Brothers, Little Richard, Chuck Berry and Eddie Cochran. Using his prowess as a wrestler to

2

good effect, on one occasion in Rome he laid out six Italian policemen intent on beating the shit out of Little Richard. Within a year he had started his own management company and taken charge of the careers of The Nashville Teens, The New Vaudeville Band, Jeff Beck and Terry Reid, running his management company from the same office at 155 Oxford Street in London's West End as his friend and partner, the record producer Mickie Most.

In January 1967 he began a long association with Jimmy Page when, on Most's recommendation, The Yardbirds' manager Simon Napier-Bell asked Grant to take over the group. Unlike many managers, Grant liked to travel with his charges, using his intimidating physical presence to ensure that promoters paid his band on time and in full. Although he made The Yardbirds more money than they had ever earned before, he couldn't keep the band together and when they fell apart in July 1968, he set about helping Page to put together Led Zeppelin. "I

always had the most respect and admiration for Jimmy," Grant later told author Ritchie Yorke. "I felt that I was closer to him than any of the other members of The Yardbirds and I had immense faith in his talent and ability. I

"The man who made it all possible. Let me tell you he never likes to be in group pictures, he doesn't like playing soccer with us, but what a manager – what a member of the group."

ROBERT PLANT ON PETER GRANT,
EARLS COURT, MAY 1975

just wanted to do whatever he felt was best for him at the time."

In effect, Grant became Led Zeppelin's fifth member and was integral to the group's commercial success.

He began by negotiating a lucrative five-year recording contract with Atlantic Records, set up the band's publishing company Superhype and encouraged Zeppelin to concentrate on albums and live shows and to ignore the singles market and television appearances, all of which only enhanced the group's mystique. He was also instrumental in 1974 in establishing Zeppelin's own record company Swan Song, going on to manage several of the acts signed to the label, including Bad Company and Maggie Bell, although he turned down an invitation to manage Queen.

Always happier when he could be on the road with his band rather than being stuck behind a desk, stories of his tenacious and often belligerent defence of Led Zeppelin's interests are legendary. The famous scene in the film The Song Remains the Same in which he gets tough with concert staff over the sale of unauthorised merchandise was tame in comparison with some of his exploits. He was arrested on at least

2

three occasions defending the interests of his band and several times he had a gun pulled on him by an irate promoter or agent. To him it was simply all part of the job.

Spotting someone holding a microphone in the audience at a concert in Vancouver in March 1970, he dragged the bootlegger back stage, smashed his equipment and delivered a beating designed to discourage him from ever repeating his misdemeanours. Except that it wasn't a tape pirate at all but a government official checking decibel levels. Grant was charged with assault and for a while was unable to return to Canada. On another occasion, he took an axe to some bootleggers, fortunately showing enough self-restraint not to use it on their persons after chopping up their recording equipment.

Occasionally he complained to tour manager Richard Cole that the band were out of control. But most of the time he regarded the destruction of hotel rooms and other associated mayhem as a legitimate way of letting off steam after a high-octane gig and never quibbled about paying up for the damage. Throwing TVs out of windows in particular became part of the routine. When Grant came to settle

Peter Grant: 'How on earth do you follow Led Zeppelin?'

the bill after Zeppelin had wrecked several suites at the Edgewater hotel in Seattle in June 1972, the manager admitted he had always harboured a secret desire to hurl a TV out of a window. Grant promptly peeled off an extra 500 dollars and said: "Have one on us."

His methods may have been unconventional but his stewardship was key in effecting a shift in the balance of financial power within the music industry in favour of the artists. Zeppelin not only made more money than any band in rock history but Grant ensured that they retained most of it, too. Taking on the American promoters who for years had grown fat on 50 per cent of concert takings, Grant insisted on a preposterous 90 per cent for the band. As Zeppelin had become the biggest draw in America, the grumbling promoters had little choice

but reluctantly to agree.

Away from Zeppelin's on-the-road madness, Grant was a contented countryman, living deep in rural Sussex with his wife and two children in a moated house. When they divorced, Grant raised the kids alone and moved to genteel Eastbourne. Eventually the years of pressure and hard living took their toll. When the group split following John Bonham's death in 1980, Grant seemed at a loss and was fighting heroin addiction. His long association with Jimmy Page ended in 1983 and he disappeared into virtual retirement. It was "a period of blackness" he later said, but he never got involved in rock management again. But then as he said in one of his last interviews before suffering a fatal heart attack on November 21, 1995, "How on earth do you follow Led Zeppelin?"

2

city's leading critic declared that Zeppelin were to rock "what Formula One cars are to road racing", while *Billboard* reckoned the way they had destroyed Iron Butterfly at the Fillmore East earmarked them as "the next big super group". The record was selling purely on the word-of-mouth enthusiasm generated by that first tour. "I think what did it for us was the live thing," Page observed. "We were unknown, we did our number and the word got out that we were worth seeing." And they now had a reputation to take back home to a previously uninterested Britain.

BACK TO BLIGHTY: FROM HEROES TO ZEROS

"They returned like victors. They were the hottest new act in the States. They had conquered America. And all of a sudden they were back on the English circuit playing to 400 people." *Led Zeppelin tour manager Richard Cole*

Strange as it may seem, when the band returned to Britain there were mutterings if not open doubts over Robert Plant's position in the band. The singer, who during the first American tour had earned the nickname 'Percy' after the British TV gardener Percy Thrower, was being singled out for criticism in some of the more negative reviews of the band, led again by *Rolling Stone*, which insultingly dubbed him "a pretty soul-belter who can do a good spade imitation".

According to Richard Cole, such comments also began to gnaw away at Page, who came to question whether he had made the right decision over his choice of singer. "It was a very touch-and-go thing whether Robert would even be in the group after that first

tour, because he didn't quite seem to make it up to Page's expectation," the tour manager recalled later. "At the time there was a possibility he wouldn't do another tour. That's the truth." Plant has also confessed to having his own self-doubts. "I was very intimidated," he recalled almost 30 years later. "Maybe I had a complex, maybe I was just neurotic or paranoid but I thought, 'This is all too much. Am I really here? Do I belong in this sketch?'"

To his credit, Page has always loyally denied in public that he ever had any doubts and has never offered anything but the highest praise for his colleague's vocal abilities, even when Plant himself has been highly self-critical of his early efforts. "I was very uncomfortable on stage and didn't know what to do with myself,'" the singer admitted to this writer in 2005. "I was really taken by the music but I was pleased when I was able to start crafting it a bit more. At the time I didn't even know what craft was. I was overwhelmed by it. There were much better singers at the time who could have brought it on home in a different way. If there had been Steve Marriott or Steve Winwood or Terry Reid, all of whom I considered to be far better singers than me, it would have had a different personality and the band would have gone a different way."

In particular, Plant has been highly critical of some of his vocal mannerisms on the band's debut album (see interview page ?).

But when the comments were reported to Jimmy Page, he offered this sterling defence of his old colleague: "I know he's not happy with the ad libs on *Led Zep* I, but I think he should be really pleased with his vocal approach. He was performing in a very inspired way, like everyone else in the band. What he did was really fitting, in terms of

2

where we were going. It was an essential element. And millions would agree with me rather than with him on how great his singing was on those first couple of records."

If Plant's position was ever in any serious doubt, the moment of crisis passed swiftly as the band settled down to

The Disc and Music Echo chart for April 1969 makes interesting reading, with the band who Zeppelin would effectively succeed, Cream, posthumously heading a field heavy with musical scores and samplers

promoting their debut album, which received a belated British release on March 28, 1969. It entered the chart two weeks later and stayed there for the next 79 weeks, peaking at number six.

If some of the reviews were negative and dwelled on the alleged hype surrounding the band, a few perceptive critics recognised that *Led Zeppelin I* represented a significant milestone in the development of British rock music. The ever-loyal Chris Welch chipped in with a brace of encouraging reviews, one in *Punch* which hailed it as the rock album of the year and another in *Melody Maker* under the headline: "JIMMY PAGE TRIUMPHS: LED ZEPPELIN IS A GAS."

In the underground magazine *Oz*, Felix Dennis wrote: "Very occasionally an LP record is released that defies immediate categorization, because it's so obviously a turning point in rock music that only time proves capable of shifting it into perspective. This Led Zeppelin album is like that." Even more presciently, he added: "Of course, as a result of this album we'll lose the group to the States and almost certainly within months the *Melody Maker* letters page will headline 'Is Page better than God?'" The band later came to play a small and unwitting part in the infamous *Oz* obscenity trial at the Old Bailey in 1971, when the line "I'd love to meet a chick who could fuck like Led Zeppelin I, but she'd wear me out in a week" was seized upon by the prosecution as evidence of the magazine's moral depravity.

The band promoted the album with BBC radio sessions for John Peel's *Top Gear* show and an R&B programme on the World Service presented by Plant's old partner, Alexis Korner, as well as virtually the only serious TV appearances of Zeppelin's career, for Swedish and German networks and on a new BBC2 show called *How Late It Is*, on which they deputised at the last minute for the Flying Burrito Brothers and played 'Communication Breakdown' and 'Dazed and Confused'.

Another short Scandinavian tour in March ended in near disaster with an emergency landing at Stansted on their return flight to Britain and the band dramatically exiting the plane via safety chutes. In an horrific imitation of the burning Zeppelin on the front cover of their debut album that might have spooked more superstitious souls, an engine had caught fire. Yet that same night Led Zeppelin were back on stage at the Marquee to commence a series of British dates which found them playing such venues as the Toby Jug, Tolworth, and Bromley Technical College. Fees were risible, one gig guaranteeing them just £60. The halls were mostly small but full, and the crowd reaction was increasingly enthusiastic, with the exception of a disastrous appearance at the Top Rank Ballroom, Cardiff, where an out-dated dress code demanded everyone wore tie-and-jacket. Stewards even attempted to apply the rule to the group itself and they were initially refused entry for being inappropriately attired. When they were eventually allowed to play, their set was brought to an abrupt end when the revolving stage whisked them out of sight, halfway through 'How Many More Times'. The set was to last exactly 45 minutes and they were not even extended the courtesy of being allowed to finish the number, as they were replaced by an inane disc jockey playing that week's top twenty.

During the first two weeks of April when not travelling between gigs, they began recording their second album at Olympic Studios, Barnes. Among the new compositions swiftly completed were 'What

Is and What Should Never Be' and 'Whole Lotta Love'. Yet once again, it must have come as something of a relief when in mid-April they left behind uptight, stuffy, class-ridden, jacket-and-tie Britain for their second tour of America, where their debut album was now flying.

LOVE & THEFT: ZEP'S DEBT TO THE BLUES

Fans will tell you that Led Zeppelin took their blues influences and transformed them into something new and unique that was all their own. Detractors argue that they robbed and stole from the blues, and were little more than a bunch of thieving magpies who seldom gave credit to those whose work they plundered. A more objective and neutral judgement would be to state that much of the band's greatest material borrowed from blues idioms, both musically and lyrically – a long-standing practice among the great bluesmen themselves, after all – but that sometimes they were strangely careless about citing the source of their inspiration. The band itself responded to the criticisms by pointing out that much of the blues derived from traditional sources and, in any case, their performances were totally different to the originals. "Bluesmen borrowed from each other constantly and it's the same with jazz; it's even happened to us," Page observed to *Guitar World* in 1998. "As a musician I'm only a product of my influences." Of course, the disputes arise over how carefully those influences are credited and where the lines are drawn between influence, borrowing and outright theft.

Zep's blues-drenched debut album included two Willie Dixon songs (both credited) and the traditional 'Babe I'm Gonna Leave You', which they rearranged

LED ZEPPELIN

2

from a version by Joan Baez. Another track, 'How Many More Times', which was listed as a group composition, lent heavily on Albert King's 'The Hunter' but the band could reasonably argue that King's song had, in turn, been based on an earlier Howlin' Wolf number.

The controvesy over the band's appropriation of the blues really started with *Led Zeppelin II*. The album included their signature tune, 'Whole Lotta Love', which borrowed liberally from the lyrics of Willie Dixon's 'You Need Love'. Yet unlike the same author's 'You Shook Me' and 'I Can't Quit You Baby' on the first album, this time the song was listed as a band composition, and Dixon failed even to get a mention. He sued, and Led Zeppelin settled out of court. Equally controversial was 'The Lemon Song'. Heavily based on 'Killin' Floor' by Howlin' Wolf, it also borrowed lyrically from Robert Johnson with its infamous "squeeze my lemon" sequence, and from Albert King's 'Cross Cut Saw Blues'. That the songwriting credit was given to Plant, Page, Jones and Bonham provoked a protest from Jewel Music, the publishers of 'Killin' Floor'; it resulted in another settlement, and a change in the songwriting credit on future copies of the album. A third song on the record, the blues-rocker 'Bring It On Home', was lifted from Sonny Boy Williamson's track of the same name.

By 1970's *Led Zeppelin III* the blues was still providing a powerful source of inspiration and material. The album included 'Gallows Pole', a trad folk tune that was popularized by Lead Belly, although Page apparently based the group's take on it on a version by Fred Gerlach. Another song on the same album, 'Hat's Off to (Roy) Harper', a tribute to the maverick English folk singer Roy Harper, borrowed from the Bukka White

tune 'Shake 'Em On Down'. *Led Zeppelin IV*, which appeared in 1971, included 'When the Levee Breaks', based on the 1929 recording by Memphis Minnie and Kansas Joe McCoy, and appeared with the hybrid writing credit Page, Plant, Jones, Bonham – and Minnie.

Even in the middle of their rock 'n' roll excess, the blues remained a source for much of Led Zeppelin's work. 1975's *Physical Graffiti* featured a version of 'In My Time of Dying', while *Presence*, released the year after, included 'Nobody's Fault But Mine'. On the record it was credited to Page and Plant, although the latter cheerfully admitted when they played it live that it had been written by Blind Willie Johnson.

The posthumously released album *Coda* featured further blues songs, this time properly credited to BB King and Willie Dixon. Since the band broke up, Plant, in particular, has remained a staunch advocate of the blues, and is an enthusiastic collector with an encyclopaedic knowledge of the most obscure recordings and artists to match.

RECOMMENDED LISTENING:

The Early Blues Roots of Led Zeppelin (Catfish)
In the absence of an official compilation of Zeppelin's blues material, this collection of the original source material from which they drew and/or stole makes fascinating listening and includes inspirational tracks by Memphis Minnie, Sonny Boy Williamson, Blind Willie Johnson, Robert Johnson, Bukka White, Lead Belly and Big Bill Broonzy.

FROM SUCCESS
TO EXCESS
1969–1970

3

"Led Zeppelin is probably the most aggressive, masculine rock group anywhere. They batter at the mind and ear, insisting they will penetrate."

LIVE REVIEW IN *THE EDMONTON JOURNAL*, MAY 1969

FROM SUCCESS TO EXCESS

3

1969–1970

In what had seemed, to both the band and their critics, an amazingly short time, Zeppelin had moved from the shadows of presumptuous obscurity to the limelight. Their almost immediate success in the States, while being coolly received in the UK, was a mirror image to the Beat Boom bands of the previous generation. Suddenly, they were the hot ticket, with a follow-up album to beat all follow-up albums to boot.

Although it was less than four months since an untried and rather green Led Zeppelin had flown to America for their first tour, it was a very different band that returned to the US in April 1969. The first album was climbing the *Billboard* chart and there was a buzz about them, at least in all of the cities where they had already played. They were no longer the support but were now either headliners in their own right, or sharing top billing with such established acts as Delaney & Bonnie and Three Dog Night, as 27 shows across North America were crammed into a six-week tour.

They were further buoyed by the new material they had started recording for *Led Zeppelin II*. Although their hectic schedule meant they would not finish recording the album until August, it was already obvious to all concerned that their sophomore effort was shaping up to be a classic. There was now a strutting, cocksure swagger about the group, both on and off stage, and Plant in particular seemed to have shed his earlier

insecurities. If they had been tentative on the first tour, they now believed not only that they were the loudest, horniest, most explosive rock band on the planet but that it was only a matter of time before the rest of the world knew it, too. With such an attitude, it was on this tour that some of the most outrageous incidents in the infamous catalogue of their on-the-road excesses took place and their reputation as 'the hammer of the gods' was first forged.

"We were hot and on our way up and nobody was watching too closely," tour manager Richard Cole later recalled. "All the Led Zeppelin depravity took place the first two years in an alcoholic fog. Seemingly overnight, we found ourselves in a position to do almost anything we wanted and there seemed to be a tidal wave of free-spirited girls who were always cooperative and compliant."

Much of the debauchery was chronicled years later in his book by a boastful Cole but more damagingly, it was also observed

LED ZEPPELIN

at the time by Ellen Sander, a journalist with *Life* magazine who went on the road with the band. She was so disgusted with their behaviour that she refused to give the band the publicity of the planned cover story. Her editors backed her and pulled the piece and her observations eventually appeared in a book in 1973, in which she accused the band of "failing to keep their behaviour up to a basic human level". She also recorded Page's callous attitude to groupies ("Girls come around and pose like starlets, teasing and acting haughty. If you humiliate them a bit they tend to come on all right after that. Everybody knows what they come for.") and detailed such stories as a plot to gang bang a pair of groupies and then stuff their orifices with cream doughnuts. She also claimed that two members of the group ripped her dress and tried to rape her before Peter Grant arrived in the nick of time and pulled them off. "If you walk inside the cages of the zoo, you get to see the animals close up, stroke the captive pelts and mingle with the energy behind the mystique," she wrote of her encounter with Zeppelin. "You also get to smell the shit firsthand."

Another who saw the hooliganism and excess at first hand was Pamela des Barres, a leading groupie known at the time as Miss Pamela. "As much as I loved Zeppelin, they kind of fucked things up in L.A.," she later observed. "Something about their energy really altered the *joie de vivre* of the scene. They thought they could get away with anything and they could, because everybody wanted to get near them. They were very debauched and the girls got younger and more willing to do anything. It got to be incredibly sick."

On their return to Britain they opened a short tour supported by Blodwyn Pig and The Liverpool Scene in Birmingham on June

Pamela des Barres, or "Miss Pamela" of the GTOs, one of a number of groupies who ligged with the Zep in LA, with Page outside Bingenheimer's English Disco

13, 1969 and reached a wider audience with no fewer than three sessions for BBC's Radio One that same month. Much bootlegged over the years, the best of the radio broadcasts were eventually officially released on the double CD *BBC Sessions* in 1997 (see page? for an account of the material).

Their two-week sojourn in Britain, during which time they conducted further work on *Led Zeppelin II*, ended over the last weekend of June with performances at the Bath Blues Festival and the Pop Proms at the Albert Hall, the band's biggest two UK appearances to date. They also garnered some of their best British reviews. "When Zeppelin came on and played at a good ten times the volume of everyone else, the audience very nearly freaked completely," *Disc* reported of the Albert Hall show. "They stormed the stage, danced in the aisles and the boxes and were screaming so hard that the band did three encores. Jimmy Page, ex-Yardbird, who's got together one of the most exciting live bands playing anywhere right now, blew some really mean and fine guitar solos." Nick Logan in the *NME* concluded: "It is boggling that in a matter of months they have achieved such a high degree of musicianship and become one of the biggest crowd-pullers around."

The tour and the radio appearances helped propel the band's debut album into the top five of the British chart. But the weekend after the Albert Hall, they were back in America again for another barnstorming two-month coast-to-coast stint and more off-stage excess – and in one instance on-stage excess when an inebriated Bonham ran on stage and stripped naked during a performance by the Jeff Beck Group at the Flushing Meadows festival, New York. He only escaped arrest when Peter Grant rugby-tackled him and then hid him from the police in a locked dressing room. Along with the booze, the endless supply of groupies also helped them unwind between shows and during the band introductions one night on stage in Toronto, Plant let the cat out of the bag when he candidly announced: "On lead guitar and as many chicks as he can find...Jimmy Page!" At the end of the tour, the guitarist went into New York studio to finish mixing *Led Zeppelin II*, before taking a holiday in Spain and Morocco while the other three members enjoyed the group's first proper break of the year with their families. Back home, the wild, out-of-control, groupie-abusing rock 'n' roll studs found little difficulty, it seems, in transforming themselves back into quiet and respectable husbands and fathers.

Virtually none of the material from the forthcoming new album had been played live during summer 1969 but after their hard-earned break, Grant lined up another assault on American concert halls to coincide with the release of *Led Zeppelin II* in October 1969. Unlike the debut album, which had

been recorded in such a tight time frame, work on the second album had sprawled over a period of almost six months, with songs written in hotel rooms while on the road and recorded in snatched studio sessions between live dates. Plant called it a "crazy" way to make an album – and yet it somehow worked to produce an era-defining record which created the template for a thousand derivative heavy rock bands to imitate. *Led Zeppelin II* marked the beginning of Plant's writing partnership with Jimmy Page but it was still the guitarist's monumental riffs that dominated. Many of them were blues based but Zeppelin's second album marked them out from the other British blues bands of the era such as John Mayall, Fleetwood Mac and Chicken Shack. Zeppelin were louder and heavier, for sure, but they were also somehow far sexier and more theatrical. As Plant put it in 2005, "It was still blues based but it was a much more carnal approach to the music and quite flamboyant."

Aside from the mighty riffs of 'Whole Lotta Love' and Bonham's drum showpiece 'Ramble On', there were gentler moments such as the acoustic part of 'Ramble On' and the lovely 'Thank You', with Plant making a major contribution as a lyricist. "I'd never really written a song until Zep got together, so the crafting of lyric and melody was developing all the time," Plant told this writer many years later. "The writing process is quite personal and intimate but working with Jimmy was very stimulating. He was my senior in every respect but the melding was good and by about the eighth song we wrote together I began to realise that I had something with this guy that was very special. I was no longer just chancing it so I was feeling better and better all the time. *Led Zeppelin II* was very virile. That was the album that was going to dictate whether

3

The double-page spread in Melody Maker *for the band's early 1970 UK tour to promote* Led Zeppelin II *was unusual for the time, and again shows how Grant forcefully and rapidly built their reputation within the first 18 months of their existence*

or not we had the staying power and the capacity to stimulate. It had changed colour completely from the first album. It had become much more creative and imaginative."

"In the early days I was writing the lyrics as well as the music because Robert hadn't written before," Page recalls. "It took a lot of ribbing and teasing to actually get him into writing. And then on the second LP he wrote the words of 'Thank You'. He said, 'I'd like to have a crack at this and write it for my wife.'" Elsewhere, however, Plant's lyrics had an unfortunate tendency to

ZEPPELIN: SINGLES

From the outset, Led Zeppelin adopted a 'no singles' policy in accord with their self-image as a serious rock band rather than a pop group. Interestingly, in this respect, the band saw themselves as a very different creature from The Rolling Stones, with whom they vied in the early 1970s for the title of the greatest rock 'n' roll band in the world. "I always thought of the Stones as a pop group who made singles," Robert Plant noted in 2005. "The whole idea of what we did competing with Bobby Goldsboro for airplay as they were wasn't where we were at. What we said was there's no point putting out a single when the album is the statement of the band. It sounds quite pompous now, but underneath it all, that was true."

According to the deal Peter Grant had struck with Atlantic, the band had the power to determine what was released under its name and therefore had an effective veto on all singles, Yet although they never released a single commercially in Britain, in America they did make several concessions to their rule. 'Good Times Bad Times' backed with 'Communication Breakdown', both taken from the first album, had appeared as a single in America in March 1969 and although it didn't chart, it did get AM radio play which helped to promote the album. Helpfully, both tracks were also short enough that they didn't require editing for the seven-inch single format.

Following the release of *Led Zeppelin II* in October 1969, Atlantic in America started pressuring the band to release another single and suggested the five-

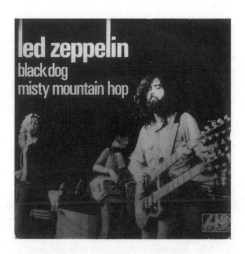

3

band eventually gave in, rationalising their climb-down by reasoning that as the edited version was already all over the airwaves, they were merely accepting what was a fait accompli. The edited single eventually sold almost one million copies, doing particularly brisk trade with jukebox companies. However, the band vetoed all plans to issue the edited single in Britain, where Atlantic had expectantly given it a catalogue number. Instead, Plant's old friend, Alexis Korner, had a top twenty hit covering 'Whole Lotta Love' with his band CCS, which also became the theme tune of the weekly TV show, *Top of the Pops.*

and-a-half-minute-long 'Whole Lotta Love'. According to an interview Bonham and Plant gave in *Melody Maker* at the time, the band agreed on the condition that the track was not edited but released in its entirety, complete with the sonic storm of its experimental middle section. However, what the band hadn't factored in was the enterprising nature of American disc jockeys. Long before the remix became a standard practice, several AM stations began playing their own edited version of 'Whole Lotta Love', omitting its unconventional middle section. Retailers then started asking Atlantic to release it commercially in edited form and the label petitioned Peter Grant to sanction it.

Grant stalled by telling them the band would record a custom-made single, although this seems to have been simply a ruse that there was never any serious intention of fulfilling. Reluctantly, the

Despite the 'no singles' policy in the UK, viewers of BBC's weekly chart round-up Top of the Pops got exposure to the band week in and week out, as Alexis Korner and CCS's cover of 'Whole Lotta Love' was adopted as the show's theme tune

In later years, the band resisted with particular vehemence sustained record company pressure to issue 'Stairway to Heaven' as a single, but the widely held idea that Zeppelin never released any singles is wide of the mark. In America, Led Zeppelin actually released ten singles between 1969–79. In addition to 'Whole Lotta Love', three more of them made the *Billboard* top twenty – 'Immigrant Song', backed with 'Hey Hey What Can I Do', the only non-album track ever to appear on a Zeppelin single (1970), 'Black Dog' (1971) and 'D'yer Mak'er' (1973).

LED ZEPPELIN

3

'borrow' without attribution from his beloved blues heroes.

This became a particularly sore point on *Led Zeppelin II* when Willie Dixon, who wrote many of Muddy Waters and Howlin' Wolf's greatest songs, subsequently sued and received out-of-court settlements for segments from both 'Whole Lotta Love' and 'Bring It on Home' which were lifted without credit from his songbook. Certainly, Led Zeppelin weren't the only white rock band of the 1960s to steal from black blues artists. But on *Led Zeppelin II* the band was more brazen than most and, as the writer Barney Hoskyns has noted, they appeared "callously indifferent to the implications of this purloining".

In later years, both Page and Plant have squirmed when questioned about it and somewhat unedifyingly attempted to blame each other. "I think when Willie Dixon turned on the radio in Chicago 20 years after he wrote his blues, he thought 'that's my song'," Plant said in 1985. "When we ripped it off I said to Jimmy, 'Hey, that's not our song.' And he said, 'Shut up and keep walking.'" Page claimed the problems were all down to Plant. "Robert was supposed to change the lyrics and he didn't always do that," he told *Guitar World.* "That's what brought us most of the grief. They couldn't get us on the guitar parts of the music but they nailed us on the lyrics. So if there is any plagiarism, just blame Robert."

Yet such arguments were still in the future when *Led Zeppelin II* was released. Not all of the reviews were ecstatic and there were carping voices from the likes of *Rolling Stone*, which for some reason had a vendetta against the band from the outset. But the critics could not prevent the album topping the charts and when *Led Zeppelin II* toppled The Beatles' *Abbey*

Road from the number one spot in America in December 1969, it somehow seemed to define the end of the 1960s and symbolise the rise of the new order. Inside a year, they had gone from earning 500 dollars a night for their first US shows to a basic minimum guarantee of 100,000 dollars. A further indication of just how fast and how far they had risen was Grant's decision to turn down an invitation to appear at the Woodstock festival in August 1969, on a bill that included Jimi Hendrix, The Who and Santana. "Atlantic were very keen and so was our US promoter. I said no because we'd have been just another band on the bill," he explained. Zeppelin now topped the bill or they didn't appear at all, it seemed.

A report in the *Financial Times* at the end of 1969 calculated that the group had generated five million dollars in US sales. It didn't earn them MBEs like The Beatles, but their contribution to Britain's balance of payments was recognised when Gwyneth Dunwoody, a minister at the Board of Trade in Harold Wilson's Labour government, presented them with gold discs at a ceremony at London's Savoy Hotel the week before Christmas 1969. "You seem to be gas rockets rather than Led Zeppelins," she told them. Plant kissed the minister on the cheek and following the ceremony Page celebrated by popping round to an up-market car dealership in Berkeley Square to buy himself a Rolls-Royce.

In America, the album's success had been helped by the release of an edited version of 'Whole Lotta Love' as a single. In Britain the band refused to sanction its release, insisting they were strictly an albums act. That may have slowed their progress but by early 1970, *Led Zeppelin II* had inexorably risen to the top of the British chart, too.

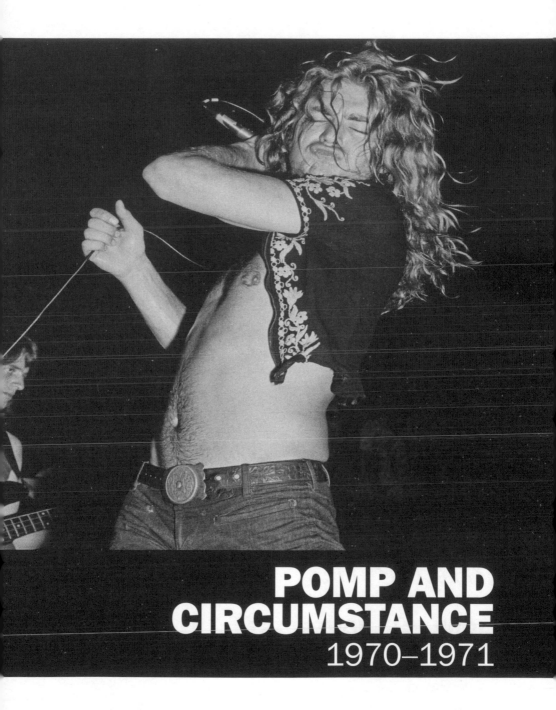

POMP AND CIRCUMSTANCE
1970–1971

LED ZEPPELIN

4

"I suppose it's a combination of a good band and the time it broke. Cream had gone and other groups had an even chance of getting in. But somehow we made it."

JOHN PAUL JONES, 1970

POMP AND CIRCUMSTANCE

4

1970–1971

With The Beatles no more, the Stones recovering from the horror of Altamont, in tax exile, and out of contract at Decca, and The Who wondering how to follow *Tommy*, 1970 was the year in which Led Zeppelin officially became the biggest British group in the world. What's more, rock's old guard didn't like being superseded one little bit. And they did their best to false-foot the young pretenders.

In early 1970, the writer Ritchie Yorke canvassed other prominent UK musicians for their views on Led Zeppelin and the replies tasted more than a little of sour grapes (see 'Sour Grapes' on next page).

The year started with a brief British tour, which went some way towards mending bridges with the more hostile elements of the British rock press and those sections of its readership that felt aggrieved that the band had turned its back on its homeland. "I think our success in America had an effect on the critique over here," Plant noted. "It was like 'They've gone and who the fuck are they anyway?' Oh well, it's overblown." Highlight of the tour was a two-and-a-half-hour show at London's Albert Hall on January 9, 1970, which Jones described as a "here-we-are type of show" to prove they hadn't deserted Britain. In fact, it was only seven months since their last British show – coincidentally also at the Albert Hall – but the statistics for once are revealing. Between December 1968 and April 1970, Led Zeppelin played 153 shows in America. During the same period, they played just 28 shows in Britain.

Just what Britain had been missing and how spectacular a live act they had become can be seen in the film of the Albert Hall show, shot for a planned documentary which never happened but which eventually appeared on the *Led Zeppelin* DVD set in 2003. In the years since, we've got used to theatrical stadium shows with dry ice and inflatables. Yet what is striking about Zeppelin circa 1970 is how simple, direct and yet intense was their stagecraft. As critic Barney Hoskyns put it, the DVD reveals a show stripped down to "just four men, barely more than boys bound together in intense rhythmic symbiosis, rooted in the most brutal, pulverising grooves ever devised".

It's also clear that there's a fair degree of spontaneity and improvisation going on. "You had to be on the ball, especially in the improvised parts," Jones says. "You'd have to watch each other for cues. Lots of things happened on stage to alter the songs. In the fast part to 'Dazed and Confused' John and I would turn the riff round backwards and Pagey would come across and shout, 'What the fucking hell do you think you are

LED ZEPPELIN

4

SOUR GRAPES: WHAT A BEGRUDGING ROCK ARISTOCRACY THOUGHT OF LED ZEPPELIN IN 1970

Keith Richards: "I played their first album quite a lot when I first got it but then the guy's voice started to get on my nerves."

Eric Clapton: "I don't know about them. I've heard their records and I saw them play. They were very loud – I thought it was unnecessarily loud. I liked some of it but a lot of it was just too much. They over-emphasised whatever point they were making."

Pete Townshend: "I'm not one of their biggest fans which doesn't mean that I don't like them, but means that I don't really get into their music a lot."

John Lennon: "From what little I've heard, they sound all right."

doing?!' That was good fun."

Plant's presence is also impressively charismatic, even when playing air guitar during Page's solos. "At that Albert Hall show I was 21 and just a black country hippie," he now says modestly. "I was hanging on for dear life, weaving my way through the three greatest players of their time. It was an absolute shock when I first saw that footage. It's so disarming – not unnerving but kind of cute and coy, and you see all that sort of naïvety and the absolute wonder of what we were doing. And the freshness of it, because the whole sort of stereotypical rock singer thing hadn't kicked in for me."

As usual, the reviews were mixed with *Disc* raving about the show and *Melody Maker* bizarrely claiming "It took them nearly the whole of their set to get the fires blazing",

which suggests that their reviewer was at a different show to the one captured on film. But it mattered not. The UK music press is not always as powerful as it likes to pretend and where Zeppelin was concerned, British rock fans had made their own minds up and no amount of sneering from critics who received their records and concert tickets for free was going to change their minds.

A mishap caused the postponement of the final date of the tour in early February, when Plant crashed his Jaguar on his way home after going to see the West Coast band Spirit playing at Mothers in Birmingham and was briefly hospitalised. But by the end of the month he was fit enough for a short tour of Europe, which produced one of the group's oddest gigs when they were forced to appear in Copenhagen under the name The Nobs. Before the show they were confronted by Eva Von Zeppelin, who claimed to be a relative of Count Von Zeppelin, who had designed the German airship that bore his name. Announcing that "They may be world famous but a group of shrieking monkeys are not going to use a privileged family name without permission," she must have been a formidable lady for the group were intimidated enough to change their name for the night – or perhaps they just enjoyed the joke. Nothing further was heard from Eva or her lawyers, and a week later they were back to being Led Zeppelin for an appearance at the Montreux Jazz Festival, promoted by Claude Nobs, whose name they had borrowed in the panic in Copenhagen.

After another, box-office-breaking America tour in spring 1970, billed as 'An Evening with Led Zeppelin' in recognition of the fact that their elongated sets now meant they had no need of a support act, work began on the third album. That it would present a different sound from the first two

4

LPs had already been telegraphed by Robert Plant when he told *Melody Maker*: "We haven't prepared much material yet but we've got a few things down and it's all acoustic, folks! You can just see it, can't you: 'Led Zeppelin go soft on their fans' or some crap like that." He also revealed that he and Page planned to rent a cottage in Wales, "where we can lock ourselves away for a few weeks just to see what we can come up with when there's no one else around".

He already had a location in mind. When he was a child, Plant had regularly spent summer holidays with his parents in a cottage called Bron-Y-Aur (Welsh for 'golden hillside' and pronounced Bron-raar) just north of Machynlleth in Powys, central Wales, near the River Dyfi, rented from friends of the family. It was rural and isolated and with no running water, heating or electricity it could not have been further removed from the

hedonistic pleasures of the Hyatt hotel on Sunset Strip or the trials and tribulations of the just completed American tour, during which a promoter had pulled a gun on Peter Grant, a show had been stopped in Pittsburgh when a brawl erupted and Bonham had vented his homesickness by systematically destroying hotel rooms. The tour had ended on another bum note with the cancellation of the final date, after Plant collapsed with exhaustion in Phoenix. In late April, a week after the band's return from America, the singer decamped to the cottage with his wife Maureen, daughter Carmen and the family dog, Strider. Page arrived with his girlfriend Charlotte Martin and two Led Zeppelin roadies, Clive Coulson

The acoustic section, which was to become a staple of the live shows after Led Zeppelin III, *gets an early outing during "An Evening With Led Zeppelin" in the USA, 1970. Jones (left) is playing mandolin*

LED ZEPPELIN

and Sandy MacGregor, were also invited along to take care of the domestic chores and ensure that the drudgery of cooking, cleaning, lighting fires and fetching water from the stream didn't interfere with the serious business of strumming guitars and writing songs.

Coulson later insisted that the roadies weren't taken for granted. "Everyone mucked in really. I wouldn't take any of that superior shit. They were wonderful people to work for, normal blokes. They weren't treated as gods," he said. Nevertheless, there was never any doubt as to who were the paymasters and which members of the party were there as hired hands. "Pagey was two people – one of the lads and the boss," Coulson admitted. "Plant's speciality was posing and telling people how to do things."

'Getting it together in the country' had already become something of a tradition in rock circles. Traffic had put together its debut album while staying in a country cottage in Berkshire and Plant was also much impressed by time spent hanging out with The Incredible String Band, who lived collectively in a row of cottages in the Scottish borders. There was also the role model of the San Francisco bands who had retreated up the coast from the city and across the Golden Gate Bridge to the more bucolic surroundings of Marin County and The Band, who had recorded both their debut album *Music from Big Pink* and *The Basement Tapes* with Bob Dylan in a communal house in upstate New York.

As a working holiday it was highly productive in more ways than one: Page and Charlotte Martin's daughter Scarlet (who later became a respected rock photographer) was conceived while there. But the songs also flowed prolifically. Page brought a portable tape recorder along so that no song

or song fragment was lost. Among the songs that began to take shape at Bron-Yr-Aur were 'Friends', 'Celebration Day', 'Gallows Pole', 'That's the Way', 'Hats off to (Roy) Harper', 'Bron-Yr-Aur Stomp' (based on a song called 'Jennings Farm Blues', named after Plant's new home, which they had started the previous December). All were further developed to appear on *Led Zeppelin III*. Also products of the stay in the Welsh mountains were 'Hey Hey What Can I Do' (a rare non-album track that was the B-side to 'The Immigrant Song', released as a single in America) and pieces that later became 'Over the Hills and Far Away' (on *Houses of the Holy*), 'Down by the Seaside', 'The Rover' and 'Bron-Yr-Aur' (on *Physical Graffiti*) and 'Poor Tom' (on *Coda*).

Plant in particular was ecstatic about the whole experience, which represented the culmination of the hippie dream he had nurtured since 1967's 'Summer of Love' and which had sustained him even when he was reduced to joining a road gang laying tarmac in West Bromwich high street. "We wrote these songs and walked and talked and thought and went off to the abbey where they hid the grail," he later recalled of their Welsh idyll. "No matter how cute and comical it might be now to look back at that, it gave us so much energy because we were really close to something. We believed. It was absolutely wonderful and my heart was so light and happy. At that time, at that age, 1970 was like the biggest blue sky I ever saw."

The sun was still shining when Page and Plant took the songs to Jones and Bonham and the four convened to begin rehearsing the material at Plant's farm in Worcestershire. In an attempt to replicate at least some of the spirit of Bron-Yr-Aur, they then decamped in June 1970 with some mobile recording equipment to Headley

4

set was sandwiched by Flock and Hot Tuna, leaving Jefferson Airplane as the nominal bill-toppers. But Grant had astutely calculated that with festival bills at the time habitually over-running by several hours, hitting the crowd when it was wide awake and ready to rock in the early evening was preferable to topping the bill in the early hours of the morning when everyone was exhausted.

The plan almost went wrong when Flock received an ecstatic ovation and were called back for two encores, but Grant ordered his roadies to start dismantling the American group's gear against the wishes of the festival organisers and Flock themselves, who were planning a third encore. His hard-ball tactics won the day. The bewildered Flock were hustled off, Zeppelin went on as dusk was falling and proceeded to play like demons. The reception was phenomenal and glowing reviews hailed their set as the highlight of the weekend. For the first time, the band's detractors in the UK music press were forced to admit that perhaps they had got Led Zeppelin wrong. Or perhaps they were simply bowing to the clamour of their own readership: in September, Zeppelin were voted best band in the annual *Melody Maker* readers' poll, displacing The Beatles from the top slot they had held continuously since 1963.

Grange, an allegedly haunted former workhouse built in 1795 to shelter paupers, orphans and illegitimate children. The sessions went well, with Jones entering the acoustic spirit by introducing mandolin, and with further work taking place in Island's London studios, the album was virtually finished by July, although other delays in the mixing and the gimmicky sleeve design with its revolving card disc delayed release until October. This meant its release missed their sixth American tour, which culminated with a brace of shows at Madison Square Garden on September 19, for which the band grossed more than 100,000 dollars. It was the day after Jimi Hendrix's death and Plant paid tribute to him from the stage, calling his demise a "great loss for the music world".

Led Zeppelin's only British appearance during the second half of 1970 came at the Bath Festival of Blues and Progressive Music in June. With Page dressed in a 'Farmer John' hat and tweed overcoat and Plant sporting a pointy, goatee beard, it was the biggest UK appearance of their career to date in front of an ecstatic 150,000 audience. Peter Grant had negotiated that the band would take the stage at sunset, which meant that their

The fans who had catapulted Zeppelin to the top tended to be slightly younger than the average rock constituency, often still at school rather than college or university, and in some quarters were disparagingly referred to as 'headbangers'. In fact, it was an accurate description of the characteristic pose adopted by many fans and the sight of the entire front row at a Zeppelin concert with their heads weaving up and down with hair flying over their faces in time to the thundering riffs made for an extraordinary sight. Were such

LED ZEPPELIN

Page in farmer's tweeds, Plant in a Charles I "full set" at Freddie Bannister's seminal Bath Festival of Blues and Progressive Music in 1970

fans ready for the subtler and surprisingly mellow sounds emanating from the Welsh cottage that were about to appear on *Led Zeppelin III.* Although they all faithfully bought the new record when it appeared in October 1970, many were undoubtedly disappointed that it was not a standard heavy rock album. The riffs that it did boast, such as the crunching opener 'The Immigrant Song', were certainly spectacular. But such moments were tempered by the acoustic material born of the Bron-Yr-Aur sojourn, such as 'Friends', 'Tangerine' and the Crosby, Stills and Nash-influenced 'That's the Way'. "What came out on our third album was a reflection of the fact that the pendulum had swung in the total opposite direction from all that *Led Zeppelin II* live thing and the energy of being on the road," Page explains. "It was like, 'Oh we're here, we're in nature, we can hear the

birds sing, there's not a car sound, there's no aeroplanes, there's no concert to do. It was just fantastic.'"

According to Plant, they were "obsessed" with change and doing something different. "*Led Zeppelin II* was something we felt good about because it would have been more obvious to use 'Whole Lotta Love' as a kind of calling card and carry on in that direction," he observed. The "simple thunder" of the heavy riffs was easier to assimilate, he conceded. "But you can't just do that, otherwise you become stagnant and you're not really doing anything, you're just pleasing everybody else." Certainly, some fans were less than delighted with the change of direction, and although the LP initially sold spectacularly and went to number one on both sides of the Atlantic, in the long term it has remained the weakest-seller

THE STORY: **POMP AND CIRCUMSTANCE**

among the band's first four seminal albums.

Yet even as the album was hitting record stores, in the autumn of 1970 Page and Plant were on their way back to Bron-Yr-Aur to repeat the cottage experiment and begin work on material for the next album. "It was just the four of us this time," Henry Smith, one of the two roadies who accompanied them, recalls. "It just felt like a good thing. Like if you want to write you need to get away and this was a great place to get away because there was nobody around. It was so off the beaten path. We were in the middle of a sheep field, I remember, and the sheep would almost come into the house while Jimmy and Robert were working on songs."

It was a shorter stay than six months earlier, but among the material they worked on was the introduction of what was to become 'Stairway to Heaven'. Then as before, the pair took their ideas to Jones and Bonham at Headley Grange, where basic backing tracks were recorded before being finessed further at Island Studios in London in December 1970. Those sessions were then followed in the New Year by a return to Headley Grange, where the band stayed for much of January and February 1971. Jones hated the place. "It was cold and damp," he complains. "Virtually no furniture, no pool table, no pub nearby." He would no doubt have preferred to record at Stargroves, Mick Jagger's well-appointed country pile, but Page – living up to his 'Led Wallet' nickname, had apparently baulked at the idea when the Stones singer had quoted a rental of £1,000 a week.

But Jones' antipathy towards Headley Grange found him in a minority. "It was really great," Plant reported. "The mics coming in through the windows and a fire going in the hearth and people coming in with cups of tea and cakes and people

tripping over leads and the whole thing in utter chaos. It was a good feeling and we did it as easy as pie." Road manager Richard Cole paints an equally bucolic picture. "There weren't any serious drugs around the band at that point. Just dope and a bit of coke," he recalls. "We had an account at a shop in the village and we'd go down there regularly and collect huge quantities of cider. They were playing at being country squires. They found an old shotgun and used to shoot at squirrels in the woods, not that they ever hit any. And there was this lovely old black Labrador wandering around which we used to feed." The beast, of course, was commemorated in 'Black Dog', the opening track on *Led Zeppelin IV*. Plant also wrote the lyrics to 'Stairway to Heaven' at the house, and if the spirit of Bron-Yr-Aur ran through *Led Zeppelin III*, it was the ambience of Headley Grange that dominated the follow-up.

With the album virtually finished, Peter Grant announced a 'back to the roots' British tour for March 1971, culminating with a return to the legendary Marquee club in London's Soho, where the band had last played in December 1968. It was a deliberate attempt to step away from huge venues such as Madison Square Garden and Grant further let it be known that the group had turned down one million dollars for a show in Germany on New Year's Eve 1970 to be relayed by satellite coast-to-coast across America. He may well have exaggerated the figure but the story helped to dissipate British resentment at the band's concentration on the US market and allowed them to claim that remaining in contact with their fans was more important than the money.

"The boys came to me just after Christmas and talked about their next tour," Grant told *Melody Maker*. "We decided to do the clubs and forget about the bread and the

LED ZEPPELIN

4

PAGE'S GUITARS

The most enduring image of Jimmy Page on stage is of him playing the solo on 'Stairway to Heaven' on his custom-made double-neck Gibson. But needless to say, he owned an army of guitars which were deployed for different purposes in the studio and in concert.

On the first Led Zeppelin album and the band's early live dates he favoured a 1958 Fender Telecaster, given to him by Jeff Beck. In 1967, he had it painted in psychedelic colours and it was this guitar rather than the Gibson double-neck that was actually used for the studio version of 'Stairway to Heaven'. The guitar was subsequently 'retired' due to problems with the pick-ups.

By the time of *Led Zeppelin II* he had switched to a sunburst-finished 1959 Gibson Les Paul. During the early days he also used a Gibson "Black Beauty" Les Paul, but this was stolen on tour in 1970. He had bought the guitar in 1962 on hire purchase for £185 and used it extensively in his session work. He was devastated to lose it and, in 1973, placed an advert in *Rolling Stone* offering a reward for its return with "no questions asked". There was no response.

The Gibson Les Paul remained his favoured instrument for the rest of the Zeppelin era, and the 1959 model was joined by a similar-looking 1958 model which he bought or was given by Joe Walsh of The James Gang and later the Eagles. It was this guitar which was copied at Gibson's custom shop to create the now discontinued Jimmy Page Signature Les Paul series.

The Gibson SG 12/six-string double-neck guitar was introduced specifically to play 'Stairway to Heaven' on stage. It was also used live on 'Tangerine', 'The Rain Song' and 'The Song Remains the Same'. He seldom played it

in the studio, the one exception being its use on 'Carouselambra'.

Towards the end with Led Zeppelin, he rediscovered his early passion for Fender guitars, playing a 1959 Telecaster in Botswana brown and a 1960 blue Stratocaster with tremolo arm. Both were used live with Led Zeppelin and remained favourites in the 1980s when Page used them with The Firm and on his solo tours.

For acoustic work, on the first Led Zeppelin album he used a Gibson J-200 that had belonged to Big Jim Sullivan. After 1970, he mostly played a Martin D28 both in the studio and during the acoustic set which became a key part of Led Zeppelin's live shows, although a Harmony Sovereign is used quite heavily on *Led Zeppelin III*. When a 12-string was required, he mostly used a Rickenbacker. The pedal steel heard to prominent effect on *Led Zeppelin III* is a Fender 10-string model.

When it came to effects units, Page used a Roger Mayer fuzz box, a Sola Sound Tone Bender, a Vox Cry Baby Wah-Wah, the Maestro Echoplex, an MXR phaser, an Eventide clockwork harmonizer and, of course, a theremin.

4

big concert halls. We're going to play the universities and clubs and restrict prices to about twelve bob a ticket. When I rang the Marquee, the manager refused to believe it was me offering him Led Zeppelin so he had to call me back to be convinced."

"The audiences are becoming bigger and bigger, moving further and further away. We are losing contact, so by going back to places like the Marquee we aim to re-establish our contact with the people who got us off the ground in the first place," Page explained. "It will give the fans a chance to see a group which in the accepted tradition would be appearing only at large auditoriums for high prices." The tour also gave fans an early chance to hear some of the material from *Led Zeppelin IV*, which would in the event not be released until November. Foremost among the new numbers was 'Stairway to Heaven', which received its debut minus the recorders but with the introduction of Page's soon to be familiar custom-made Gibson SG double-neck at Belfast's Ulster Hall on March 5. The song was described by *Melody Maker's* Chris Welch as "an excellent ballad" which displayed Plant's "growing lyricism", a favourable enough response but one which gave no indication that it was to become one of rock music's most epic and enduring landmarks. 'Black Dog' and 'Going to California' were the other new songs unveiled on the tour, but although the band played well, the smaller venues cramped the theatrical swagger Zeppelin had developed on their American tours and the entire exercise left many feeling oddly under-whelmed. Richard Cole also suggests that after being treated like gods in America, they were unimpressed by the meagre backstage hospitality at such venues as the Nottingham Boat Club and the Belfry in Sutton Coldfield.

By the end of the tour, which took in a dozen dates in 17 days, Plant was also having voice problems, which resulted in the postponement of the recording of a BBC Radio 1 *In Concert* session. When it was rescheduled for April 1, the band put in a bravura performance that compensated for any disappointments on the tour and gave the broader listening public its first taste of 'Stairway to Heaven' when the show was broadcast in an hour-long edited version three days later.

The fourth album had originally been planned for a late spring or early summer release, to coincide with European dates and set up the band's seventh assault on North America, beginning in August. Unfortunately, a cock-up with the mixing nixed this plan and when Page returned from Sunset Sound in Los Angeles with what was meant to be the finished album and played it to the rest of the band at Olympic in London, the entire group was in for a shock. They knew they had made a great album but nobody could understand why it sounded so terrible. The answer was a purely technical one: a mismatch between the tape machines on which the music had been recorded and mixed. Only the Sunset Sound mix of 'When the Levee Breaks' could be rescued and the laborious process of mixing the album's other seven tracks had to begin all over again.

It was a morale-sapping blow and another followed when they arrived in Italy for a show on July 5 in Milan's Vigorelli Velodrome. With more than 2,000 Milanese police on duty in anticipation of trouble, confrontation became almost inevitable and trouble started well before the concert when left-wing demonstrators chanting slogans outside the stadium were charged by riot police firing tear gas and water cannon. The skirmishes moved inside the auditorium but

LED ZEPPELIN

4

MAGICK MOMENTS: PAGE AND ALEISTER CROWLEY

Of all the lurid tales surrounding Led Zeppelin, none has provoked more controversy over the years than the sinister rumours that the group were 'Satan's own band'. The rumours began in the early 1970s as a direct result of Jimmy Page's growing interest in the magician and sexual libertarian Aleister Crowley (1875-1947). Dubbed by the press in the 1930s "the most evil man in Britain", Crowley conducted black magic rituals and sex orgies at his 'satanic temple' on London's Fulham Road and styled himself 'The Great Beast'.

In the most extreme rumours, it was held that three members of Zeppelin (with John Paul Jones as the dissenter) had signed a pact with the devil. It was claimed that the words 'Here's to my sweet Satan' could be heard if you played the 'If there's a bustle in your hedgerow' verse in Stairway to Heaven backwards. The disasters and mishaps that dogged the latter part of the band's career were all attributed to their liaison with Lucifer and one theory even claimed that John Bonham's death in 1980 was retribution for Page's occult obsession.

Total nonsense, of course. But Page's interest in the realm of magic was a matter of record. He had the phrases "Do What Thou Wilt" and "So Mote Be It" scratched into the run-off matrix at the centre of the original vinyl release of *Led Zeppelin III*. Both were derived from the sayings of Crowley. He was also a collector of rare books and manuscripts connected with the magician and even bought the robes in which he had conducted his magic rituals. In 1975, he purchased the Equinox occult bookshop and publishing house, located in Kensington High Street, London, and used it to publish a facsimile of a 16th-century magical text edited and annotated by

Crowley in 1904. He also collected Crowley's paintings of magical subjects and pictures from his collection were displayed at London's October Gallery in 1998.

In 1971 Page also purchased Crowley's former home, Boleskin House, on the shores of Loch Ness in Scotland. The house had an evil reputation but Page was intrigued by its history. It was said to have been built on the site of a church that had been burnt to the ground with all its parishioners inside. A man had been beheaded there, according to local legend and, of course, his head was said still to roll around the halls at night. A lodge keeper had also gone berserk there and tried to murder his family.

Page had the house redecorated by a Satanist called Charles Pierce and the ill-repute of the place continued to grow as one

'The Great Beast': mad as a hatter

4

caretaker committed suicide and another was claimed to have lost his sanity. Page had his rather sinister fantasy sequence in the movie *The Song Remains the Same* filmed near Boleskine House in 1973. He eventually sold the property in the late 1980s but as far as is known, he still has his Crowley memorabilia, said to constitute the most extensive collection in the world.

On stage with Zeppelin, Page often appeared with astrological symbols embroidered into his clothes, representing Capricorn, Scorpio and Cancer, which are Page's sun, ascendant and moon signs. His 'Zoso' symbol for *Led Zeppelin IV* was also derived from occult sources (see separate box) while the painting of the hermit he commissioned for the album's inside cover was based on the tarot.

Another devotee of Crowley was the filmmaker Kenneth Anger, who asked Page to compose the soundtrack for his film *Lucifer Rising*. Page's music for the project was never completed, with the director publicly calling the guitarist a mere "dabbler" in the occult and accusing him of "having an affair with the White Lady" and being too strung out on drugs to complete the project. Page's soundtrack was eventually replaced in the film by music written in prison by Bobby Beausoleil, a member of Charles Manson's notorious 'family' and a convicted murderer.

When asked about his interest in the occult by interviewers in later years, Page has invariably been cautious and taciturn. Yet in the first flushes of his enthusiasm, he was quite open, telling one journalist: "You can't ignore evil if you study the supernatural as I do. I have many books on the subject and I've also attended a number of séances."

He also called Crowley "a misunderstood genius of the 20th century" and in a 1972 interview with *Disc and Music Echo*, he

The zodiac trousers

made clear his interest in Crowley's 'sex magick' – and appeared to confirm the criticisms that Zeppelin's attitude towards women was deeply misogynistic. "Magic is very important if people can go through it," he said. "I think Crowley is completely relevant to today. We're seeking for truth: the search goes on. Crowley didn't have a very high opinion of women – and I don't think he was wrong. Playing music is a very sexual act, an emotional release, and the sexual drive comes in along with all the other impulses."

None of the rest of the band shared his fascination with the occult and he appears to have made no attempt to share his interest with them. "No one really delved into what Jimmy did," Richard Coles says. "He didn't really speak about it much. It was as much of a mystery to us as it was to everyone else." Plant was equally dismissive in 2005. "I've never shared those preoccupations with him and I don't really know anything about it," he said.

LED ZEPPELIN

the band decided to go ahead with the gig in the mistaken belief that their music would have a calming effect. It might have worked on the 15,000-strong crowd, but the band's appearance seemed to have the opposite effect on the police. As soon as sections of the crowd jumped to their feet to applaud Zeppelin's arrival on stage, the forces of law and disorder charged, wielding batons and hurling more tear gas. Plant appealed for calm but it was hopeless. Within a few numbers a full-scale riot had broken out and when a tear gas canister exploded close enough to the stage to make the band's eyes water during Bonham's drum solo on 'Moby

Dick', Grant ordered them off stage. In anticipation of trouble, he had perceptively demanded the money and the return first-class air tickets up-front. According to Bonham's drum technician Mick Hinton, "The roadies stayed on to protect the stage. I got hit on the head with a bottle and the next thing I knew I was on a stretcher. I remember we lost the hi-hat, but aside from that the kit was OK, incredibly."

Plant still sounded disturbed by the event when he described it to this writer almost a quarter of a century later. "We escaped down an access route and the troops pumped gas canisters at us," he recalled.

READING THE RUNES

Page   Jones   Bonham   Plant

Strictly speaking the band's fourth album is not called *Led Zeppelin IV*. Like The Beatles' *White Album* and The Byrds' double LP widely known as *Untitled*, it was the band's intention that their fourth LP should have no title at all. The only marking it bore on the cover was the four runes or hieroglyphs that appeared both on the label and the spine of its cover. "I think *Four Symbols* was how it was referred to by us at the time," Plant says.

On Page's suggestion, the runes – or at least two of them – came from a book called *The Book of Signs* by Rudolph Koch. "At first I wanted just one symbol but since it was our fourth album and there were four of us, we each chose our own," Page explained.

"Jimmy showed me this book he had and said we should all choose a symbol from the book to represent each one of us," John Paul Jones remembers. The symbol he chose depicted a circle inlaid with three interlocking semi-circular arcs which, according to Koch's book, was used to ward off evil. According to Page, the bassist chose it because of the "precision and dexterity" required to draw it.

Bonham chose a simpler emblem of three overlapping rings, like a simplified version of the Olympic symbol and which represented his family. "I suppose it's the trinity of man, woman and child. I suspect it had something to do with the mainstay of all people's belief," Plant observes. However, the down-to-earth

"We managed to get in a dressing room and I barricaded the door with a medicine cabinet and got everybody in there with wet towels around our heads. Then they broke the windows and popped a couple of canisters in from the street."

The band never played in Italy again and when their seventh American tour opened in August, their personal backstage security had been discreetly doubled. In the wake of what had happened in Milan, the habit of American audiences to let off volleys of firecrackers in the auditorium caused some understandably jumpy moments and there were stage invasions in New York and Honolulu and serious crowd trouble in Boston. According to Richard Cole, there were also death threats and the band's collective sense of isolation and paranoia had never been higher. Despite such problems the tour was deemed a success. Peter Grant had been desperate for Led Zep to return to the US. Ludicrous though it may sound now, he feared that in the 11 months since the band had last toured there, the pedestrian but briefly huge Grand Funk Railroad were on the point of stealing the band's thunder. Grant was satisfied that the band had reasserted its supremacy and GFR were sent down the track into oblivion.

Bonham was far from disappointed when they subsequently discovered in Pittsburgh that it also resembled the symbol for Ballantine's beer.

Plant and Page's symbols did not actually come from Koch's book, but were custom-designed. The singer's feather in a circle was inspired by native American symbolism. "My choice involved the feather, a symbol on which all philosophies have been based," he explained. "For instance, it represents courage to many Indian tribes. I like people to lay down the truth. No bullshit. That's what it was all about."

Most mysterious of all was Page's symbol, which appeared to read 'ZoSo', although the guitarist insisted it was never intended to resemble a word. "It's just a doodle. Although it looks more like writing than the other three, that wasn't the intention," he explained. There has been speculation that it was a reference to the work of the occultist and self-proclaimed 'sorcerer' Austin Osman Spare, who started a mysterious cult called Zos and designed a series of magical symbols or 'sigils', with which it is almost certain that Page was familiar. According to the writer Kenneth Grant: "When vividly visualised, the emblem or sigil mysteriously stirs the subconscious and a corresponding image, or set of images, arises in the mind. In proportion to the power of belief in the sigil, so is the clarity of the image which it evokes. If the sigil taps a layer of ancient or cosmic memory, some astonishing images surge into the mind and the skilful sorcerer is able to project them into the astral mind-stuff of other individuals, so that they imagine the image to be a palpable presence." Such theories may well have influenced Page's thinking when he came up with the idea of the four symbols for the fourth album.

Another possible influence is a 1557 antique tome about alchemy called *Ars Magica Arteficii*. A symbol similar to 'Zoso' was reproduced and credited to this 16th-century source in The *Dictionary of Occult, Hermetic and Alchemical Sigils* by Fred Gettings, published in 1982.

LED ZEPPELIN

4

The fourth album was still not out, but the band unveiled much of the new material, with the triumphant 'Stairway to Heaven' as the jewel in the crown. Plant repeatedly told audiences that the new album would be out in three weeks – which proved to be a hopelessly optimistic forecast while they battled with Atlantic over their desire not to put the band's name on the cover or to give the LP a title.

Frustratingly, there was still no sign of the new record when the band undertook its first ever tour of Japan at the end of September. Although they played just five shows in three cities, it was a memorable trip in several ways. On the first night in Tokyo, Plant complained about their recent American tour, which he compared unfavourably with the way they had been "having a ball" since their arrival in Japan. On stage the band seemed relaxed and the sets were full of ad libs and improbable improvisations. For some reason, Plant dedicated all the new songs to Cliff Richard and sang a snatch of Simon & Garfunkel's 'The 59th Street Bridge Song (Feelin' Groovy)'. Page responded by throwing in a few licks from 'Honky Tonk Women'. On another night, the 'Whole Lotta Love' medley included Cliff's 'Bachelor Boy', while elsewhere Plant offered up snatches of 'The Lady Is a Tramp' and 'Smoke Gets in Your Eyes'.

It was clear they were relaxed and having fun – which made the fight that erupted between Plant and Bonham in Osaka all the more strange. During the row, Bonham gave Plant a split lip and then refused to return to the stage while the singer led the crowd in a chant to persuade him to return and apologised: "Japan is a wonderful place and you're too much. You're putting up with a lot. We don't usually do things like this."

When Bonham finally reappeared, he initially refused to play his 'Moby Dick' showcase. Bootleg tapes reveal him saying: "I don't want to play it. I'm fed up playing it!" Grant later attempted to explain the problem: "It was over some dispute over some money from some tour. He still owed Bonzo some petrol money, seventy quid or something, but that's how it was." Bonham and road manger Richard Cole were also involved in one of the most infamous tales of Zep's on-the-road excess when they used two samurai swords to slash everything in their hotel rooms to shreds at the Tokyo Hilton. In another misjudged prank, in Osaka the band invited Atlantic Records' UK boss Phil Carson to play bass while Jones was on keyboards. The band then disappeared, leaving Carson alone on stage – which Page, Plant, Jones and Bonham thought was a hilarious in-joke but which left the audience feeling short-changed. On a more sombre note, in Hiroshima, where the Americans had dropped the first atom bomb 25 years earlier, the band visited the Peace Gardens and played a benefit concert, donating all proceeds to the bomb's victims, and received peace medals from the mayor in return.

At the end of the tour Bonham and Jones returned via Moscow while Page and Plant stopped off in Thailand and India. "In Bangkok all the kids followed us calling 'Billy boy, Billy boy', which means queer, because of (our) hair, but they're laughing and happy all the time," Plant recalled. The pair spent much of their time in local brothels and other houses of ill repute. But in Bombay they also checked out the local music scene and the possibility of recording with Indian musicians, laying the groundwork for their return to do just that a year later.

Back in Britain, *Led Zeppelin IV* was finally ready for release – almost. Further wrangling over the artwork meant that it was November before it finally appeared,

Plant in full flight at the Empire Pool, Wembley – the Electric Magic event

eight months later than originally intended. "The record company hierarchy aren't into the fact that covers are important to a band's image," Plant grumbled. They knew it was a great album, heavier than *Led Zeppelin* with more riffs on the likes of 'Black Dog', 'Rock and Roll' and their astonishing version of Memphis Minnie's 'When the Levee Breaks', but tempered with the ethereal 'Battle of Evermore', featuring Fairport Convention singer Sandy Denny, and the epic 'Stairway

to Heaven'. Bonham told *Melody Maker* it was the best album they had ever made and Plant concurred. "It's strong stuff and exciting and the flame is really burning higher and higher," he said just before its release. He hadn't changed his view 35 years later when he told this writer: "I think it was beautifully written in most areas. It wasn't overstated. It was crafted."

The sense of mystery created by the four, strange runic symbols which were the

LED ZEPPELIN

THE TEN BEST-SELLING ALBUMS OF ALL TIME

29 MILLION

1=. EAGLES: *THEIR GREATEST HITS* (1971–1975)

29 MILLION

1=. MICHAEL JACKSON: *THRILLER*

23 MILLION

3= BILLY JOEL: *GREATEST HITS VOLUME 1 & VOLUME II*

23 MILLION

3=. LED ZEPPELIN: *LED ZEPPELIN IV*

23 MILLION

3=. PINK FLOYD: *THE WALL*

22 MILLION

6. AC/DC: *BACK IN BLACK*

21 MILLION

7. GARTH BROOKS: *DOUBLE LINE*

20 MILLION

8. SHANIA TWAIN: *COME ON OVER*

19 MILLION

9=. THE BEATLES: *THE BEATLES (WHITE ALBUM)*

19 MILLION

9=. FLEETWOOD MAC: *RUMOURS*

* BASED ON US

SOURCE: RIAA WEBSITE (SEE 'TOP TALLIES' TAB)

album's only identification only helped to sell the record, particularly when they were used full-page in a strong press advertising campaign. The four symbols were also displayed prominently on stage when the band celebrated the album's belated release with a 16-date British tour, of which the centrepiece was two dates at London's Empire Pool. Billed as 'Electric Magic', the five-hour extravaganza included circus acts and even some performing pigs, dressed in hats and ruffles. The swine were something of a disappointment but the band were not, earning some spectacular reviews for a bravura performance. "This was no job, this was no gig. It was an event for all," Roy Hollingsworth wrote in *Melody Maker*. "So they get paid a lot of bread. Well, people paid that bread and I reckon they got every penny's worth."

It was a fitting end to a fraught year and *Led Zeppelin IV* topped the British chart, although the success of *Santana III*, Sly and The Family Stone's *There's a Riot Goin' On* and Carole King's *Tapestry*, all of which topped the American chart over the winter of 1971–72, meant that it failed to rise above number two in America. Nevertheless, it stayed on the American chart for two years and ultimately went on to become the fourth best-selling album in musical history (see box). As John Paul Jones succinctly put it, after *Led Zeppelin IV*, no one ever again compared them to Black Sabbath.

HAMMER OF THE GODS
1972–1973

5 *"Give an Englishman 50,000 watts, a chartered jet, a little cocaine and some groupies and he thinks he's a god."*

ROLLING STONE MAGAZINE ON LED ZEPPELIN

"I was settling into insanity. It was wonderful. I was the golden god."

ROBERT PLANT

HAMMER OF THE GODS

1972–1973

The trappings of success were mixed: financial and domestic security, respect from many of their peers and indeed adulation from their ever-growing number of fans. But manager Peter Grant was aware that the momentum had to be kept up, which meant more touring and all that this entailed.

Away from the madness and mayhem of touring, Led Zeppelin enjoyed playing the part of devoted dads and respectably settled family men. With the band's fourth album riding high in the charts on both sides of the Atlantic, the beginning of 1972 found all four band members relaxing at home and enjoying the sweet contentment of domesticity. Plant was ensconced on his Worcestershire farm, where his wife Maureen was about to give birth to their son Karac, joining their daughter Carmen. Bonham had bought a farm nearby where he bred Hereford cattle and his wife Pat was expecting their second child. Jones, the most private and self-contained member of the band, was at home with his wife Mo and their three children in their comfortable house in Rickmansworth, Hertfordshire, where he had built a home studio. Page, the only unmarried member, now had a daughter by girlfriend Charlotte Martin and had sold his Pangbourne boathouse and bought a country estate in Sussex called Plumpton Place, complete with its own moat. He would shortly add to his property portfolio with Tower House in London's Kensington, which he bought from the actor Richard Harris.

The idyll did not last long for Peter Grant had lined up their first visit to Australia and New Zealand, starting in February 1972. Things got off to an inauspicious start when a planned concert in Singapore was cancelled due to the reactionary nature of the government, which refused admission to males with long hair. Around the same time, the British bubblegum group Middle of the Road, who had enjoyed a British number one with 'Chirpy Chirpy Cheep Cheep', cheerfully agreed to an enforced short-back-and-sides in order to play in Singapore but Led Zeppelin felt the prospect of beginning their first Antipodean tour looking like a bunch of skinheads was too high a price to pay. When their flight stopped in Singapore for refuelling en route to Australia, they sensibly stayed on the plane.

Initially, it wasn't much better once they reached Australia. After a first gig in Perth, which was marred by running fights between fans and police, their hotel was raided by the local drugs squad. Astonishingly, nothing was found and the rest of the tour was wildly received by Australian audiences unused to visits from rock royalty. On the way back, Page

LED ZEPPELIN

5

and Plant again stopped off in Bombay to tend the seeds they had sown a year earlier. Hiring a local studio, the Bollywood composer Vijay Raghav Rao assembled a group of string players and they recorded experimental East–West versions of 'Four Sticks' and 'Friends'. It wasn't entirely successful and the results were never officially released, but the experience was to have a long-lasting influence on the musical development of both Page and Plant.

Back in Britain, thoughts turned swiftly to writing and recording the fifth album with initial sessions taking place both at Olympic studios in London and Mick Jagger's country pile, Stargroves, with Page this time agreeing to the high rent. A dozen new tracks were soon in various stages of completion and with out-takes from the previous two albums also available, thoughts turned to the possibility of a double album. However, work was interrupted by the start of their eighth American tour in June 1972.

It was this tour that more than 30 years later was commemorated on the live album, *How the West Was Won*, and the recordings reveal that Zeppelin were on fire, as plenty of new material from the uncompleted fifth album, including 'Over The Hills' and 'Far Away', 'The Crunge', 'Dancing Days' and The Ocean, was incorporated into the set alongside often stunning versions of the now established repertoire classics. It was also a huge success commercially. "We finally saved up the air fare to get back," Plant told the crowd. The irony was delicious for, in fact, for the first time Grant had hired them a private jet to fly around America. It was also the first tour on which he insisted on 90 per cent of the takings going to the band, leaving just 10 per cent for the promoter. The traditional split had been 50:50 but Zeppelin were such a draw

The Zep tearing it up over Australia in 1972. Bonzo's distinctive rune now appears on his bass drum, but in comparison to the Stones' elaborate stage outfits of the period, the boys retained considerable street cred by still looking as if they could have wandered onto the stage from the crowd

THE BATTLE OF THE BANDS

5

The rivalry between The Rolling Stones and The Beatles in the 1960s is legendary – but by the early 1970s, it was Led Zeppelin they were vying with for the title 'greatest rock 'n' roll band in the world'.

Although the Stones released chart-topping albums in Let It Bleed (1969) and Sticky Fingers (1971), after their 1969 American tour had ended in the disaster of Altamont, they stayed off the road for the next three years, leaving Zeppelin to rise to the top on the back of their relentless touring of the US.

Following the release of the double LP Exile on Main St in May 1972, the Stones embarked on their first American tour since 1969. It was a spectacular trek. Between June 3 and July 26, they played 51 shows in 32 venues, drawing an audience of 750,000 people and grossing four million dollars. They also took a leaf out of Peter Grant's book in demanding a high percentage of the takings, although not quite as high as Zeppelin's 90 per cent. "There was a 100 per cent gross due to advance sell-outs for every concert," tour manager Peter Rudge told Billboard. "The Rolling Stones took between 60 and 70 per cent of that amount, but that was a gross figure. All expenses came out of

the Stones' earnings. And they spent a lot of money to put on good shows everywhere."

Every gig seemed to be followed by a celebrity-packed party with a guest list that extended far beyond the rock' n' roll set to draw in the great and the good of the literary, art, film and social worlds, and a string of beautiful women from Jackie Kennedy's sister to Zsa Zsa Gabor.

"They could play three months in San Francisco and probably six in New York and sell out every seat," the promoter Bill Graham asserted. "They are the biggest draw in the history of mankind. Only one other guy ever came close: Gandhi."

Zeppelin's tour, which took in 19 dates between June 6 and 28, was spectacular in its own right and musically it was arguably the best they had ever played. Yet there's no doubt they were totally eclipsed by the Stones. Melody Maker's Roy Hollingsworth, who covered both tours, noted of their date at New York's Nassau Coliseum: "It was one of the most amazing concerts I'd seen from any band at any time." But he topped his own hyperbole when he caught up with the Stones a week later and wrote: "This tour is going to go down as the rock 'n' roll tour of all

time."

Once the tour was over, Zeppelin could not disguise their bitterness. "We've just toured the States and done as well if not better than the Stones but there was hardly anything about it in the British press," Bonham complained to NME. "All we read was 'the Stones this' and 'the Stones that' and it pissed us off, made us feel what the hell, here we are flogging our guts out and for all the notice being given to us we might as well be playing in bloody Ceylon. Because the kids in England didn't even know we were touring the States."

A couple of years later Plant was still sore enough to complain to Rolling Stone Magazine's Cameron Crowe: "We knew full well that we were doing more business than them. We were getting better gates in comparison to a lot of people who were constantly glorified in the press."

Perhaps what hurt most, however, was not the respective column inches or even box office receipts, but the simple fact that while the Stones were being lionised by the likes of Andy Warhol, TrumanCapote and American chic liberal society, Led Zeppelin were still regarded as the hooligans at the gate.

LED ZEPPELIN

5

that despite loud grumbles, promoters had little choice but reluctantly to agree.

The one problem was that the press chose virtually to ignore the tour. This was largely due to the fact that at exactly the same time, The Rolling Stones had returned to the road for their first American tour since 1969, which had ended with the horror of Altamont. Unveiling the famous tongue logo for the first time and with a galaxy of celebrities in tow, including Jack Nicholson, Goldie Hawn, Hugh Hefner, Andy Warhol, Truman Capote, Princess Lee Radziwill and Norman Mailer, the Stones gobbled up all the column inches, both in America and back home in Britain, while Zeppelin's record-breaking tour went virtually unreported (see box). Perhaps it was payback for the hostility that had existed between Zeppelin and the media from the outset but the band felt slighted and were furious. As Keith Shadwick puts it: "Zeppelin wanted their media egos massaged and were intent on throwing their toys out of the pram if no one listened." To try and make them listen, Grant hired as the band's official publicist BP Fallon, whose previous clients had included T Rex, whose *Electric Warrior* had just a few months earlier dislodged *Led Zeppelin IV* from the top of the British chart. Plant, with typical wit and bravado, later explained the band's change of tactics in its media relations: "We thought it was time that people heard something about us other than that we were eating women and throwing the bones out the window."

With the tour over, at the end of June 1972 the band briefly went into Electric Lady studios in New York to do some work on the album that would become *Houses of the Holy*, before returning to Britain and their families. While Plant, Bonham and Jones relaxed, Page continued to work on the new album, determined not to repeat the mixing errors that had delayed *Led Zeppelin IV*. However, there were other delays as he overdubbed parts while the sleeve design also caused the usual headache. He also became distracted by accepting a commission from the film director Kenneth Anger to write the soundtrack for his film *Lucifer Rising*. The project would prove to be a disaster, with Page completing less than half-an-hour's worth of music and being unceremoniously sacked. But at the end of 1972, he was still working hard and was enthusiastic about the project. "I wanted it to sound timeless in a way, not to sound dated by anything. I used a synthesiser on it but I tried to use it in such a way that it didn't sound like a synthesiser, just that all the instruments didn't sound like what they ought to sound. You don't quite know what it is at any point."

Jones was also starting to use a synthesiser – or rather a mellotron, an early and somewhat temperamental machine that The Beatles had deployed on 'Strawberry Fields Forever' and which the likes of The Moody Blues and King Crimson had also used to good effect. It can be heard on 'The Rain Song' on *Houses of the Holy* and Jones also took it with him when the band headed back to Japan for a second Far Eastern tour in October 1972. When he used the mellotron during *Stairway to Heaven* on stage, Plant habitually quipped: "John Paul Jones was the rather cheap orchestra."

True to form, the new album still wasn't ready by the time of the Japanese dates, which went well – although, if Richard Cole is to be believed, a stopover in Hong Kong on the way back was later to have serious ramifications for the band when they were introduced to heroin for the first time. According to Cole, he had tried to obtain them cocaine but was given heroin instead. He didn't bother telling them and they snorted rather than injected it and were violently ill.

5

There was still no sign of the new album when they returned home and commenced a 24-date British tour, the longest they were ever to play on home soil and for which ticket prices were pegged at £1. The tour opened at the end of November in Newcastle, and with a 10-day break over Christmas carried on until the end of January. Needless to say, it was not without incident. In Glasgow, the band's new publicist BP Fallon was beaten up by fans who had been sold counterfeit tickets and were looking for a scapegoat. In protest, the group refused to play an encore, a strange decision to punish a crowd that presumably did not contain the miscreants, who would have been unable to obtain entry without proper tickets.

Fallon's attempts to make the band more media friendly included lining up an interview during warm-up gigs for the British tour in Montreux between Plant and *Melody Maker's* Chris Charlesworth, who in his report then dared to suggest that the band's popularity was waning. Plant then took great delight in sarcastically relaying the comment to the crowds, which gave them standing, stomping, storming ovations every night. Fallon also invited *NME's* Nick Kent to accompany the band around the UK. He filed favourable copy at the time, but years later claimed that in all his years as a rock journalist he had never seen anyone behave worse than Bonham and Richard Cole. "I once saw them beat a guy senseless and then drop money on his face," he wrote. "It makes me feel sick when I hear Plant talking about what a great geezer Bonzo was, because the guy was a schizophrenic animal."

While Zeppelin travelled around America by private jet, in Britain it was a different story with band members driving themselves to and from gigs. On the way to a date at Sheffield City Hall on January 2, Bonham and Plant broke down in the drummer's Bentley and were forced to hitchhike in the rain. The singer caught a cold, and although the show went on that night, the following two dates had to be postponed.

Almost unbelievably, the much-delayed new album – which had now been given the title *Houses of the Holy* – was still not ready when Zeppelin began a European tour in March 1973. On their French gigs, the band were accompanied by Benoît Gautier, an executive from Atlantic Records' Paris office whose recollections offer a fascinating insight into the mentality of the Zeppelin touring party at the time. "It was obvious that some of them were using drugs but they were very discreet," he reported. "They never asked for grass or anything; they asked for legal things, mostly girls. Prostitution is legal in France. They wanted good booze, nice parties and amusing people. Peter Grant would say, 'I want everybody to have a good time tonight; can you find six beautiful girls?' On one occasion, he claims he was asked to arrange a lesbian sex show for the band to watch at their hotel, the swanky George V in Paris.

Equally revealing are his observations on the band's individual members. Page he described as "the mastermind of it all and very much in control", but he was shocked by the amount of cocaine he was taking. Plant, he noted, "never harmed anybody, had good manners, was always smiling". He found Jones "bright, intelligent and cultured" and reckoned the bassist was the smartest member of the group. "He never got caught in an embarrassing situation," he remarked. "He would always show at the very last minute for anything. You'd never even know where he was staying. He drove himself and was independent from the rest of the band. Peter and the band were always saying, 'Where the fuck is he?' It upset them that they couldn't manipulate him."

The picture he paints of Bonham, however, is deeply disturbing. At one point the drummer offered Gautier a line of cocaine. He was about

LED ZEPPELIN

5

The 1973 US tour was the pinnacle of the band's touring excess

to snort it when he realised it wasn't cocaine at all but heroin. "He thought that was the funniest thing, offering you coke and giving you smack. He would take a chance of killing you!" On the other hand, he says that when he admired a particular shirt Bonham was wearing, he took it off and gave it to him. "Bonzo would cry when talking about his family," he recalls. "Then the roadies would start to push him to do something and he'd go crazy. He would throw drinks or dump food on somebody if Jimmy told him to. He had no natural defence against being manipulated and nothing to protect him."

Houses of the Holy finally hit record stores towards the end of the European tour, 17 months after *Led Zeppelin IV*. Predictably, it went to number one the world over but it was an oddly unsatisfying affair. In some ways it found the band commendably attempting to break new ground, often going for mood rather than raw excitement. But the atmospheric power of the best tracks such as 'Dancing Days' and 'The Song

Remains the Same' was offset by the throw-away frivolity of 'D'yer Mak'er' and 'The Crunge', which Page freely admitted had been recorded as "just a giggle". If the purpose of such songs was for Led Zeppelin to show the critics that they had a sense of humour, arguably they worked. But musically they were lightweight and dragged the album down.

Page seemed to recognise this, too, when he told *NME*: "I'm deaf to the album because we made it such a long time ago but I know there's some good stuff there." Which, of course, there was, but which is quite different from saying it's a great album. As a follow-up to the power and glory of *Led Zeppelin IV*, it was a disappointing and heavily flawed exercise that betrayed the fact that it had been so long in the making that much of the joy and spontaneity had been squeezed out of the grooves. Reviews at the time were mixed and history has not been particularly kind to *Houses of the Holy*, either. Ultimately, it's hard to argue with Keith Shadwick's conclusion: "If it had been released closer to the unfolding success of *Led Zeppelin IV* the line-up of songs would have been different and more tightly co-ordinated. The feel may well have been different, too, for there is a palpable air in the songs towards the end of the album of a band who have arrived, big time, and are surveying their domain."

Barney Hoskyns perceptively compares *Houses of the Holy* to The Rolling Stones' *Goats Head Soup*. Both bands had made acclaimed masterpieces in *Led Zeppelin IV* and *Exile on Main St*; both had taken the best part of a year-and-a-half to follow it up – and after the long wait both bands managed to miss the mark. However, there was at least one fundamental difference. After *Exile on Main Street*, the Stones' best work was already behind them. Led Zeppelin still had the triumph of *Physical Graffiti* to come, which many regard as their crowning glory.

Whatever the failings of *Houses of the Holy*, they were still dynamite on stage. "We're playing better than we've ever played before," Plant insisted. "It's working that does it. It's easy to get stale and some bands reach a peak and think that's it – the old country house bit and a year off. It doesn't work that way. There's only one way to function and that's on stage. We've reached a high and we ain't going to lose it. And no bad album review is going to change that."

As if to prove it, their ninth American tour which opened in May 1973 set about redefining the parameters of rock as extravaganza – or as the estimable Dave Lewis put it, "With this tour Led Zeppelin graduated from being a mere rock band to something of an institution in America." Perhaps spurred by the previous year's disappointment at being out-done by the Stones, they added lasers, dry ice, backdrops,

mirror balls, exploding cannon, smoke bombs and giant screens relaying pictures to the more distant parts of the huge stadiums in which they played. "We felt the denim jeans trip had been there for a long time. It was time to take the trip a little further and these ideas fit perfectly with the mood of the new songs and the excitement of the old," Plant explained.

Chartering their own private jet again, they set about breaking attendance records set by The Beatles seven and eight years earlier on a marathon coast-to-coast trek split into two legs. Opening on May 4 and closing 87 days later on July 29, with most of June taken off in the middle for their batteries to be recharged, by the end they had also topped the four million dollars grossed by the Stones on their 1972 tour, setting another record.

A new addition to the touring party was American PR Danny Goldberg, who immediately proved his prowess as a spin doctor by 'leaking' to *Rolling Stone* that Grant anticipated the biggest-grossing US tour of all time with box-office receipts in excess of five million dollars, and then extracting a quote from the mayor of Atlanta, where the tour opened, that Zeppelin were "the biggest thing to hit America since the premiere of *Gone with the wind*." In their early days, Zeppelin had been attacked in the British music press as all hype and no substance. The band were hurt by such criticisms, which they felt were unfair and ignorant. Now here they were paying Goldberg to hype to the heavens in the most calculated and cynical way. Perhaps it was a case of 'if you can't beat them, then join them'.

But it wasn't merely hype, of course. In Atlanta, they played to a crowd of 50,000. The next day in Tampa, Florida, they topped that with a paying crowd of 56,800 – the largest ever concert attendance for a single act, breaking a record set by The Beatles in 1965, even without counting an estimated 6,000 gatecrashers. Peter

LED ZEPPELIN

5

Grant later joked: "I didn't tell them really how big it was going to be, but when we drew up, Robert was going 'Fucking hell, where did all these people come from?' And I just said: 'Don't worry son. I know you're still on probation with the band, but you'll be all right.'"

Playing three-hour sets featuring material ranging across their entire career, the band also used their sound checks to work up new material that would eventually appear on *Physical Graffiti*, including 'The Wanton Song', 'The Rover' and 'Night Flight'. Off stage, there were the usual debauched goings-on, and for once the usually reticent Jones was caught out, passing out drunk in his hotel room in New Orleans with a pretty young woman, who, to the general hilarity of his fellow band members, turned out to be a transvestite. Bob Hart, a journalist from the British tabloid *The Sun*, chronicled some of the excesses but kept his own counsel about the band's huge drug intake intact. It was only several years later that he admitted: "I saw quantities of coke on that tour that were truly remarkable. There was an English girl I'll call Jane who travelled on the tour and she was the coke lady. This was so that nobody else ever carried or touched the coke. When she was summoned she would apply the coke with the little finger of her right hand, then follow that up with a sniff of cherry snuff and, as a final touch, she'd dab the nostrils with Dom Perignon 1966, which was the signature drink of the tour."

Hart also noted that in San Francisco, alongside the lavish backstage food, drink and other refreshments, promoter Bill Graham provided a table "bearing a large pile of a certain white substance" as an unofficial extra on the band's rider. Despite Goldberg's efforts, press reaction was once again mixed. *Rolling Stone* typically sneered, reporting from the San Francisco show that "Zeppelin are back doing what they do best: converting heavy

mental into dollars." However, the British music press had long got over its reservations about the band. Charles Shaar Murray, reviewing the same show for *NME*, wrote: "Led Zeppelin and 50,000 San Francisco people got together to provide one of the finest musical events I've ever had the privilege to attend. There may be bands who play better, and there may be bands who perform better and there may be bands who write better songs, but when it comes to welding themselves and an audience together into one unit of total joy, Zeppelin yield to nobody. Altogether a magical concert. I suppose legions of die-hard Zep freaks have known this all along, but for me it was a revelation."

After enjoying most of June off, during which time some of the band vacationed in Hawaii, the tour resumed in Chicago on July 6, 1973 for an equally successful second leg. After experiencing problems with the small private jet they had chartered for the first leg, they now had their own Boeing 720, known as the Starship with LED ZEPPELIN emblazoned on the fuselage, and which Cole had managed to hire at a bargain 10,000 dollars a week. At Chicago's O'Hare Airport they proudly showed it off to the party of travelling journalists and were particularly pleased that it dwarfed Hugh Hefner's private jet parked alongside.

During the second leg of the tour, filmmaker Joe Massot filmed the band over three sold-out nights at Madison Square Garden in New York for what was to become *The Song Remains the Film*. He asked the band to wear the same stage clothes each night so the footage could be edited together and all complied with the request except Jones, who perversely wore something completely different each night. Yet it would be another three troubled years before the unsatisfactory film was finally finished and released.

The New York gigs made a fitting finale to a landmark tour, although the band's triumph

THE STARSHIP

5

Hiring the Boeing 720 wasn't merely about celebrity one-upmanship. On a practical level, the Starship meant the band did not have to change hotels every night but could base themselves in large cities such as New York, Los Angeles, Dallas and Chicago and fly back in luxury on a plane fitted with revolving armchairs, a bar, club room, bedrooms and a shower. There was even an organ. After a gig, a fleet of limousines ensured that the band were frequently in the air before the audience had even exited the venue. NBC News was invited to film on board the Starship and footage showed Page and Plant singing along to 'I do Like to be Beside the Seaside' accompanied by Jones on the plane's organ. In an accompanying interview, Plant complained: "I'm a bit upset there's not a pool table."

John Bonham, a notoriously uneasy and reluctant flyer, found that if he sat up front in the cockpit in the co-pilot's seat, some of his nerves evaporated. However, Grant's claim to journalist Chris Charlesworth that the drummer had once taken the controls to fly the band from New York to L.A. was probably a wind-up.

After Zeppelin had started using the Starship in 1973, it was subsequently used by The Rolling Stones and Elton John. By Zeppelin's 1977 tour, however, the Starship was out of commission. It was replaced by 'Caesars Chariot', a Boeing 707 chartered from the Caesar's Palace casino in Las Vegas.

was marred by a couple of off-stage incidents. First, just before the third gig, 180,000 dollars in brand new notes from the Madison Square Garden promoter went missing from the band's safe deposit box at the Drake Hotel. Tour manager Richard Cole discovered the theft and after getting the road crew to search all the suites in the hotel booked to the band and cleansing them of drugs, with particular attention to the rooms occupied by 'Jane the coke lady', he called in the police. For his pains, he was then interviewed as a suspect,

5

although he was not charged after taking a lie detector test. The band later sued the hotel and received a settlement from the Drake's insurance company. It left a sour note but also put the band in a quandary. As Bonham put it, "If we make like we care too much, they'll say we're only in it for the money. If we say we don't care, they'll say it's because we're too rich." Asked by the press why the band carried so much cash, Grant claimed it was to pay off the cost of hiring the Starship, although that still left 150,000 dollars in spare change.

The police also got involved in a second incident at the Drake when Grant was arrested for assaulting *New York Daily News* photographer Charles Ruppman and ripping the film out of his camera.

The day after the final New York concert, the band flew back to Britain. They were wrecked, probably in equal parts by the hard work and by the hedonistic excesses that followed when the night's graft had been done. Page was in a particular bad way, described by Stephen Davis as "exhausted, malnourished, sleepless, raving". The guitarist's alarmed family suggested he went to a sanitarium and he admitted he felt he probably belonged in a mental hospital at the time. "I was thinking 'What the hell am I going to do?' because it seemed like the adrenaline tap wouldn't switch off," he told one journalist. "During those concerts to that many people, there was so much energy being stored up. I felt like a kettle with a cork in the top. I'd stay up for five nights on the trot. It didn't seem to affect my playing but I'd come off stage and I was not levelling off at all, not turning off the adrenaline. I couldn't. I felt I needed to go somewhere there was a padded cell so I could switch off and go loony if I wanted. I was quite serious about it."

On tour, of course, staying up for five nights was aided by the copious amounts of cocaine

he was taking. On his return, it may well be that this was where Page's problems with heroin started. Rather than the padded cell the drug became his way of turning off the adrenaline.

Jones responded in a different but equally extreme way. He went to Peter Grant and told him he was leaving the band. "He told me he'd had enough and said he was going to be the choirmaster at Winchester Cathedral," he revealed. Jones says that the choirmaster line was a joke, but confirms the gist of the story. "I did consider leaving after our 1973 tour of America. I'd just had enough of touring and I did go to Peter and tell him I wanted out unless things were changed. There was a lot of pressure on my family, what with being away so long." Grant asked him not to do anything rash or hasty but to go away and reflect upon it and to think again. "It was kept low key," Grant added. "I told Jimmy, of course, who couldn't believe it. But it was the pressure. He was a family man, was Jonesy. By that time the security thing in the US was getting ridiculous. We started getting death threats. It got very worrying after that and I think that's how we lost a little of the camaraderie." Jones sought further assurances that things were going to change, and having received satisfactory answers from Grant, decided to stay.

Meanwhile, Plant was having voice problems and in 1988 he confessed: "Fifteen years ago I had an operation on my throat and couldn't speak for three weeks." At various times during the 1973 American tour he had sounded hoarse and strained and it seems almost certain that the operation he alluded to took place in the late summer or autumn of 1973. Clearly Led Zeppelin desperately needed a rest. Yet few could have guessed that it would be another 18 months before the band would be seen on a live stage again.

WEARING AND TEARING
1974–1976

6

"I realised I really missed the unity of the four of us. I realised that above everything else, above record companies, above films, we were Led Zeppelin."

ROBERT PLANT 1975

WEARING AND TEARING

6

1974–1975

Six years on the road, a load of cash in the band's account and tax exile beckoning, things were getting tough. Everybody – the Inland Revenue, record labels, movie producers, roadies and groupies – wanted a piece of the action. But then a few nights at Earls Court did the trick. Can you fly any higher? For the faithful, probably not.

During the long sabbatical from live appearances that followed the 1973 American tour, Led Zeppelin were hardly inactive. There was a film to finish, a record label to launch – and without the interruption of endless live dates, a record to make that would see them realise the double album they had long talked about and which would match The Beatles' *White Album*, The Who's *Tommy* and The Rolling Stones' *Exile on Main St* as a heavyweight statement of their abilities.

It should have swiftly become apparent to a man as astute as Peter Grant that the film was a folly. He had been a stuntman and bit-part actor before he went into rock management and perhaps his previous experience had coloured his vision for he was besotted with the idea. After filming the Madison Square Garden shows in 1973, it was decided that each band member should have his own fantasy vignette. Instead of telling them not to be ridiculous, Grant decided that he, too, should have his own fantasy scene, one of the few times he ever actively courted or encouraged the idea of himself as the 'fifth member' of the band. That the model for their cinematic venture was T Rex's film *Born to*

Boogie only seemed to emphasise that they were courting potential disaster: Led Zeppelin so despised the notion of being a pop band that they refused to release any singles in Britain. Yet here they were using the biggest teenybopper band in the land as a template. "They wanted to show themselves as individuals but not in the traditional way of interviews," director Joe Massot said. "They wanted more symbolic representations of themselves." From the moment this misconceived decision was taken, the film was doomed to resemble a self-indulgent home movie rather than a serious documentary about the greatest rock 'n' roll band in the world.

The band and Grant each dreamed up their own sequences and Massot spent the latter part of 1973 shooting their ideas, however weird and whimsical. Only the down-to-earth Bonham avoided pretension by choosing to be filmed with his family and on his farm with his tractor and his cows. In a way, it was his fantasy but at least it was real and he was actually living it. By March 1974, the inexperienced Massot had been sacked – ironically not due to the ineptitude of the fantasy sequences but following a

LED ZEPPELIN

screening of the rough cut of the live footage from Madison Square Garden. The band didn't like what they saw and Massot later famously quipped: "They thought it was my fault Robert Plant had such a big cock. It took them another year to recuperate." In his place came the more experienced Peter Clifton, who inherited not only a complete mess of a film but all the internal complications of the band's politics, which meant that like Massot, he was never completely in charge of the footage.

At least in launching their own label, Led Zeppelin were on surer ground. If what they knew about film-making could be written on the back of a postage stamp, nobody could deny that they certainly knew how to sell records. With their contract with Atlantic Records expiring at the end of 1973, Grant wasted no time in negotiating a new deal under which Zeppelin would administer their own still unnamed label and have complete control over artistic direction and signing policy, but which would be distributed worldwide by Atlantic. Crucially, Zeppelin would be the label's main act and this time the model was not T Rex but The Rolling Stones, who had established a similar deal with Atlantic following the expiry of their original contract with Decca Records (London in America). The deal was announced jointly by Grant and Atlantic founder Ahmet Ertegun in January 1974, but it was May before Swan Song was up and running, launched with a double celebration at the Four Seasons in New York and the Bel-Air hotel in Los Angeles, where Groucho Marx was among the unlikely guests.

The name took some time to resolve. Only a month before Swan Song's launch, Plant was still saying the matter was unresolved. "We went through all the usual ones, all the ones that twist off your tongue right away, like Slut and Slag, the sort of name one would associate with us touring America. But that's not how we want to be remembered. We want

something really nice." The logo was based on the 1869 painting Evening, Fall of Day by William Rimmer, depicting a winged Apollo, although it has often been misinterpreted as representing Icarus or Lucifer.

The British launch of Swan Song did not come until October, with a launch party for The Pretty Things' album Silk Torpedo on Halloween night in Chislehurst Caves in Kent. It was one of the few occasions that Britain got a taste of the Zeppelin school of debauchery with which America had grown so familiar, with stripper nuns and all manner of other excess.

Unfortunately, the label's signing policy proved to be rather conservative. Instead of searching for fresh talent – and perhaps running the risk of discovering a new band that might eventually eclipse them – they created a rest home for their old friends and contemporaries, The Pretty Things, who had been around since the mid-1960s, being a case in point. The most successful of their signings was Bad Company, fronted by former Free singer Paul Rodgers. But, whether as a deliberate act of policy or not, they never ran the risk of taking on anyone who might rival let alone outstrip them. Essentially, Swan Song was a plaything, but with Zeppelin themselves as the label's guaranteed multi-million-selling lead attraction, it was an indulgence they could easily afford. However, to Plant's never-ending disappointment, when both the Chess and Sun back catalogues were up for sale, he and Page were over-ruled when they proposed buying them, with Jones, Bonham and a particularly hostile Grant out-voting them.

Yet both the American and British launches of Swan Song had unexpected bonuses. While in Los Angeles, Zeppelin received an invitation to meet Elvis Presley after the band had been to see him perform at the L.A. Forum. Meanwhile, The Pretty Things' performance at Chislehurst Caves, according to Plant, reminded the band that the main purpose for their existence was not to make films or run record labels but to create music in front of as big an audience as possible. As a result, Grant was asked to put together a major touring schedule for 1975.

There was also the follow-up to 1973's *Houses of the Holy* to concentrate minds. One might have thought that with their own label, the logistics of putting out an album would have been simpler but it wasn't the case. Sessions for the new album had actually begun at Headley Grange in late 1973. The band reconvened there in February 1974, and even though they were now thinking about a double album, they were optimistic about getting it out that spring. By May, the sessions had been concluded and a track listing agreed that combined new material and some of the backlog of unreleased tracks from previous albums. "What we talk about is creating something as notable as Beethoven's Fifth. Not just something that would still be remembered in 50 years but something so mammoth that it would last forever," Plant even told one interviewer. Ominously, however, he also joked: "We haven't got around to our six-month decision on covers yet."

In the event, it took almost another year for the cover and other assorted problems to be ironed out and *Physical Graffiti*, their first double album and their debut release on Swan Song, did not appear until February 1975.

The clever jacket art was intriguing enough, but the music inside – from the Arabesque thunder of 'Kashmir' to the cataclysmic bottleneck blues of 'In My Time of Dying' – was, and remains, simply awesome. There was no unifying theme to the album, but it really didn't need one. Drawing on material spanning four or five years, it summed up everything that had taken Zeppelin to the top and at the same time mapped out new vistas and horizons for them. As with the Stones' double album *Exile on Main St*, some critics took their time to take it all in, but the reviews were positive

and the album topped the charts in both Britain and America, where it stayed in the number one spot for six weeks.

By the time *Physical Graffiti* hit the shops, Zeppelin were already back on the road for their tenth American tour and they would not return to live in Britain for the next 12 months. Three weeks before the tour was due to begin, the band's accountant Joan Hudson informed Grant that there would be "massive problems" with the Inland Revenue and a gargantuan tax bill to pay unless the band took a prolonged absence from UK shores. It was the price of rock 'n' roll fame: like The Rolling Stones three years earlier, Led Zeppelin were now tax exiles.

Their tenth American tour was not a bad way to begin a year in exile. Like its 1973 predecessor it was split into two legs, running from mid-January to the end of March, with a 12-day break in the middle. In its early stages there were health problems. Page had damaged a finger in a train door which restricted his dexterity on the fretboard. Plant caught flu (allegedly after arriving bare-chested at Chicago's O'Hare Airport in January!) and Bonham complained of stomach pains. Page's injury in particular created a few changes in the set list but any shortcomings were covered up by Zeppelin's most successful stage presentation to date, with a neon-lit backdrop, a massive light show and laser effects to heighten the drama of Plant's violin bow interlude.

By the second leg, which opened at the end of February, *Physical Graffiti* was finally out, the band were in much better shape and the tour ended triumphantly in Los Angeles at the end of March with, bizarrely, *Deep Throat* porn star Linda Lovelace introducing the band on stage. Off stage, heroin had been added to their usual list of debauched pastimes. "Although alcohol and cocaine were still much more prevalent, I frequently nourished my own smack habit, and

6

LED ZEPPELIN

6 THE SWAN SONG FAMILY

THE PRETTY THINGS

Veterans of the British beat boom of the 1960s, The Pretty Things are one of the great hard-luck stories of British rock. Cast in the same mould as The Rolling Stones, they played an even dirtier, tougher form of rudimentary R&B but despite a couple of classic hit singles with 'Don't Bring Me Down' and 'Rosalyn' (both later covered by David Bowie) they were swiftly eclipsed by Mick, Keith, Brian, Bill and Charlie. In 1967, they reinvented themselves as a 'Summer of Love' psychedelic band and the following year released the classic S.F. *Sorrow*, widely recognised as the first 'rock opera'. Yet it was virtually ignored at the time and all of the plaudits went instead to Pete Townshend for The Who's *Tommy*. Even the endorsement of Led Zeppelin failed to bring them commercial success and after two albums on Swan Song, founder member Phil May left in 1976, effectively bringing the band to an end. The remaining members changed their name to Metropolis and there was talk of Jimmy Page producing them, but nothing ever materialised.
Swan Song albums:
Silk Torpedo (1974)
Savage Eye (1976)

BAD COMPANY

Formed in late 1973 by ex-members of Free, Mott the Hoople and King Crimson as an instant supergroup, Bad Company were by far the biggest success on Swan Song other than Led Zeppelin themselves. With the voice of Paul Rodgers as the main attraction but ably backed by Mick Ralphs on guitar, Boz Burrell on drums and Simon Kirke on bass, they were one of the progenitors of stadium rock, with the likes of Foreigner and Bon Jovi taking their cue from the band's power chords and testosterone-charged lyrics. Managed by Peter

Grant, unlike his other charges they were very much a singles band, hitting the higher echelons of the charts with 'Can't Get Enough', 'Good Lovin' Gone Bad' and 'Feel Like Makin' Love'. They split in 1982 and Rodgers went on to form The Firm with Jimmy Page.
Swan Song albums:
Bad Company (1974)
Straight Shooter (1975)
Run with the Pack (1976)
Burnin' Sky (1977)
Desolation Angels (1979)
Rough Diamonds (1982)

DAVE EDMUNDS

Like his close friend and collaborator Nick Lowe, Edmunds had a brilliant ability to recreate classic rockabilly, rock 'n' roll and country styles without ever descending into the realms of pastiche. He first came to prominence in the late-1960s with the blues-rock trio Love Sculpture, who scored a top ten hit with 'Sabre Dance' and then enjoyed a chart-topping solo single in 1970 with 'I Hear You Knocking.' His band Rockpile supported Led Zeppelin at Knebworth and he recorded four albums for Swan Song that included such hit singles as 'I Knew the Bride' and 'Girls Talk'. After building his own studio, Rockfield, in his native Wales, he became a top producer, helming albums by the likes of the Flamin' Groovies and Shakin' Stevens. Robert Plant has used his Rockfield studios regularly over the years.
Swan Song albums:

Get It (1977)
Trax on Wax 4 (1978)
Repeat When Necessary (1979)
Twangin'... (1981)

MAGGIE BELL

Coming on like a Scottish Janis Joplin, Maggie Bell's raw and earthy voice graced Stone the Crows until the band split in 1973. She then signed to Swan Song as a solo artist, but despite her debut album being produced by the legendary Jerry Wexler and featuring the cream of America's session players, she enjoyed little commercial success. She subsequently fronted the band Midnight Flyer, who were also signed to Swan Song, releasing just one album.
Swan Song albums:
Suicide Sal (1975)
Midnight Flyer (with Midnight Flyer) (1981)

DETECTIVE

Discovered by Jimmy Page in a club in Los Angeles in 1976, Detective were fronted by ex-Silverhead singer Michael des Barres and also featured former Yes keyboard player Tony Kaye, Michael Monarch on guitar, Bobby Pickett on drums and Jon Hyde on drums. Clearly modelling their sound on Led Zeppelin, Page himself produced their debut album under the pseudonym Jimmy Robinson. Fame eluded them despite their illustrious champion, although it did land them roles in an episode of the American TV comedy *WKRP In Cincinnati*.
Swan Song albums:

Detective (1977)
It Takes One to Know One (1978)

WILDLIFE

Discovered by Simon Kirke around the time of Bad Company's demise, Wildlife was a band based around the two young Overland brothers, who played music broadly in a style similar to Journey or Styx. "I was looking for a band to either join as a drummer or produce. I heard the tapes and thought, 'There's some really good stuff here'," Kirke recalls. In the end he became the drummer and their sole album was produced by Mick Ralphs. With Swan Song barely functional and on the point of winding up, the album and the band sank without trace.
Swan Song albums:
Wildlife (1983)

Artists signed to the label but whose work was never released included New York singer-songwriter Mirabai, The Message (featuring future Bon Jovi members Alec John Such and Richie Sambora), and Itchy Brother. The label also had lengthy discussions about signing Roy Harper, but despite the close friendship between the singer-songwriter and members of the band, negotiations broke down. Swan Song ceased operations in October 1983, and when the offices were cleared out, demos from Iron Maiden and Paul Young's Q-Tips were found unplayed in a filing cabinet. On Swan Song's demise, Robert Plant started his own label, Es Paranza, and Jimmy Page and John Paul Jones reverted to Atlantic Records.

LED ZEPPELIN

6

at one time or another Jimmy, Robert and Bonzo tried some, too," Richard Cole recalled.

Unable to return to Britain for tax reasons, Grant decided to use the limited number of days they were allowed into the UK for a series of five dates at London's Earls Court in May 1975 – their first concerts on home soil since January 1973. With the full panoply of their American stage set on show, they played a series of barnstorming shows which included a fine acoustic set, as can be seen on footage included on the 2003 DVD. Plant couldn't help having a jibe one night at Chancellor of the Exchequer Denis Healey, whose tax policies had forced them into exile. "We're about a foot away from the chain gang with our dear Denis," the singer noted on the first night before ironically dedicating 'In My Time of Dying' to the Labour politician. At the very end of the last show as the band took their bow, Plant quipped: "If you see Denis Healey, tell him we're gone!"

With hindsight, the Earls Court dates were "the last of Led Zeppelin's glory days before they were beset by tragedy", as Dave Lewis wrote in *Led Zeppelin: The Concert File*. After taking off with Page on a holiday to Morocco – "hunting in the jungle for new words and new songs for a new album", as Plant put it from the Earls Court stage – the singer and his wife Maureen and three children continued their vacation on the island of Rhodes in Greece. It was there on August 4, with the band's next American tour due to start three weeks later, that the car in which Plant and his family were travelling collided with a tree.

Plant's wife, who was driving, broke her pelvis and leg and fractured her skull and required an immediate blood transfusion. She had a

For British fans, the extended run at London's Earls Court in 1975 (above and right) probably remains the high point of Zeppelin's achievement

THE DAY ZEP MET ELVIS

6

By 1974, when Led Zeppelin got to meet Elvis, there was some confusion about who was now the 'King'. Presley and Zeppelin shared the same American promoter, Jerry Weintraub, and so all concerned knew that outside of Las Vegas, in terms by pulling power the British group was the hotter ticket.

When Zeppelin turned up to see his show one night at the Forum in L.A., Elvis was intrigued to meet this bunch of long-haired English barbarians who were selling out venues faster than he was. After singing 'Love Me Tender', he told the audience: "I want to let everyone know my favourite band Led Zeppelin is here tonight. I'd like to have the spotlight put on them and I hope you'll join me in welcoming them." According to the not-always-reliable account of the band's road manager Richard Cole, when the lights came up, they revealed drummer John Bonham to be fast asleep.

Afterwards the band were shown up to Presley's penthouse suite at the Inglewood, over the street from the venue. Determined to show who was the real star, he kept them waiting until the room was full before making his entrance. While Bonham attempted to engage him in conversation about hot rods and Peter Sellers movies, Elvis asked if the wild stories about Zeppelin on the road were true. Robert Plant mumbled something about them all having families and how easily rumours were spread. Presley laughed – and the ice was broken.

"The four of us and him talked for a couple of hours," Plant recalls. "We all stood in a circle and discussed this whole phenomenon, this lunacy. You'd have to go a long way to find someone with a better idea of what it was all about. He was very focused." Despite the mishap of Peter Grant sitting on Elvis's father Vernon ("He was perched on the end of the settee and I just didn't see him"), they got on so famously that Plant and Presley were soon trading lines from 'Treat Me Like a Fool'. When they left, Elvis asked Led Zeppelin for their autographs. Bonham was intensely embarrassed and only partly reassured when Presley explained that the signatures were apparently for his daughter, Lisa Marie.

For Plant the meeting was a particular thrill, for his entire youthful desire to become a singer had been down to the first time he had heard Presley's voice. "It was the blue note, that mournful dip in the scale that you didn't hear in English music," he recalled in 2005. "It was the whole deal of that emotional delivery he borrowed from Arthur Crudup and Johnnie Ray. I was eight or nine and I didn't know anything about the technical ability of it. I just heard this sound that wasn't anything to do with childhood. I recognised the conviction, although I didn't even know it was called conviction. I didn't know anything about sexuality or the innuendo or that it was part of a movement called rock 'n' roll. I just knew the call, the pleading in that voice."

LED ZEPPELIN

6

rare blood type which might have caused a life-threatening delay in locating supplies, but fortunately her sister, Shirley, who had the same blood group, was travelling behind in a second car with Page's girlfriend and their daughter Scarlet. The children, who had been sitting in the back, suffered only minor cuts, bruises and shock, but Plant in the front passenger's seat broke an arm and both his legs.

Charlotte Martin contacted Richard Cole back in London, who immediately flew private doctors out to Greece. After emergency treatment there, Cole managed to get the entire party on a plane back to London for further surgery. The day after the crash, Grant cancelled all plans for the American tour and the band would not tour again until 1977.

In addition to his broken bones, Plant, however, had a further pressing problem. As a tax exile he could only spend the bare minimum of time in Britain and within days he had to be moved again. While his seriously ill wife remained in hospital in London, he was flown in a wheelchair to Jersey, a British island near the coast of France with offshore tax status. There he spent a month in recuperation isolated from all those he loved when they needed him most – and vice versa. What was to become known as 'the curse of Led Zeppelin' had officially begun and the band would never shake it off for the rest of their career.

By September 1975, Plant had been moved again, this time to Malibu, California, where he met up with Page. The singer was still in a wheelchair but keen to resume some kind of work, if only to take his mind off what had happened. They were soon joined by Jones and Bonham to rehearse the new material that was taking shape for the album that was to become *Presence*. "The whole band really wanted to play and had wanted to do that tour," Plant explained. "The same effort was put into the album."

Certainly, the new record was coming

together surprisingly quickly by Led Zeppelin's standards, but there were still problems. Page complained that Jones was never around in L.A. and after nearly quitting in 1973, it seemed that the bass player was still feeling somewhat semi-detached. Bonham was missing home and taking exile hard. His reaction was all too predictable: he went on the rampage, drinking and fighting his way up and down Sunset Strip. American tax laws, however, meant that they couldn't stay too long in the US either, so the band decamped to Munich, Germany, and the Musicland studio, located in the basement of the Arabella Hotel. Working faster than at any time since the first album, *Presence* was done and dusted in two weeks. Plant's problems seemed to have focused the band. "It was really like a cry of survival," the singer said. "There won't be another album like it. It was a cry from the depths, the only thing we could do." Years later he was to tell this

THE STORY: **WEARING AND TEARING**

ZEPPELIN GOES PUNK?

The Clash's Paul Simonon probably spoke for most punks when he said that he only had to look at the cover of a Led Zeppelin album to feel sick. After all, flying around America on a private jet playing three-hour-long shows in 50,000-seater stadiums with dry ice and lasers flashing represented just about everything that punk, with its three, chord DIY ethos, was against. In turn, most prog-rockers hated punk as heartily as punk despised rock's old guard. However, Led Zeppelin – or at least some of its members – were rather taken with the bratish upstart, even claiming to hear an echo of their own humble origins in its anger and energy. "Punk kind of woke us up again," John Paul Jones reckoned. "Oh yeah, I remember what we are supposed to be doing here."

All four members of the band went to see The Damned at the Roxy in London's Covent Garden. "They were the best initiation one could have had," Page said. "So powerful and tight. Exactly what rock

'n' roll is all about: sheer adrenaline music. I think that new wave is the most important thing that's happened since Hendrix." He also checked out Eater and Generation X while Plant was bold enough to turn up to a Sex Pistols gig at the Roxy, only to be mercilessly parodied by Johnny Rotten from the stage. Today Plant talks – without irony – of his "joy" at the advent of punk. "It was marvellous, especially if you discounted the lack of originality in most of it!" he says. "But there was creativity and a vibrancy. Some of them were only intent on burning out. But some of them had a skill and a craft. The Damned were always imaginative rather than venomous." He even claims to have understood the 'year zero' mentality that held that everything that had gone before musically was crap, merely by dint of being old. "It wasn't that much earlier I'd felt exactly the same," he reasons. "And it was true that groups as big and effective as Pink Floyd and Led Zeppelin had, to all intents and purposes, vanished. You

don't always know you're becoming remote and missing the point. You get comfortable and you think that's it so there had to be some spit and some sputum."

But what about his infamous confrontation with Johnny Rotten at that Sex Pistols gig? "He fawned at my feet in mock respect, but as I pulled my foot back to kick him in the head, I was grabbed by a pal of mine who said 'That'll be the last thing you ever do, if you do that'," Plant recalls.

Zeppelin's support for punk did not extend to signing any of its bands to Swan Song – or perhaps none of them wanted the stigma of being associated with such 'old farts'. But Plant claims Zeppelin's own music was influenced by punk rock: "Listen to Wearing and Tearing on *Coda*. That was our contribution to the whole thing, saying 'yes, you've got it right.'" But you can't be in the youth club forever. "Punk grew up very quickly, and when you see these punk reunions today they look worse than Barclay James Harvest, don't they?"

LED ZEPPELIN

6

LUCIFER RISING

Jimmy Page began working on the soundtrack for Kenneth Anger's film *Lucifer Rising* in 1973, when the pair found themselves bidding against each other for a rare Aleister Crowley manuscript at a Sotheby's auction. Their shared interest in magic and the occult promised a fruitful collaboration.

Page was initially enthusiastic about the project, declaring that he felt it was "quite an honour that he asked me". He also enthused about early rushes of part of the film which Anger gave him: "It's just so arresting. I had a copy and while I was in the US I hooked it up to a big stereo and frightened the daylights out of everyone. I was on the sixth floor and there were complaints from the twelfth. There's a real atmosphere and intensity."

Yet by 1976 their relationship had gone horribly wrong. Anger complained that Page had produced just 28 minutes of completed music in three years. Page countered that Anger hadn't given him enough material to work with. "I just wanted to see the bloke finish the bloody film," he said. "All I can say is that Anger's time was all that was needed

to finish that film. Nothing else. I told him that he must put the music on after he put the footage together, so I was just waiting for him to contact me. I never heard anything."

In a full-frontal media assault on the guitarist in September 1976, Anger announced: "I haven't laid eyes on Jimmy Page since early June". I've been trying to get in contact with him since then; I've fixed meetings through his office and been stood up half-a-dozen times. I've left messages on his Kafka-esque answering machine. All I've had is promises that the soundtrack is on its way, but nothing's materialised. I've got a fucking film to finish."

He went on: "The way he's been behaving is totally contradictory to the teachings of Aleister Crowley and totally contradictory to the ethos of the film. Lucifer is the angel of light and beauty. But the vibes that come off Jimmy are totally alien to that – and to human contact. It's like a bleak lunar landscape. By comparison, Lucifer is like a field full of beautiful flowers, although there may be a few bumble bees waiting to sting you if you are not careful. I'm beginning to think Jimmy's dried up as a musician. He's got no themes, no inspiration, no melodies

writer: "*Presence* has got some of the hottest moments Led Zeppelin ever had – agitated, uncomfortable, druggy, pained."

The album's speedy completion came despite a growing dependency on heroin, described by Richard Cole. "Bonzo, Jimmy and I used smack during the daytime hours in Munich and none of us seemed the worst for it," the tour manager later wrote. "No one ever talked about the possible risks and we probably didn't think about them, either. We felt trapped indoors by Munich's frigid air. Heroin, it seemed, made the time pass more quickly."

The year ended optimistically with the album finished and a one-off gig in Jersey on December 10 before a lucky audience of just 350 souls at Beehan's Park West, a nightspot in the island's capital, St Helier. Plant was still in a wheelchair, and although he took his first steps unaided shortly afterwards, he soon scotched any hope of a swift return to touring when he told a journalist: "I could do with just sitting down with all my family and thanking the gods," he said. "That doesn't mean to say I've lost the grease at the bottom of my shoes. It means I've got to go back to my corner for a while."

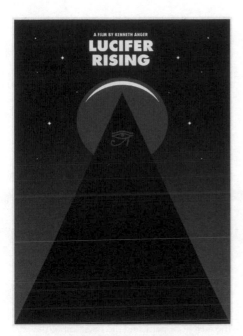

along." Asked whether he felt vindictive towards Page he said: "You bet I do. I'm not a Christian, turn the other cheek kind. In fact, I'm all ready to throw a Kenneth Anger curse." He further suggested that the 'problem' that was dragging Page down was an addiction to heroin.

Page hit back: "What a snide bastard. I've got to get my side across because now it's just gone too far. His stuff was just all over the place. I had a lot of respect for him. As an occultist he was defiantly in the vanguard. I just don't know what he's playing at. I'm totally bemused and really disgusted. It's truly pathetic. I mean, he is totally powerless – the only damage he can do is with his tongue. He started writing silly letters to everyone he thought I knew. The whole thing about "Anger's curse", they were just these silly letters. God it was all so pathetic."

Anger eventually turned to Bobby Beausoleil to finish the soundtrack. A member of mass murderer Charles Manson's notorious 'family', Beausoleil wrote the music while in prison.

Page's partial score, haunting and disturbing, was eventually released on vinyl only in 2012.

to offer. He has this problem dragging him down. He's been acting like Jekyll and Hyde, and I have to have someone who's 100 per cent. I really don't think he has the zing – the capabilities to do it. If he'd have said he was bored with the project I'd have understood, but he's just strung me

The end of the band's year-long tax exile helped. Plant talked enthusiastically of getting back to what he called 'the Isle of the Blessed' and joked that once reunited with his wife he didn't plan on getting out of bed for the first three months. With a return to the road ruled out, *Presence* appeared in March 1976 to some of the most positive reviews of the band's career as critics recognised the edge and urgency of tracks such as 'Achilles Last Stand'.

Needless to say, it went to number one on both sides of Atlantic, although it lacked the sustained selling power of some of its

predecessors. The long-running sage of the film was also reaching its end, although by now both the band and even Grant were heartily sick of the entire project. Plant was the most outspoken, declaring: "The attitude and the antics of the people involved with film, the way they follow their own odd trips are really beyond my comprehension." As *The Song Remains the Same* was the only film of which he had any knowledge, it was clear he was talking about director Peter Clifton. "The idea of the solitary man standing in front of the camera repeating himself time and time again to some irate lunatic

LED ZEPPELIN

6

sitting in a chair with 'director' written on the back – yuk." Page was equally disillusioned. "It's so time-consuming. It's a horrible medium to work in. It's so boring," he complained.

Even Grant had grown sick of the film and made his feelings plain by failing to turn up when Clifton met Warner Bros. in America to thrash out a distribution deal for the film. In his place he sent Richard Cole and another roadie, who arrived totally off their faces on booze and cocaine and looking and smelling like they hadn't been to bed in days. Nevertheless, a deal was struck and the film and accompanying soundtrack album were scheduled for an autumn 1976 release.

In the meantime, Grant sacked Clifton, as he had sacked Joe Massot before him. Only this time it turned nasty, with Zeppelin heavies being ordered to search Clifton's premises for 'stolen' negatives or out-takes. To the director's fury, Grant then left his name off the film's posters and publicity. When the film eventually opened the reviews were poor, and after the briefest of runs disappeared from sight. The fantasy sequences in particular were widely dismissed as risible – or worse. The highly-respected Dave Marsh wrote in *Rolling Stone*: "While Led Zeppelin's music remains worthy of respect – even if their best songs are behind them – their sense of themselves merits only contempt."

The soundtrack fared better. Although they certainly weren't Zeppelin's best performances, fans had long been demanding a live album and – bootlegs aside – *The Song Remains the Same* was the best they were going to get. "As regards the actual gig that was used in the film, it wasn't a terribly good night and it wasn't terribly bad. Certainly it wasn't a magic one, but it wasn't tragic," Page noted. He also admitted that "there are loads of howling guitar mistakes on there". Whatever its strengths and weaknesses, it was snaffled up gratefully and in sufficient quantities for the double album to go to number one in

Britain and number two in America, where Stevie Wonder's *Songs in the Key of Life* kept it from pole position.

If the reception that greeted *The Song Remains the Same* was a disappointment, Page had another film-related shock in store when, in September 1976, director Kenneth Anger launched a very public attack on the guitarist, who was supposed to supply the soundtrack to his film, *Lucifer Rising* (see page 104).

While Zeppelin was off the road for the duration of 1976, the musical landscape was changing dramatically, particularly in Britain where the punk revolution launched itself with a mission to sweep all the 'dinosaur' bands and 'old farts' into the dustbin of history. In September, the annual *Melody Maker* poll found Zeppelin relegated to second place as best band, Page in second place in the guitarist poll and Plant losing out as top British singer. Not that this was anything to do with the advent of punk and the rejection of the 'dinosaurs': the band that beat them were ultimate triple concept album prog-rockers Yes, whose singer Jon Anderson and guitarist Steve Howe also topped their respective sections. Zeppelin's problem was that due to circumstances beyond their control, they had simply been off the road and out of the swim for too long.

While many of the prog-rockers viewed punk with as much distaste as its safety-pinned disciples had for rock's old guard, Zeppelin's relationship was more ambivalent. Page and Plant expressed their admiration for its spirit and energy, although with Zeppelin's reputation for rock 'n' roll decadence, there was little chance of much reciprocation (see page 103). What was clear was that in order to reconnect with the changing musical climate, Led Zeppelin desperately needed to return to the road.

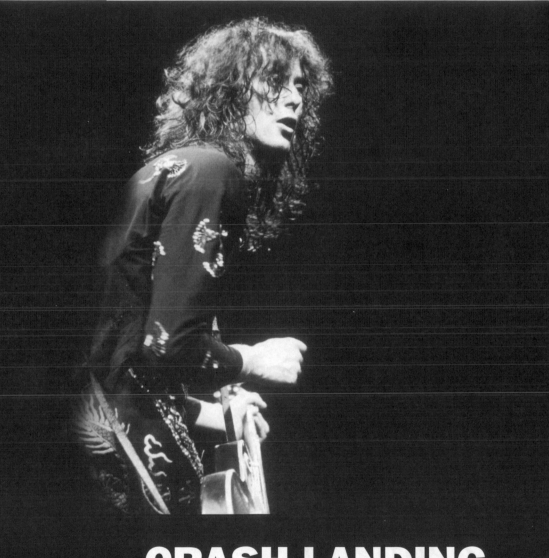

CRASH LANDING
1977–1980

7

"Fate is already written. I tried to pick myself up and as I did so slowly, I realised my family was way more important than the luxurious life I'd been living in Led Zeppelin."

ROBERT PLANT

CRASH LANDING

7

1977–1980

For the last three years of their life as a band, it seemed all four members were dogged by misfortunes, some self-inflicted, some way beyond their control. Conspiracy theorists pointed to Page's interest in the occult, Plant blamed fate, and times and audience tastes were changing, while more pragmatic critics saw the inevitable tensions between the high life and substance abuse, and the attractions of a more sober domestic existence as the factors lying at the heart of the problem. By no means a spent force, the arc of the Zeppelin's astonishing flight had passed its zenith, and little could be done to stop the inevitable descent.

By the time Led Zeppelin's return to active service was announced in early 1977, they had already spent much of the previous November and December rehearsing for a new tour in Emerson, Lake & Palmer's Manticore studio in Fulham, west London. Their eleventh American tour was scheduled to take in 49 dates in 30 cities in three legs across seven months with extended breaks. The anticipated gross was a mind-boggling 10 million dollars – in financial terms double the business they had done in 1975.

Yet misfortune dogged the tour from the outset and those of suspicious disposition might regard some of the events that occurred before they had even played a note as doom-laden portents. With the tour due to open in late February, Plant contracted laryngitis, resulting in the start being delayed

until April. Then they were unable to hire the Starship, their usual means of transport around America, because one of its engines had fallen off. Instead, they chartered a Boeing 707 owned by the Caesar's Place casino in Las Vegas which, of course, was dubbed Caesars Chariot.

Fitting them all on the flight became a problem, too, for by now Zeppelin's entourage of personal assistants, bodyguards, physicians and other flunkeys had grown to bloated proportions. "The entourage had grown to ridiculous numbers, which was one of the problems during that spring and summer tour," according to Richard Cole. "Cliques were formed and a very tight organisation became fragmented."

Cole himself hired John Bindon, who had served a jail sentence for murder, as

LED ZEPPELIN

7

head of security. He argued that the death threats that had accompanied Zeppelin on recent American tours meant that they required some serious muscle, but it was indicative of a culture of casual violence that now seemed to hover over the band, although apart form Bonham's occasional participation, none of the group's members sanctioned or liked it. However, it could be argued that even by turning a blind eye to what was being done in their name made them culpable. The promoter Bill Graham would certainly maintain so as a result of a vicious incident during the third leg of the tour and Grant, suffering under a dark cloud of depression brought on by his marital break-up and further destabilised by heroin addiction, was not really in any fit state to keep his unruly crew in any semblance of good order.

When the tour finally opened in Dallas on April 1, 1977, the band were understandably nervous. "We had to postpone a lot of dates and reshuffle them and I didn't touch a guitar for five weeks," a bone-thin Page noted. "I got a bit panicky about that – after two years off the road that's a lot to think about." Although Plant was fully recovered from the injuries he sustained in the car crash, during the first few gigs he experienced considerable pain in his right foot, which was permanently enlarged as a result of his accident.

The fifth show in Chicago had to be cancelled after 65 minutes because Page was visibly ill. The official reason was given as food poisoning but his drug habit had obviously weakened his never robust constitution. After this slow start, the band eventually moved into top gear with a set that reinstated a full acoustic segment for the first time in several tours. Partly it was to allow Plant a chance to sit down but it

was an artistic success, particularly with the introduction of 'Battle of Evermore' into the set for the first time, with John Paul Jones singing Sandy Denny's part. Surprisingly, only 'Achilles Last Stand' and 'Nobody's Fault But Mine' from the current album *Presence* were included – but on the other hand, as the record had been out for more than a year it wasn't actually that 'current'. Elsewhere, material from every album but their debut was featured plus a Page tribute to Jimi Hendrix with a version of 'Star-Spangled Banner', along the lines of the one the guitarist had played at Woodstock. Even into the second leg a self-critical Page continued to complain that he was "still only warming up" and not operating at full capacity, but by the time the first leg ended at the end of April in front of 76,229 people at the Pontiac Silverdome in Michigan, it was clear that Zeppelin were almost back to their best.

During the two-week break before the next leg, Page took a short vacation in Egypt but he was back in London by May 12 to collect – with the rest of the band – an Ivor Novello award for their 'outstanding contribution to British music'. The second leg of the American tour opened in Birmingham, Alabama, six days later and continued through to the end of June, taking in six nights at New York's Madison Square Garden and another half dozen at the L.A. Forum. Their triumph was only marred by a disastrous open-air appearance in front of 70,000 fans in Tampa, Florida, which had to be abandoned after three songs due to torrential rain, a decision which resulted in a riot which put 60 fans and several policemen in hospital.

By the time the third leg opened in mid-July, the band seemed tired and oddly dispirited. Despite the lengthy breaks in between the various legs, perhaps having been on the road since the beginning of April was simply too much. Whatever the reasons, the first two gigs in Seattle and Tempe were lacklustre. They then moved on to Oakland for two fateful concerts that would prove to be their last on American soil. On the first night, a local security guard had his head banged against a wall by Zeppelin's crew over some slight, real or imagined. Then Peter Grant's son Warren was apprehended by a security guard who tried to prevent him from removing a wooden 'LED ZEPPELIN' sign from the band's backstage dressing room. Cole, John Bindon, Grant himself and John Bonham then waded into the fracas that left security guard Jim Matzorkis in need of hospitalisation.

Promoter Bill Graham – who had been putting on Zeppelin shows in the San Francisco Bay area from the beginning and The Yardbirds before that – was furious, but refrained from immediate counter-action in order not to jeopardise the second night's show. The following morning, however, he filed charges and police arrived at the band's hotel to arrest Bonham, Cole, Bindon and Grant. "I watched those guys walk through with their hands cuffed behind their backs. That

The 1977 US tour, climaxing with a string of dates at Madison Square Garden and the L.A .Forum, revealed a band whose glory days were fading

LED ZEPPELIN

Promoter Bill Graham filed charges against the band after one of his security guards was attacked and hospitalised in the band's dressing room

was worth everything," Graham later said. "I saw them with their heads bowed down and their tails between their legs. As far as I was concerned every one of those guys in the band was accountable for that shit, because they allowed it to go on. We weren't the only ones it happened to. We were just the last ones."

All four were subsequently found guilty, fined and given suspended sentences. They didn't contest the case against them but the closest Grant came to admitting culpability was that the incident had been "regrettable". Graham declared that he would never book Led Zeppelin again – not

knowing that even if he had wanted to, the chance would never arise again.

While some members of the entourage, including Zeppelin's attorney Steve Weiss, stayed in California to sort out the mess, on the day after the arrests, Robert Plant and others flew on to New Orleans, where the band were due to play in front of a crowd of 80,000 at the Superdrome on July 30. As soon as they checked in to the Royal Orleans hotel, the singer received a phone call from his wife Maureen back in England. She told him the devastating news that their five-year-old son Karac was near death after failing to respond to treatment for a respiratory infection. What followed must have been the worst two hours of his life, until a second call came through from Maureen informing him that Karac had died.

Cole, Plant and Bonham took the next available flight back to Britain while Grant stayed behind to cancel the remainder of the tour. Plant's father was interviewed in the British press and declared: "All this success and fame, what is it worth? It doesn't mean very much when you compare it to the love of a family. Karac was the apple of my son's eye. He was a strong child, mischievous, bright and full of life. He had never been ill before. His death seems so unreal and so unnecessary."

In a way, Plant never got over his loss: what parent could? The realisation that his fame and money and being the golden god of rock did not make him immune from the most appalling personal tragedy shook him to the core and changed his outlook forever. "The perspective of that, losing one's child, is the bitterest pill to take," he told this author almost 30 years later. "I've got two more boys now who are gems – different kinds of guys but really good friends of mine. But at that time nothing was in my favour at all." He was further hurt by "the sensationalism and the cheap shots that followed it" as the more irresponsible sections of the media suggested Page's interest in magic and the occult had brought down some sort of demonic curse on Led Zeppelin. "The comments about it at the time all connected it to Jimmy's dalliances and preoccupations with the dark side and whatever. I've never shared those with him and I don't really know anything about it. Fate is already written. I tried to pick myself up and as I did so slowly, I realised

my family was more important than the luxurious life I'd been living in Zeppelin."

It was a terrible, shocking price to pay for such a realisation and his disillusionment with his old rock 'n' roll life was no doubt deepened further when Page, Jones and Grant failed to make it back to Britain for the funeral. Nothing would ever be the same again – in more ways than one. "I haven't taken a drug since that day," Plant told *Uncut* in 2005. "I thought 'How am I ever going to deal with the next moment and put my shoulders back and be a man?' I thought I'd better refocus the whole deal."

Inevitably, the rumour mill that Led Zeppelin were breaking up went into overdrive, while adherents of the curse theory claimed further dubious 'evidence' when a month after the death of Karac Plant, Bonham crashed his Jensen car and broke two ribs. Page kept his spirits up by talking to *Melody Maker* about plans for the next album. In truth, there was virtually no communication between Plant and the rest of the Zeppelin camp throughout the winter of 1977–78. Sensibly, his colleagues realised that he needed time and space and that any pressure on him to resume his career would probably be counter-productive.

The go-between was John Bonham and the rest of the band relied on him to judge when the time was right to try to lure the singer back into the fold. "He encouraged rather than coaxed me back," Plant says of the drummer's role. "He was very gentle because Bonzo was my pal and we had a lot of love for each other. We'd known each other since we were 16 and he spent a lot of time coming over to see Maureen and me with his missus, Pat. I really didn't want to go back. But eventually he said 'Give it

7

LED ZEPPELIN

7

a whirl again. You've got to sing. You're a big head.'"

The reunion came after Grant eventually convened a band meeting at the end of April 1978 at London's Royal Garden Hotel. "That was after a long uphill battle to get him to work again," Grant later recalled. "Robert kept saying he'd do it and then back down, but Bonzo was a tower of strength. We had a meeting and they started talking about Bad Company and Maggie Bell and all that with their Swan Song hats on and I said: 'What the fuck are you talking about? You should be worrying about your own careers.' So I suggested Clearwell, because Bad Company had been there. So Robert says he'd just like to do some jamming, so that's what they did."

Clearwell Castle was situated in the Forest of Dean on the English/Welsh border, conveniently near Plant's own home, but it swiftly became clear that the singer was still not ready to concentrate on music again. "I felt quite remote from the whole thing," he recalls. "Everybody was very gentle and respectful, but it still felt very tenuous. They knew that after you've had an event like that in your life you start measuring your time and what you do with it and your focus is changed forever. But I wasn't comfortable in the group at all, then. We'd gone right through the hoop and because my hoop was on fire, I didn't know if there was enough in it any more."

In the end, it was October 1978, some 15 months after the death of his son, before Plant finally felt able to face the prospect of working again. After rehearsals in London the band had 10 new songs ready to record and moved to Stockholm where they took over ABBA's studio and wrapped up the sessions in just three weeks, with group members

commuting back to Britain each weekend. Although they worked fast, the recording was not without its problems. Page was clearly hampered by his heroin addiction and the band divided into two factions, with drugs the dividing line between them. In the 'clean' corner were Plant and Jones; in the narcotics corner were Page and Bonham.

Many of the tracks began with Jones and Plant recording keyboards and guide vocals as the bass player increasingly stepped into Page's shoes in the songwriting stakes. An unhappy Page complained that Jones was also "trying to take over as producer", but the simple truth was that he was stepping into a vacuum of the guitarist's own making. According to Dave Lewis, throughout the sessions the guitarist was "distant, less enthusiastic and not entirely comfortable" and showed a particularly antipathy to Plant's more mellow songs such as 'All My Love'.

Despite such problems, the album was finished 10 days before Christmas. In fact, the band had more than enough material and three of the strongest tracks, 'Wearing and Tearing', 'Ozone Baby' and 'Darlene', were omitted from the album's running order with the idea that they would appear instead on a souvenir EP intended to coincide with the band's return to the live stage. However, in early 1979, Maureen Plant gave birth to another son and her husband's determination to give his family priority complicated Zeppelin's live plans. The singer simply didn't want to tour, particularly in America, which would have taken him away from home for too long. On the other hand, a tour of Britain and/or Europe hardly offered the venues to stage the barnstorming return Grant desired. "It seemed logical to me that if we were going to regain our position as the world's top group, we'd better play the biggest place possible," he said.

In the end he came up with the idea of the band headlining a major summer festival, extracting an asking price of £1 million for two appearances over consecutive weekends in early August 1979 at Knebworth House, near Stevenage in Hertfordshire. Zeppelin's long-awaited return to the stage was announced exclusively by Annie Nightingale on BBC television's *Old Grey Whistle Test* on May 22, and by the end of June the band were already rehearsing at Bray Studios, near Maidenhead, Berkshire.

On stage and on screen and in new outfits at Knebworth, August 1979. Page felt the sheer scale of the event meant that the Zeppelin had met its match

Although long finished, various delays meant the new album was still not yet in the shops and it was decided its release should coincide with the Knebworth appearances. After album titles such as *Look* and *Tight But Loose* had been considered and rejected, the band eventually settled on *In Through the out Door* because, as Page put it, "that's the hardest way to get back in". In the event, they just missed the deadline to get the

LED ZEPPELIN

7

album out for Knebworth but it hardly mattered. A festival triumph was almost guaranteed to catapult the album to number one, anyway – and so it proved.

As they hadn't played live in two years, before appearing in front of more than 200,000 fans a brace of low-key warm-up gigs were arranged for late July in a Copenhagen theatre seating just 2,000. Despite obvious and understandable nerves and some equipment problems, the shows went well enough, although *NME*'s reviewer was vitriolic. "They appeared sloppy and unrehearsed, sometimes seeming awkwardly lost, bewildered, stiff and reluctant to play," Eric Kornfeldt wrote. "They were no more than a quartet of uninspired old men, a relic from the past. There was so little feeling inherent in the set that it was like watching a fully automated factory producing an endless string of chords that neither musicians nor audience cared about." It was the sort of review that frankly told you more about the politics of *NME* at the time than how Led Zeppelin actually played and many of the ripest phrases smacked of having been written even before the gig started.

Despite such predictable sneering, all was set fair for an emotional return to the UK stage after a four-year absence. Before the gig, Plant observed: "We're not heroes anymore. Heroes are in books – old books." That wasn't how the fans saw it and on August 3, the night before they played, Plant toured the festival site in a jeep and was overwhelmed by the enthusiasm he found. "People had pushed down the stone pillars to get in early. It was a phenomenally powerful thing," he reported.

The tension rose throughout the day on August 4 as a support bill that included Chas & Dave, Fairport Convention,

Commander Cody, Southside Johnny and The Asbury Dukes and Todd Rundgren's Utopia did their best to entertain the impatient crowd. When Led Zeppelin eventually took the stage, they looked quite different from the four hippies who had last played on a British stage at Earls Court in 1975. Page wore white chino-styled pants and a smartly tailored shirt, Jones wore a white suit and Plant looked sharp in cords and an expensive designer shirt.

The set had its high points and its failings. Page was not always on top of his game and Plant was clearly on edge. "That was a very twitchy time for me. I was wracked with nerves," he confessed many years later. "We could have gone back to the Queen's Head pub. Instead we went back to hundreds of thousand of people. Nobody's big enough to meet those expectations, It didn't work for us. We played too fast and too slow and it was like trying to land a plane with one engine. But because there was some chemical charge in the air, it was fantastic for those who were there. It was definitely intense."

The following weekend was inevitably something of an anti-climax, even if Zeppelin arguably played better and were more relaxed. Plant sniped from the stage about some of the less than adulatory press reviews that had greeted the previous weekend's gig but the crowd was far smaller, which had unfortunate consequences. Led Zeppelin's guaranteed fee was renegotiated and reduced but it still wasn't enough to prevent promoter Freddie Bannister's company from going into liquidation.

In Through the out Door was eventually released the week after the second Knebworth date, packaged in a brown paper bag with a series of six different sleeves inside. The trick was that the purchaser didn't know which sleeve they were getting and the somewhat cynical hope behind this marketing ploy was presumably that diehard Zeppelin fans would try to collect all six covers. Ultimately, the packaging suggested confusion and the music inside similarly lacked cohesion or unity, although album sales were more than respectable and spectacular in America.

Yet instead of building on Knebworth and the release of *In Through the out Door*, Zeppelin retreated once more. Page hinted at all kinds of touring plans and Plant had promised from the stage at Knebworth that fans would get an opportunity to see them again before Christmas. Yet in reality there was little will within the band to take to the road again. The mood in the camp wasn't helped by the continuing escalation of Page's drug problems, and in October 1979 a 19-year old boy died of an overdose at his house in Sussex. All of the band minus Page appeared as guests at a London benefit concert for UN relief in Kampuchea at the end of December, but 1980 arrived with still nothing scheduled in Led Zeppelin's empty diary.

Grant's determination to get them back to America met with implacable resistance from Plant. Eventually he got the singer to agree to a short European tour and the band reconvened to rehearse at the Rainbow in north London in April 1980.

Symbolically, Page suggested that they tried to capture their early fire and enthusiasm by rehearsing the old Yardbirds number 'Train Kept A-Rollin'', the first number they had ever played together back in 1968. It subsequently opened every show on what was to be their final tour.

When the tour commenced in Germany in mid-June, it was for the first time without Richard Cole. Grant had finally had enough of his increasingly unreliable tour manager and decided that his spiralling heroin habit had made him a liability. "I'd paid for the doctor's bills and all that and it just wasn't getting better," he said. "He had a massive problem so I thought the only way to shake him up was to blow him out. So I told him I wouldn't want him in Europe and he says: 'You can't do it without me.' I said 'Well, we've got to.'" He was replaced by Phil Carlo from Bad Company's road crew, much to the relief of the now firmly anti-drug Plant, who had lobbied Grant to have Cole removed. "There were personalities I didn't take kindly too in the end," the singer said. "I found it very difficult to be a doting father on the one hand and to deal with people like Richard Cole on the other."

With 14 dates inside three weeks across Germany, Belgium, Holland and Switzerland under the slogan 'Over Europe 1980', in venues with an average capacity of around 4,000 and using a much reduced PA system, the tour was intended to have a 'back to the roots' feel that would recreate the excitement of the early 1970s. Grant also hoped that it would rekindle Plant's taste for performing and lead to an American tour that autumn. "I hoped being up there would give him the necessary lift to do it," Grant confessed.

The gigs, with the acoustic set reduced only to Page's guitar showcase 'White Summer'/'Black Mountain Side' and some of the longer pieces dropped in favour of a tighter, leaner approach, were mostly excellent. Plant was fighting fit and in great voice after his long lay-off and Jones too was in good shape. Page, dressed in baggy suits that looked even baggier as the tour went on and his frame even more

LED ZEPPELIN

7

emaciated, was erratic, either inspired or sloppy depending on his drug intake, and Bonham was his usual self, equally capable of playing up a storm or falling off his drum stool dead drunk, as he did in Nuremberg. The tour wound up on July 7 in West Berlin, as it was then still known. Is it just misty-eyed nostalgia and hindsight to suggest that there was a renewal of the old camaraderie at what proved to be Led Zeppelin's final ever gig? It's impossible to say unless you were there but many like to think so. Certainly, it was the longest set of the tour, as if they genuinely didn't want it to end, Page playing a lengthy and lyrical solo in 'Stairway to Heaven' that extended the song to 14 minutes, while 'Whole Lotta Love' clocked in at more than 17 minutes. Plant's final words from the stage as the front man of the mightiest rock 'n' roll band in the world were: "Thank you very much everybody who's worked with us and put up with us and all those sort of things and goodnight!"

Not, of course, that anyone knew it was the end. In fact, quite the opposite for just as Grant had hoped, as they landed back in England, Plant told him walking across the tarmac that he would tour America again, but only for a maximum of four weeks. Grant immediately set about arranging a tour that he optimistically dubbed 'Led Zeppelin the 1980s – Part One'. He swiftly had a 19-date itinerary in place that would begin in Montreal on October 17 and wind up with four nights in Chicago, ending on November 15.

The band dispersed for summer holidays and Page spent August moving out of Plumpton Place in Sussex and into the Old Mill House, a mansion on the River Thames at Windsor, which he had just purchased from Michael Caine. They

agreed to convene there on September 24 in preparation for rehearsals at the nearby Bray Studios, which they had used before the Knebworth gigs.

The week before they did so, Page visited Swan Song's London offices to look at a model of the stage set and lighting rig it was proposed they would use. He also began to draw up a potential set list, which showed a greater sense of adventure than that summer's European dates, and included a number of songs never previously played live, headed by the epic 'Carouselambra' from *In Through the out Door*.

On the morning of September 24, Plant and Bonham arrived in Windsor together and, according to the singer, the drummer was in a dark mood. "Bonzo was in one of those periods where he thought he was no good," he recalled. "We drove down to rehearsals together the morning before he passed away. He was saying, 'I don't want to do this. You play the drums and I'll sing.' We got to the studio and that's what happened. I played the drums and he sang a bit."

Bonham had been drinking since early in the day and it was an unsatisfactory rehearsal. Nevertheless, it seemed to have blown a few cobwebs away and the entire band returned for a celebration at Page's house, where Bonham continued drinking heavily. By midnight he was in a drunken stupor and roadie Rex King carried him upstairs and laid him on a bed. They had seen him in a similar state many times before and nobody was particularly worried. Two roadies apparently checked on him on different occasions the next morning. When he hadn't appeared by the afternoon, Jones went to "kick him out of bed" – and swiftly realised that he was dead, having choked on his own vomit. He went downstairs to break the news to Page and Plant. "I think he had been drinking due to some problems in his personal life but he died because of an accident," the bassist said later. "He was lying down the wrong way, which could have happened to anybody who drank a lot. At first the main emotion for me was anger. It seemed such a waste."

The coroner subsequently concluded that Bonham had drunk the equivalent of 40 measures of vodka in the 24 hours before his death. He was just 32. "It could have happened to any one of us," Jones concluded. Ironically, on the day he died the first adverts were appearing in the American press with mail-order ticket application forms for the shows that were being cancelled even as the papers were rolling off the presses.

There was never any question that Bonham's death meant an end to Led Zeppelin. Two years earlier The Who had lost Keith Moon in not dissimilar circumstances. The rest of the band pronounced him "irreplaceable" – and two months later replaced him with Kenney Jones of The Faces. This time, there would be no repeat of such behaviour. "I always say to Roger Daltrey, 'how could you do that?'," Plant said in 2005. "We desperately needed to come together again and create a new direction, which we might have been able to do. We may well have made it better and

John Bonham was so integral to the band that all of the remaining members agreed that to continue would be not be desirable. A replacement would make it 'more like a tribute band playing Led Zeppelin songs'

more constructive and focused again. But as it happens we couldn't. For me there was no debate."

Nor indeed, was there any desire elsewhere in the Zeppelin camp to carry on. "We had to stop as a mark of respect to John's contribution," Page said. "We could not have gone on without him. It would have been dishonest. Nobody else could have fitted into his role." According to Jones: "He was so integral, to have gotten someone else would have made it more of a tribute band if you were playing Led Zeppelin songs, because anyone else would have to be in his shadow all the time."

After the funeral, held at Bonham's local parish church on October 7, the band took a swift break in Jersey while they tried to come to terms with what had happened. When they returned, Grant summoned a meeting at London's Savoy Hotel. "They all looked at me and asked me what I thought," he recalled. "I said it just couldn't go on because it was the four of them and they were all relieved because they had decided the same. For Led Zeppelin to make that music it needed the four of them to do it. And now that was gone."

Despite speculation in the press that Bad Company's Simon Kirke, Cozy Powell, Aynsley Dunbar, Carmine Appice and Roxy Music's Paul Thompson were all in the frame as Bonham's replacement, on December 4 Grant issued a statement in the names of the three remaining members which read: "We wish it to be known that the loss of our dear friend and the deep respect we have for his family, together with the deep sense of harmony felt by ourselves and our manager, have led us to decide we could not carry on as we were."

AFTERMATH AND THE SOLO YEARS
AFTER 1980

8

"Ahmet Ertegün always used to say to me, 'Hey man, if you want to do well, you got to put the band back.' I had to tell him, 'This isn't a movie.'"

ROBERT PLANT

AFTERMATH AND THE SOLO YEARS

After 1980

Although their millions of fans fervently expected some form of reunion, the fact of John Bonham's untimely check-out meant that for Plant at least this was never really going to happen. The remaining band members' paths have crossed at various times, but with a powerful royalty-earning backlist none of them needed to work, and all could afford to pursue their own interests, some more fruitfully than others.

Since the death of John Bonham, the remaining three members of Led Zeppelin have been unswervingly true to their word and resisted all attempts to put the band back together. In 27 years, there have been just three one-off reunions – at Live Aid in 1985, the Atlantic Records 40th birthday party in 1988 and their induction into the Rock and Roll Hall of Fame in 1995. Of the three of them, only Robert Plant's solo career has really fired, but then with the royalties still flowing profusely from one of the mightiest and most enduring back catalogues in rock, none exactly needs either the money or further celebrity and fame.

As rock music – once imagined to be a totally disposable and transitory form – has grown as a 'heritage industry', so, too, has Zeppelin's stock. Arguably, their influence is as strong today as it was 30 years ago and their back catalogue continues to sell to new generations of fans. Every new format, from CD to DVD, has offered an opportunity to re-package and re-sell some of rock music's most memorable moments all over again.

When the band announced they were folding, Atlantic Records were swift to point out that they still owed the label one more record under the contract Swan Song had signed for five albums in 1974. Plant, Page and Jones spent some time in early 1981 debating what to do, with the guitarist keen on a chronological live double album, featuring performances from the Albert Hall in 1970 through to Knebworth and the final European tour. It was a project Page had been talking about ever since the disappointments of the soundtrack album to *The Song Remains the Same*, but for some reason Plant was against the idea and effectively vetoed it.

However, Swan Song's lawyers could find no way around the fact that they still owed an album and, determined to resist the personal pressure Atlantic founder Ahmet Ertegün was exerting for the group to reform with a new drummer, Plant compromised on an album of unused studio out-takes. Page set to work and rescued the three tracks from the *In Through*

LED ZEPPELIN

8 | WHAT WOULD A 1980s LED ZEP HAVE SOUNDED LIKE?

The American tour for which the band was beginning rehearsals when John Bonham died was to be called 'Led Zeppelin the 1980s: Part One'. What they might have sounded like during that generally dire decade for music we shall never know – but the surviving members agree that they were in a good frame of mind and optimistic about finding a new approach that reflected the changing spirit of the times. "We desperately needed to come together again and create a new direction, which we might have been able to do," Plant says. "We may well have made it better and more constructive and focused."

Page claims that he had already discussed a new direction for the next album with Bonham. "We said we were going to resort to some really intense riffing. I don't want necessarily to call it

heavy, but you know what I mean by that," he told this author in 2005. "That's the way I figured the next album should be because the music had started to lighten up on In Through the out Door and I wanted to get back to that sort of urgent intensity we managed to evoke. That was the discussion I had with Bonzo, anyway. Who knows? But the potential was definitely still there."

One strong possibility is that they would have stripped away some of the pomp and circumstance and returned to a more raw and simple approach under the belated influence of punk. "I don't know where it would have gone or for how long, but it certainly had gotten a new lease on life," reckons John Paul Jones. "Morale was very high. We were in really good spirits. Punk had

severely embarrassed us. We'd stripped it down and just went, 'OK, right. This is over, off we go again.' It was a very hopeful time."

Another possibility is that Zeppelin might have gone the other way and drowned themselves in synths and drum machines, as so many of their contemporaries did in the 1980s. By 1982, Page was experimenting with a Roland guitar synthesiser on the *Death Wish II* soundtrack and Plant also admits that he was fascinated by "all that strange questionable technology that was coming on the scene", and which led to him using a drum box on Pictures at Eleven. Given that it was a decade in which even the likes of Bob Dylan and Neil Young lost their way, perhaps with hindsight Zeppelin broke up at exactly the right time....

the out Door sessions that had been kept back for the aborted EP plus further material from the *Led Zeppelin III* and *Houses of the Holy* sessions. As a tribute to the band's departed drummer he also added 'Bonzo's Montreux', a percussion track recorded in 1976. Ironically, however, the best two tracks were probably the two live takes from the Albert Hall in 1970 which were used to fill out the album and which left Zeppelin fans salivating for an official full-length live recording, a desire that

would not be fulfilled until 2003. The album eventually appeared in November 1982, making number four in Britain and number six in America. Finally, with contractual obligations fulfilled and tax bills paid, Led Zeppelin were able to rest in peace. While Page, Plant and Jones pursued separate lives and their own careers, Swan Song was wound up and Peter Grant relinquished all management responsibilities and retreated into what he later described as "a period of blackness".

8

Of course, that didn't stop the rumours and wishful thinking or former band members running into each other via guest appearances with mutual friends such as Foreigner, Roy Harper and The Pretty Things. They even helped out from time to time on each other's projects, Page playing on a couple of tracks with Plant's Honeydrippers project and on Jones's *Scream for Help* soundtrack. Then in late 1984, the BBC broadcast a report by Michael Buerk on the plight of starving children in Ethiopia. The film prompted Bob Geldof to put together the largest benefit concert ever organised, with simultaneous events in Britain and America to be televised around the world.

In early 1985, Robert Plant rang Bob Geldof and offered his services for the American leg of *Live Aid*. The timing fitted neatly with his *Shaken 'n' Stirred* tour and the initial plan was for Plant to perform with Eric Clapton. Yet when he realised how big the event was going to be, he began to wonder whether a grander gesture was required. "It seemed to be one of the two or three times in my life when I should consider it," he said. "The event was far more important than my determination to steer clear of something, so I called Jimmy up and said 'let's do it'," he recalls.

Jones also readily agreed, and ex-Chic drummer Tony Thompson, who was on the road in America with The Power Station, was asked to fill the sensitive John Bonham role. It was also decided to add bassist Paul Martinez so that Jones could play keyboards and a second drummer in Phil Collins, who flew the Atlantic by Concorde to become the only artist to perform at both the British and American concerts.

With Plant in the middle of a tour and booked to play in Detroit the night before, the line-up was unable to rehearse until the morning of the gig. When they came to

perform it showed, but it hardly mattered. After Collins had finished his solo set, he announced that he would like to introduce "some friends of mine" – and there were Page, Plant and Jones together again on a stage for the first time in five years. Plant's voice was hoarse, Page's Gibson was out of tune and the sound wasn't working properly. Plant shouted "Good evening!" only for Page to respond with: "There'll be a short intermission while I get some monitors."

Plant later recalled: "It was so much like a lot of Led Zeppelin gigs. One-and-a-half billion people and Page is swanning around with no guitar and I'm wondering how my voice is going to stand up and thinking 17 years and we still can't get it right!" With two drummers pounding away to replicate Bonham's thunder, they opened with 'Rock and Roll', and it was an irresistible choice as Page sang the opening line "It's been a long time since I rock and rolled..."

When they'd finished Plant teased the crowd by asking for requests, at which Page broke into the riff of 'Heartbreaker' before switching into 'Whole Lotta Love', played in shortened form along the lines of the edited American single. "OK, that was kind of uptempo. This is something that takes the mood down a little, and yet, then again, lifts everything up, maybe. Who knows?" Page strapped on the famous double-necked guitar and it could only be 'Stairway to Heaven'.

In all honesty, due to technical problems and an understandable rustiness, it was not a good performance – so poor, in fact, that when *Live Aid* eventually appeared on DVD 20 years later, Led Zeppelin were the only act to refuse to allow their contribution to be included. At the time, the sheer emotion carried them through. "I'd be lying if I said I wasn't really drunk on the whole event. The rush I got from the audience, well I'd

LED ZEPPELIN

8

forgotten how much I missed it. I'd also forgotten how Led Zeppelin and Bonzo could never be replaced. The fact that they were still chanting for us 15 minutes later and that people were crying all over the place was something more powerful than words can say." Their performance aided the cause, too, for the monies being pledged by telephone increased dramatically following their appearance.

Once the emotion had subsided, Plant was far more critical. "*Live Aid* was a fucking atrocity for us," he claimed in 1995. "It made us look like loonies. I was hoarse and Pagey was out of tune. We had no monitors and the idea of playing 'Stairway to Heaven' with two drummers while Duran Duran cried on the side of the stage, there was really something quite surreal about that." He went on to liken the performance to Frank Sinatra singing 'My Way' and so it came as no surprise when they refused to allow the

footage to be used in the DVD, released in 2005 to raise money for refugees in Sudan. Inevitably, the decision brought a hail of criticism down on their heads, forcing them to issue a statement which read: "Jimmy Page, Robert Plant and John Paul Jones are in absolute full support of the fundraising project for the people of Sudan. However, Jimmy, Robert and John Paul found that both the sound and general reproduction of their performance at *Live Aid* Philadelphia was sub-standard." They then pledged financial support for the campaign in other ways.

Despite the shortcomings of their set, the emotional power was undeniable and they began to think about playing together again. On finishing his American tour in September, Plant sacked the band he had

The Live Aid appearance in Philadelphia, 1985, with Phil Collins in one drum seat, fresh from his transatlantic Concorde flight

8

been touring and recording with since 1981. By January he was in rehearsals with Page, Jones and drummer Tony Thompson at a village hall near Peter Gabriel's Real World studios near Bath, reputedly trying out new music with Jones on keyboards and Plant taking over the bass. However, the singer almost immediately got cold feet and when, on the second day, Thompson was involved in a car crash, all the singer's worst suspicions seemed to be confirmed. Plant had never subscribed to the 'curse of Led Zeppelin' theory, but Thompson's mishap brought unwelcome memories of former such catastrophes flooding back. "The second day we got to play, it really started to cook," Page recalls."And that very night Tony Thompson was injured in a car accident. I just thought, 'Wait a minute, this just isn't meant to be.' We tried playing along with a drum machine after that and then a roadie took over the drums for a bit. I just felt completely, 'What's the point, y'know?'"

In truth, the guitarist himself was not in great shape, as Plant obliquely acknowledged. "Two or three things were quite promising, a sort of cross between David Byrne and Hüsker Dü," he remembers. "But for it to have succeeded I would have to have been far more patient than I have for years."

Nevertheless, both Page and Plant made cameo appearances on each other's next albums and in 1988 came the second Led Zeppelin gig of the decade, when they reformed for an appearance at a 12-hour concert to mark Atlantic's 40th anniversary at New York's Madison Square Garden. This time, the familiar name of Bonham was back on drums once again – Jason Bonham, the 20-year-old son of the late drummer. Like *Live Aid*, it was Plant who first put his name forward. The most reluctant to turn the clock back, his reticence basically meant

that Zeppelin reunions only happened on his instigation. Page and Jones readily agreed and, with the *Live Aid* fiasco much in mind, were determined this time to rehearse fully. With Plant on tour in America, Page, Jones and Bonham spent a week rehearsing in London's Nomis studio, running through between 15 and 20 old Zeppelin numbers. Jones was particularly impressed with how much Bonham had absorbed of his father's playing. "I went in to a very old fill I used to do and he's right there with me," Jones marvelled. "It's one of those things that a bass player and a drummer only do when they've been married for 10 years but we just went straight into it."

The trio finally met up with Plant for a day's rehearsal in New York prior to the concert on May 14, 1988. Yet once again, the gig, which was broadcast live on HBO, was a bit of a mess. Subsequently, Page and Plant publicly blamed each other for the show's disappointments. The only thing they could agree on was that Jason Bonham had acquitted himself with great credit. "It was Jason's dream to play with Led Zeppelin. It was so important to him, something he'd always hoped for," Page said. "I was looking forward to it, too, because I knew how good a drummer he'd become. Jones and I had rehearsed with Jason and it had gone particularly well. We'd agreed on what we wanted to play and the sound check at the Garden sounded really good. Then at the 11th hour, Robert decides he doesn't want to do 'Stairway', so there's this running confusion and harsh words between us right up to literally the last minute and that shook me up quite a bit. The whole thing was one big disappointment, especially since I knew I wasn't playing well. It was so upsetting because we really put work into it and it should have been really good. All the last-

LED ZEPPELIN

minute dramatics about not doing 'Stairway' suddenly threw the whole thing up in the air. I was trying to cool it out at the end but it was like, 'thanks a lot, pal!'"

According to Plant: "Page and I had our usual touchy vibration-filled moment when I didn't want to sing 'Stairway to Heaven' and he said it was a necessity for the Western world and I said that I didn't think it was that important. So the rehearsal was good, the sound check was good – and the gig was foul. However, I must say that Jason Bonham was stunning. I've always tried to clip him around the back of the head and tell him to get his act together and stuff, but he really was the kingpin of the whole delivery."

In the end, Plant did sing a perfunctory 'Stairway to Heaven' at the end of a 28-minute set in which the singer had messed up the lyrics to 'Kashmir' and Page had played a limp solo in 'Heartbreaker'. 'Whole Lotta Love' and 'Misty Mountain Hop' were better, but it was far from the triumph that it should have been.

Oddly, the row and the erratic performance did not drive an insurmountable wedge between them. Behind closed doors and strictly for family and friends, they were more than happy to play together. Plant, Page and Jones all jammed together at the 21st birthday party of the singer's daughter Carmen in late 1989. After the harsh words of the previous year, this time Plant said: "Pagey was playing so good, I had a big lump in my throat. That little time of playing with him gave me something I hadn't had for a long time." Without the pressure, it seemed the

The Plant/Page Unledded world tour outing in 1998. Page elegantly coiffed, Plant less so

8

chemistry was still there and the following year they did it again at Jason Bonham's wedding reception.

A more public reunion between Page and Plant in June 1990 took place at Knebworth, the scene of Led Zeppelin's final British gig 10 years earlier, with the guitarist joining Plant's band for 'Misty Mountain Hop', 'Wearing and Tearing' (never previously performed live) and 'Rock and Roll'. Once again it led to feverish speculation that a full-scale reunion was on the cards and Page himself did everthing he could to make it happen. Plant was, as usual, reluctant, but agreed to consider it when told an offer worth several million dollars was on the table for an American tour. The singer even suggested Faith No More's Mike Bordin as a drummer – but then, according to Page, changed his mind again "the very next day" and threw himself back into his solo career.

Atlantic Records were particularly keen on a reunion because it would have helped to sell the digitally remastered, 54-track four CD box set Page spent the spring and summer of 1990 compiling for them. It included one previously unreleased item, Page's acoustic 'White Summer'/'Black Mountain Side' sequence from a 1969 BBC radio broadcast. Even without the support of live gigs, the box set sold a million, the highest-selling such project until EMI began raiding its archives for the Beatles *Anthology* series five years later. A second box set followed in 1993 and included 'Baby Come on Home', a 'lost' out-take from the first album, plus a gargantuan, 10-disc *Complete Studio Recordings* set the same year.

In late 1993, Plant was approached to contribute a Led Zeppelin-based set to MTV's highly successful *Unplugged* series. At first he was uncertain. "Then mysteriously Jimmy turned up at a gig I was playing in Boston and it was like those difficult last

days of Led Zep had vanished and we had this understanding again without doing or saying anything. We talked about the MTV thing and decided to see if we could present Zeppelin's music in a broader light. It would have been incredibly facetious if I thought I could carry any thread of the Zeppelin history on my shoulders outside of a live gig. The only answer really was to see if I could team up with the one bloke who knew where I was coming from. I felt very good about it." Page, too, was delighted at the prospect, ditching the singer David Coverdale, who he was working with at the time, and throwing himself wholeheartedly into the project. "The MTV thing was a catalyst," he said later. "It gave Robert time to think about things and get in contact. It was really the first time we had a chance to think about the future constructively – to kick it around, see how to do it and how not to do it."

In February 1994 they began working in a studio in London's King's Cross, with looped backing tapes prepared by French world music producer Martin Meissonnier. Other musicians were added, including bassist Charlie Jones and drummer Michael Lee from Plant's backing band, and an Egyptian ensemble led by Hossam Ramzy. Asian singer Najma Akhtar, hurdy gurdy player Nigel Eaton and ex-Cure guitarist Porl Thompson also joined the party, although there was no call to John Paul Jones. "Nobody rang me to tell me they were doing it, which I found a little odd," he later complained. "I saw it in the papers and called somebody up and said, 'God, I see all of the rumours are all starting again. Here we go', 'because it happened regularly. I thought it was just more rumours. And this person said, 'Haven't they told you?'

"Told me what?" I asked. 'Oh, they're going out on the road again together.'

LED ZEPPELIN

8

In early August 1994, Page and Plant flew to Morocco to record and film a sequence for the upcoming *Unplugged* show. The full recording of the show took place over two nights in a TV studio on London's South Bank at the end of the month. The new arrangements of songs such as 'Thank You', 'Battle of Evermore', 'Gallows Pole', 'Friends' and 'Kashmir' were radically different from the originals but in their way quite inspired. The show was broadcast on MTV two weeks later and the resulting album, *No Quarter: Unledded*, made the top ten in Britain and in America.

In February 1995, Page and Plant launched a year-long tour, during which they played 115 shows in 19 countries and performed new versions of 34 Led Zeppelin songs. Some fans were disappointed at the non-inclusion of Jones in the 'reunion' and the bass player himself made his disgruntlement known when a month before the tour started, Led Zeppelin were inducted into the Rock and Roll Hall of Fame at the Waldorf Astoria hotel in New York. "Thanks to my friends for finally remembering my telephone number," he quipped from the stage, although his annoyance didn't prevent him from joining in a jam session with Page and Plant, along with Neil Young. It was only the third time all three surviving Zeppelin members had played together in public in 15 years.

Without Jones, the Page and Plant tour went well enough for them to consider further collaborations. For Page it was the most creatively satisfying project he had been involved in since the demise of Zeppelin. "It's fucking great and it comes from a good chemistry and a lot of straight talking now," Page enthused. "There's a sensitivity that we've got between ourselves which I think has taken a while to kindle in these new times. But it's good stuff and there's no

better place to be." For Plant, it was the first time he had felt totally at ease with his past. "There's still an extraordinary energy, it's just that it's a bit more manageable and a bit more enjoyable. There aren't so many loose cannons or grey areas," he observed. "We know where we are and what we're doing."

The pair spent much of 1997 writing *Walking into Clarksdale*, although the album was then recorded at Abbey Road in just 35 days. Sadly, their first full songwriting venture together since *In Through the out Door* was a disappointing effort with few outstanding songs and was easily outsold by *Led Zeppelin: The BBC Sessions*, a two-disc compilation of their early radio recordings which had been much bootlegged but was not given an official release until 1997.

When they took the new record on the road in 1998 on the *Walking into Everywhere* tour, playing another 89 gigs in 18 countries, including eastern Europe, audiences showed little or no interest in the new songs and they fell back increasingly on Zeppelin classics such as 'Rock and Roll', 'Babe I'm Gonna Leave You', 'Gallows Pole', 'Heartbreaker' and 'Whole Lotta Love', although they were now mostly being played as straight rock songs again rather than in the intriguing *Unledded* arrangements. By the end of the year, to the surprise of nobody, a disenchanted Plant pulled the plug and plans for a 1999 tour of Australia and the Far East were cancelled. "Jimmy and I were kind of marooned. We were still surrounded by the protective shield of who we were and it meant we were playing big arenas around the world and I realised again there had to be another way of singing than doing it in front of a great black abyss," Plant later explained. "It was when we did an Amnesty International benefit in Paris with Bruce Springsteen,

Radiohead and the Dalai Lama that I knew it was getting absurd again. Only the Laughing Policeman was missing. Then it was suggested we played New Year's Eve in Guam and then on to Hawaii and I knew I had to get back to playing clubs and remembering what the pulse was all about. To sell 200 million albums with Zeppelin was chance. But to say goodbye to the large arenas I played with Jimmy was a very purposeful move. I just didn't think there was anything left for me to project to the back of an ice hockey arena. So I had to go off and play little places on the Welsh borders. And that gave me a new life."

In public, both sides claimed there was no animosity but it was noticeable that when the two were booked to appear separately at a charity concert organised by Roger Daltrey at the Albert Hall in February 2002, Page jammed with Paul Weller and Ocean Colour Scene but not with Robert Plant. It was the first time the pair had not played together when sharing the same bill.

At the Rock and Roll Hall of Fame presentation, with Pat Bonham and Aerosmith

Page meanwhile turned his attention to putting together *Led Zeppelin the DVD*. He had begun assessing the archive of film material as early as 1997 but it took the rapid development of DVD as a format before the project took full shape, and in 2002 he hired director Dick Carruthers to help with the task of digitalising the available material. He even swallowed his dislike of bootleggers and put out a call for audience-shot cine footage, an appeal that produced further interesting material. The two-disc DVD set appeared in May 2003 and became the biggest-selling music DVD up to that time. During his trawl through the archives, Page also came across the multi-track tapes of Zeppelin's L.A. performances from the 1972 tour, which he cleaned up and issued as the live double CD *How the West Was Won*.

Jones, Plant and Page all attended special premiere screenings in London and New York but typically, guitarist and singer

LED ZEPPELIN

8

derived different messages from watching the old footage. "If we got back in a room and played a Zeppelin number and there were smiles behind our eyes, then maybe it could happen," Page said with a considerable degree of wishful thinking. "It could be possible. I wouldn't discount it. I just don't know." Plant, however, was far more decisive. "The DVD really opens and closes the issue because it's so explicit of what it's about," he said forcefully. "It's the epitaph of Led Zeppelin – stunning, a lot of energy, a roller-coaster ride, four guys melding in this great fusion of music. And it's gone."

EPITAPH...

If there were any lingering hopes that Led Zeppelin might get together again they appeared to have been dashed in 2005 when the band significantly failed to come together to receive a lifetime's achievement award at the Grammys in Los Angeles, with only Page and Jones attending while Plant stayed home. The guitarist was clearly delighted with the award, which he felt represented long overdue recognition by an American music record industry that had always seemed to begrudge Led Zeppelin its success. "I'm sure people thought we'd been nominated in the past," he told *Uncut*. "But you know, we never even got a single Grammy nomination until now. I never thought it would happen, so of course I really enjoyed it." But he was spitting blood at Plant's failure to show. "I'm sure he had his reasons," he grumbled moodily. "But it wouldn't have taken much for him to pop over and meet everybody, would it?"

The morning after the Grammys, Robert Plant was sitting several thousand miles away drinking tea with this writer in the kitchen at Peter Gabriel's Real World Studios

in Box, Wiltshire, where he was rehearsing with his band The Strange Sensation. "I saw Jimmy had a bit of a go at me for not being there," he said. "But what can you do? What I'm doing now is more important to me. This veneration of one period of one's life is pointless. It's great to look back and smile. But middle-aged self-congratulation is very dangerous."

Yet rumours of a Zeppelin reunion continued to grow throughout 2007. Plant, as ever, had his own projects on the go and spent the early part of the year in America, finishing the album he had begun recording in Nashville the previous year with Alison Krauss.

Behind the scenes, however, he was coming under enormous pressure to agree to one final flight in the 'mothership', the title of a new Zeppelin 'best of' album. By the time the album appeared in November 2007, Plant had finally agreed to team up with Page, Jones and Jason Bonham, following some tortuous negotiations, for a one-off Led Zeppelin reunion at London's O2 Arena.

The announcement was made by promoter Harvey Goldsmith on September 12, 2007, and despite an eye-watering £135 price tag, the ballot for the 20,000 tickets was vastly over-subscribed, with fans from as far apart as America and Japan flying in for the occasion.

Given his longstanding and trenchant opposition to a reunion, many wondered what had made Plant change his mind. That proceeds from the concert went to the Ahmet Ertegün Education Fund, a charitable trust in the name of the respected founder of Atlantic Records, undoubtedly made it harder for him to resist. He may also have felt that he owed it as a favour to Page, who has still produced no new music since 1998's Page/Plant album *Walking into Clarksdale*. Perhaps he also calculated that allowing Led Zeppelin

8

one last grand hurrah would finally put the beast to bed once and for all. If so, he could hardly have been more mistaken.

Characteristically, there was the usual Zeppelin drama in the run-up to the concert when rehearsals were disrupted after Page injured the little finger on his left hand and the original November 26 date had to be postponed for two weeks.

When Led Zeppelin eventually took the stage on December 10, 2007 for their first full-length concert in 27 years, there was no new material and few real surprises – other than a genuine sense of wonder at how magnificent they still sounded, given that the three original members of the band totalled 183 years between them. Over a two-hour show, they performed 16 Zep classics. Plant even graciously sang 'Stairway to Heaven', triumphantly reclaiming the song from a thousand dodgy covers.

Yet even before the last strains of the final encore of 'Rock and Roll' had faded away, feverish speculation was abroad that such a mighty triumph had to be followed by a full-length tour. An alleged 200 million dollars was said to be on offer for a string of American dates but Plant was swift to nip such expectations in the bud, making his distaste for the idea evident by insisting that he had no intention of touring "like a bunch of bored old men following The Rolling Stones around".

He seemed far more enthused by his work with Alison Krauss. Aided by the Zep brouhaha, their *Raising Sand* album – felicitously released in the gap between the reunion announcement and the concert – became the most successful recording by any former Zeppelin member since the band's demise. It went on to win a clutch of Grammy awards, including 'Album of the Year', and Plant further shut the door on

the prospect of continued Zep activity by announcing an extensive set of tour dates with Krauss that kept him occupied through much of 2008.

For a while, his colleagues seemed determined to cash in on the revival of Zep-mania, with or without him. Jones told an interviewer that the rest of the band were in the market for a new singer and commentators cited the precedent of the reformed Queen with Paul Rodgers in the Freddie Mercury role. Thankfully, the ridiculous notion of a Plant-free Zeppelin came to nothing. Possibly his former colleagues were merely trying to twist his arm, and when he continued to resist, it was announced that the new Page/Jones/Bonham project would not be called Led Zeppelin after all. A few months later, Page's manager let it be known that all plans had been quietly abandoned because none of the singers who had been tried had "worked out".

A disappointed Page took himself off to the 2008 Beijing Olympics to perform an embarrassing version of 'Whole Lotta Love' with Leona Lewis and it seemed that Led Zeppelin really had flown for the very last time.

The film and audio recording of the 2007 reunion concert eventually appeared as a CD and DVD package in 2012 under the title *Celebration Day*. In December that same year, Page, Plant and Jones were named recipients of the Kennedy Center Honors, and all three attended a weekend of gala events in Washington, DC, the highlight of which was a reception at the White House, where US President Barack Obama hung ribboned awards around the necks of the three tuxedoed former Zeppelin hell-raisers.

Following the release of *Celebration Day*, Page announced that he was remastering the

LED ZEPPELIN

8

Led Zeppelin back catalogue, and that each album would be individually reissued with a second disc of "substantial stuff" left on the cutting room floor, including "different versions of things, different approaches to the mixes". The expanded reissues of the first five Led Zeppelin albums appeared in 2014. Meanwhile, the spatting between Page and Plant over a Zep reunion continued unabated. When Page grumpily told the *New York Times* that he was "fed up" with Plant for not committing to a reunion tour, Plant tetchily responded by telling *Uncut* magazine: "I'm not my brother's keeper. And he, really, as a pro, should know better than that."

SOLO FLIGHTS

JIMMY PAGE

It would be fair to say that Jimmy Page found the demise of Led Zeppelin harder to take than either of his surviving colleagues. Plant was full of ideas and threw himself swiftly into a busy and productive solo career, determined to prove that the most significant part of his life was not over at 32 years of age. The self-contained John Paul Jones was more than content to disappear into obscurity, spend time with his family and tinker for his own amusement in his home studio. Page, it seemed, simply didn't know what to do, although he was able to delay thinking about his post-Zeppelin future for a while as he set about compiling the posthumous *Coda* album.

Living in the house where Bonham had died can hardly have helped his state of mind and rumours were rife that his health was in a perilous state as a result of his heroin addiction. "There was a period after John died that I didn't touch a guitar for ages. It just seemed to relate to everything that had happened," he admits. When he eventually asked his road manager Tim

Marten to retrieve his favourite Les Paul from storage, the guitar case was found to be empty. "I thought, 'That's it, I'm finished.'" Fortunately, it transpired that the guitar had been borrowed not stolen, and it was swiftly returned. In March 1981, he made his first post-Zeppelin appearance on stage, jamming with Jeff Beck during the encore at a gig by his old Yardbirds sparring partner at London's Hammersmith Odeon.

Meanwhile, at his Sol studio in Cookham, Berkshire, he was working with Chris Squire and Alan White from Yes. Seven tracks were recorded but never released amid rumours that he was trying to get Plant to sing with them and the band would be called XYZ (ex-Yes and Zeppelin). Such plans came to nothing but in the late summer of 1981, he was approached by the film director Michael Winner, who was a near neighbour, to provide the soundtrack for the film *Death Wish II*. Despite his disastrous experience over the *Lucifer Rising* soundtrack, he accepted and, working with alacrity, the soundtrack album, which found him experimenting with the Roland guitar synthesiser for the first time, was released in February 1982. "I was at a very low ebb but then a great challenge came up to do a film score," he recalls. "I had eight weeks on that project, that's all I had to deliver the whole thing. That's what got me back into it without a doubt."

If so, his return to the fray wasn't immediately evident. A drug bust in 1982 was depressing proof of his continuing problems and it was well into 1983 that there was any serious sign of further activity when he performed music from *Death Wish II* and an instrumental version of 'Stairway to Heaven' at a brace of benefit concerts at London's Albert Hall that September for the multiple sclerosis charity ARMS. They were successful

8

enough for Page to agree to nine similar shows in America. Steve Winwood had sung with him at the Albert Hall, but with the former Traffic man unavailable for the American dates he turned to Paul Rodgers, footloose and fancy-free after the break-up of Bad Company. It ushered in a far more productive period in Page's post-Zeppelin life and 1984 found him appearing at folk festivals with Roy Harper, playing on albums by Harper and Stephen Stills and aiding both John Paul Jones and Robert Plant on their respective solo efforts.

The big news, however, was the band he was putting together with Paul Rodgers. Rehearsing under the name The McGregors (Page was also introduced by Roy Harper during their joint appearances as 'James Macgregor'), among those who came and went during early rehearsals were Rat Scabies, drummer with The Damned and Bill Bruford from Yes. However, the line-up eventually included Chris Slade on drums and Tony Franklin on bass and the quartet made their live debut in Stockholm in November 1984 under the name The Firm. British gigs and an American tour followed, with a set that largely avoided old Zeppelin and Free material, but many of the dates were less than sell-outs, hardly helped by a lacklustre debut album with few stand-out songs. A second album was even less well received, and after a further American tour the band split in May 1986. "The Firm was originally going to be a one-album project and then it went to two and then Paul and I agreed it had run its course, really," Page commented. Given the talent involved it was all rather a waste, but even a guitarist and singer of the ability of Page and Rodgers could not carry a band that displayed such a chronic inability to write memorable songs.

Uncertain what to do next and with the attempted Zeppelin reunion with drummer

Tony Thompson having collapsed in early 1986, Page decided to record his first proper solo album. Originally intended as a double LP with one side of rock 'n' roll, one of blues, a third of acoustic material and a fourth experimental side, it was eventually cut back to a single album, in part because demos of some of the material were stolen from Page's home. *Outrider* eventually appeared in June 1988 and featured a guest appearance by Robert Plant. Page later admitted that the album sounded "a bit like a glorified demo" but it was better received than the misconceived efforts of The Firm and Page toured the record successfully in Britain and America, also taking the opportunity to reprise favourites from the Led Zeppelin songbook. He also seemed at last to have laid some of his demons to rest, having married and become the proud father of a son, James Patrick.

After the *Outrider* tour had wound down, he talked about another album project and suggested he was putting together a new band with "a lot of young blood". Yet he put all such thoughts to one side when Atlantic asked him to oversee the remastering of the band's back catalogue. Frustrated by Plant's vetoing once again of another attempt to reunite Led Zeppelin, in 1992 Page took the surprising step of teaming up with the former Deep Purple and Whitesnake singer, David Coverdale. It was also provocative, due to a long-running feud between the singer and Plant, who regarded him as a shameless copyist. "I'd been looking for a singer to work with and gone through scores of demo cassettes with no luck. Then someone from my record company, Geffen, suggested I team up with David," Page explained. "Initially we tried a few ideas and then the stuff began pouring out. We knew we had something good."

LED ZEPPELIN

8

A routine heavy rock album followed but a planned tour of America in 1993 was cancelled, allegedly due to poor ticket sales. They did play seven dates in Japan at the end of the year but a proposed second album was scrapped when Page teamed up again with Plant for the MTV *Unledded* project. There were more than a few who believed that his dalliance with Coverdale had been deliberately conceived to rile Plant and force him, like a jealous lover, back into resuming their old partnership.

Page and Plant worked together again for the best part of the next five years, producing two albums, 1994's *No Quarter/ Unledded* and *Walking into Clarksdale* three years later, and touring extensively. However, when Plant tired of the reunion at the end of 1998 and pulled the plug, Page took it badly. His response was to go on the road in America with The Black Crowes, a liaison that lasted into 2000 and produced a live album full of old Led Zeppelin material.

Since then Page has once again gone quiet. Now in his sixties, at an age when most are settling down as grandparents, he has three young children by his current partner, Jimena, and enjoys taking and collecting them from school and fulfilling his paternal duties in a way that he wasn't always able to with his two children by previous relationships. Impressively, his extended family, which includes three different mothers and five children, are all on good terms. "Every Christmas we are all together, all the mums and all the children. We are a close-knit family," he told the *London Evening Standard* in 2004.

Musically, he remains happiest when working on Zeppelin-related projects such as the 2003 DVD, which he spent hundred of hours assembling. While Plant is terrified of being seen to rest on the laurels of Led Zeppelin, Page can't think of anything grander. He's delighted every time Zeppelin are given some new honour or award and invariably turns up to accept in person, beaming with pride and pleasure. When asked in 2005 if he was frustrated that the media were obsessed with his role in a band that had split up a quarter of a century earlier, he seemed baffled by the question. "Not at all, because if you look at it from my point of view, it was a great life in Zeppelin," he responded. When it was pointed out that his time in the band constituted less than one-fifth of his life and had come to an end when he was just 36 years old, he answered: "But it's what Led Zeppelin means across the board – the playing, the writing and the fact that we made so many groundbreaking statements at the time." Implicit in the reply was a recognition that nothing he had done since had come close to matching it.

Yet in the same interview, he insisted that there would be a new Jimmy Page solo recording. "What I need to be doing is trying to make a new musical statement," he said. "My main intention this year is to get up to speed. The way to look at it is that I took a year out. I had some things to sort out and that's done and now it's time to get back on a serious roll this year. And hopefully there will be some music. Now's the time to do something that makes people say, 'I didn't think you'd do that, but I can really see why you've done it.' We'll see what we come up with. I'm not retired yet if that's what you're thinking."

A couple of years later, the world was still waiting for the promised new music; but by then Page was otherwise engaged, having finally coerced, cajoled or otherwise persuaded the reluctant Plant to agree to the Led Zeppelin reunion that he had

8

long craved. After the 2007 reformation proved – to Page's disappointment – to be a one-off, he busied himself with other Zeppelin projects, preparing a DVD and CD release of the O2 concert and the issue by Genesis Publications in 2010 of a 'pictorial autobiography' in a hand-crafted, limited edition of 2,150 copies. There were few words in the book other than the captions, but Page himself selected the 650 photographs, arranging them in a narrative sequence. The edition swiftly sold out and in 2012 a copy was sold on eBay for 1,750 dollars.

Accolades continued to come his way, with the first-ever Global Peace Award by the United Nations' Pathways to Peace project in 2010 and the even more prestigious Kennedy Center Honor, awarded to Page alongside Plant and Jones in Washington, DC, in 2012. One honour that eluded him was a knighthood, despite Conservative MP Louise Mensch launching a parliamentary campaign for him to be dubbed Sir Jimmy.

Stage performances became increasingly few and far between, but there was a brief flurry of guest appearances in 2011 when he played unannounced at concerts by The Black Crowes, Donovan and Roy Harper.

In 2012 he finally released new 'product' – except that it was hardly new as *Lucifer Rising and Other Sound Tracks* contained the music he had produced for Kenneth Anger's 1972 film, *Lucifer Rising*, but which was never used or released at the time. Issued on vinyl only, the record was available exclusively through Page's web site. Around the time of its release he told BBC6 Music: "I'm starting to work next year, to be seen to be playing live. I'll definitely be doing an album at that point in time."

In 2013, *Billboard* reported that he had made no progress on a new solo album and was instead busy preparing another set of Led Zeppelin reissues, which would include "never-before-heard recordings". The first five reissues appeared in 2014, when Page also claimed he was keen to get back on a live stage and was planning to assemble a new touring band to play old Zeppelin material. "If I was to play again it would be with musicians ... some of them might be new to you," he said. "I haven't put the musicians together, I'm going to do that next year."

ROBERT PLANT

Devastated as he was by John Bonham's death, Robert Plant could hardly wait to launch his solo career. A new band and a new method of working in which he called the shots were his way of wiping the slate clean and putting behind him both the pain of losing his friend and what he has called the "psychosis" that surrounded Led Zeppelin. The details of the launch of his solo career were imbued with considerable symbolism: on March 9, 1981 he turned up with a bunch of local blues players dubbed The Honeydrippers at a wine bar in Stourbridge and played a set of vintage R&B and blues standards with not a Zeppelin number in sight, other than a reinterpretation of Sonny Boy Williamson's 'Bring It on Home'. The contrast with his last performance on British soil at Knebworth could not have been greater.

During the short club tour that followed, Plant began writing new material with guitarist Robbie Blunt, an old friend from the Midlands and a veteran of several bands including the criminally underrated early-1970s roots-rockers Bronco. Before long they were at Dave Edmunds' Rockfield studio in Wales, recording with a new band that included Paul Martinez on bass and Black Sabbath drummer Jezz Woodroffe. Released in June 1982, Plant's solo debut *Pictures at Eleven* represented a deliberate break with the past as he experimented with a drum

LED ZEPPELIN

machine and other programmed elements and supported the album with singles and videos, activities that had been anathema to Led Zeppelin. There was a new look, too, although Plant had already hinted at a change of image at Knebworth. Gone were the hippie threads to be replaced by smart designer labels while, the once unruly hair was expensively coiffed 1980s-style.

Pictures at Eleven made the top five on both sides of the Atlantic and proved to Plant's delight that there was life after Led Zeppelin. A second album, *The Principle of Moments*, followed in 1983 and included the hit single 'Big Log', which he even performed on *Top of the Pops* "with a lemon in the trouser pocket of my silk jump suit", he recalls. "In fact there were lemons in both pockets and they were swinging around. Big bollocks. And that's exactly what it was. Big bollocks. Going along with those funny hair-dos and mohair jumpers! But there were some fantastic moments." With a band that initially included Phil Collins on drums, he also toured the album in Britain, Australia and Japan, although he assiduously avoided Led Zeppelin material.

Before recording his third solo album proper, *Shaken 'n' Stirred*, Plant indulged himself on a handful of vintage R&B standards with a stellar pick-up band that included Nile Rodgers, Jeff Beck and Jimmy Page. Released at the end of 1984 as *The Honeydrippers: Volume One*, the five-track mini-album was a huge success in America, where 'Sea of Love' was a surprise top five single, although it fared less well in Britain. *Shaken 'n' Stirred*, however, found Plant moving in the opposite direction on his most 1980s-sounding set. The album has not stood the test of time well, but the supporting tour, which included his first American dates since 1977, was a more engaging affair,

incorporating a Honeydrippers sequence and an inflatable Cadillac car as a backdrop.

In the middle of the 1985 tour he reunited briefly with Led Zeppelin at *Live Aid*, but after vetoing plans to reform on a more permanent basis, the following year he ended his three-album partnership with Blunt, broke up his band and went back to the drawing board. He didn't re-emerge until early 1988 with the release of the album *Now and Zen*, which included a guest appearance by Jimmy Page and sampled Zeppelin on the track 'Tall Cool One'. It was an indication that he was beginning to come to terms with his past, and on the accompanying Non Stop Go, tour as it was labelled, for the first time he incorporated Zeppelin material into his solo shows, including 'Rock and Roll' and 'Communication Breakdown'. "I guess I'm eating a sizeable portion of my own words," he confessed at the time. "But these are great songs and I think enough time has now elapsed. Some of them are sacred still, but if I want to romp through 'Misty Mountain Hop' again, well it's my prerogative." Predictably there was no 'Stairway to Heaven', which he now regarded as nothing but an albatross around his neck. Indeed, he showed what he thought of the song by having an easy-listening cocktail version played as the outro music as the lights went up at gigs where sections of the audience had irritated him by calling for him to sing it.

His fifth solo set, *Manic Nirvana*, appeared in 1990 and was a harder-edged affair that echoed the relief of many that the 1980s were over. The accompanying tour included half-a-dozen Zeppelin numbers as rumours of a reunion reached fever pitch. Instead, Plant assembled a new band for 1993's *Fate of Nations* and the accompanying tour found him visiting South America and Mexico, as well as the more usual European and North American venues. It was the last time he would be seen as a solo artist

8

The Priory of Brion ensemble. Plant's shorts (but not his hair) show that this is a very different gig from the good old days

for six years, when in 1994 Zeppelin fans finally got their wish and he teamed up with Jimmy Page again.

It was a very different Robert Plant who returned to the stage in 1999. Just as in 1981 when he had picked up his solo career playing R&B with a bunch of local musicians he dubbed The Honeydrippers, this time he assembled Priory of Brion, featuring a bunch of part-time musicians which included his former Band of Joy colleague Kevyn Gammond. The repertoire consisted entirely of covers of late-1960s psychedelic classics by the likes of The Youngbloods, Buffalo Springfield, Tim Buckley, Love and Jefferson Airplane, mostly delivered from a seated position. Promoters were forbidden to advertise his name as the band made its way around tiny pubs and clubs, mostly near the Welsh border. The only publication he invited to cover the venture was the specialist *Folk Roots*. When the magazine's interviewer turned up backstage at a gig at the Cheese & Grain in Frome, Somerset, Plant quipped: "It's a long way from the golden god of cock-rock, eh?" *Folk Roots* duly featured him on its cover with a long interview in which he talked about his desire to get back to his roots and his love of Arabic music and singers such as the late Egyptian diva Umm Kulthum.

In 2000, Priory of Brion played festival dates at Glastonbury, the Cambridge Folk Festival and Fairport Convention's annual Cropredy get-together, where Plant had guested several times over the years. In all, he played more than 70 gigs with the band in an 18-month period, much to the exasperation of his manager Bill Curbishley, who wanted him back in a studio and doing something a little more high profile. "Bill said it was like Arkle pulling a milk float or Seb Coe running down the chip shop," Plant

LED ZEPPELIN

later observed. "But Priory of Brion was a bit like musical sorbet. It cleared my palette for the next thing that was going to happen."

In 2001 he dispensed with Priory of Brion's part-timers and assembled a more serious band of seasoned professionals he dubbed The Strange Sensation. Key to the line-up was Justin Adams, a guitarist who had worked with Jah Wobble but whose interests in North African music provided a strong foil for Plant's own world music passions, Others on board included keyboardist John Baggott, who had worked with Massive Attack, drummer Clive Deamer, from Portishead, Charlie Jones on bass and second guitarist Porl Thompson. Citing Julian Cope as an influence, Plant's debut album with the band, 2002's *Dreamland*, was a modest return, consisting mostly of covers done with a decidedly psychedelic twist.

After travelling to Mali in 2003 with Adams to perform at the Festival in the Desert, where he also jammed with African musicians, Plant began recording a second album with The Strange Sensation. *The Mighty Rearranger* appeared in 2005 and was his most significant statement in years. In an echo of *Led Zeppelin III*, most of the lyrics, which found him both commenting on the post 9/11 world and reflecting on his own past, were written in a remote cottage in Snowdonia. Musically the album was a thrilling fusion of styles. "I've spent time in northern Mali and in Morocco and I've got this wanderlust and muse that is part of my being now," he said, sounding more enthused than in years. "It could have been cabaret, singing ballads at the Albert Hall. Instead we have a collision of western rock and roll with this Malian/Tuareg rhythmic stuff where neither element of the music is compromised. It's an absolute collision without trying to make it a cosmic progressive rock album. It's a new place to go."

On tour the band worked up almost a dozen Led Zeppelin numbers, which took their place comfortably alongside the new material and covers. "I can now sing 'hey hey mama said the way you move' without feeling bad about it," he noted. "It's no longer sexist or tired. Strange Sensation has created an environment where the door is always open to adventure so there's a whole new shift to a song like that. We've found all the combinations."

With The Strange Sensation, Plant also instituted a policy of attempting to play in places he had never performed before, taking the band to the Arctic Circle and playing gigs in Estonia, Latvia, Ukraine and Tunisia. One rock critic disparagingly described the latter-day Plant as resembling "a middle-aged back-packer". Plant himself would surely regard the comment as a compliment.

The end of 2006 found Plant in Nashville recording with T Bone Burnett and bluegrass singer-fiddler Alison Krauss. "We were pushing ideas around. The combination of my voice with Alison's voice and T Bone's spookiness – well, I'll just say it's very encouraging," he told *Rolling Stone* at the time. The resulting album, *Raising Sand*, was credited jointly to Plant and Krauss and was released in 2007 to great critical acclaim.

After Nashville, Plant took a pilgrimage to the Delta to visit the birthplace of the blues and played his harmonica at Sonny Boy Williamson's grave. "Now I'm free," he announced. "I can drive through Mississippi, use my credit card and nobody even looks at it. And it doesn't matter to me if things are successful or not. Because I can walk away feeling I haven't wasted my time."

Following the Led Zeppelin one-off reunion at the end of 2007, Plant returned with evident relief to his solo career, turning up at bluegrass, folk and world music festivals with Krauss, playing songs from *Raising Sand* and to generally enthusiastic reviews and was nominated for two Grammy awards. That same year BBC2 aired a documentary film titled *Robert Plant: By Myself.*

In 2012 he formed Sensational Space Shifters with former Strange Sensation members Liam "Skin" Tyson, Justin Adams, Billy Fuller and John Baggott, along with Dave Smith and the African traditional musician Juldeh Camara. Patty Griffin also appeared as a special guest at several Sensational Space Shifters gigs and rumours began to emerge that Griffin and Plant had secretly wed. Plant subsequently revealed that they were not married, but were living together and dividing their time between homes in Britain and in Austin, Texas.

By the time Plant released his next solo album, 2014's *lullaby...And The Ceaseless Roar* on which he was backed by the Sensational Space Shifters, he and Griffin had separated and he was back living in Britain full time. "I'd been in the same village most of my life and I'd never really struck out," he said. "I really did like the whole idea of West Texas." Yet it seemed he liked the lure of his Albion home even more, and many of the songs on *lullaby...And The Ceaseless Roar* were about homecoming and full of references to his "island home" and his continuing fascination with the old, mystical England of Arthurian legend. "At this time of my life I'm trying to slow it all down, slow down the movement of the seasons so I can devour them," he noted.

a few suitably reworked 'quiet storm' takes on old Led Zeppelin tunes.

Together again for the launch of the DVD. Your time is gonna come...

Away from music, to his delight in 2009 he was appointed a vice-president of Wolverhampton Wanderers, the football league club he had supported since boyhood. There was talk of a second album with Krauss, but instead he found a new foil and partner when he met and fell in love with American country singer-songwriter Patty Griffin. Nostalgically reviving the name of his pre-Led Zeppelin outfit Band of Joy, in summer 2010 he began touring with a line-up that included Griffin, Nashville guitarist Buddy Miller, multi-instrumentalist Darrell Scott, bassist Byron House and drummer Marco Giovino. A studio album, also titled *Band of Joy*, was released in September 2010

JOHN PAUL JONES

After Led Zeppelin, John Paul Jones slipped back into the anonymity he had enjoyed pre-1968. Based initially in Devon where he had built his own studio, he spent the post-Zep years in happy obscurity, only reappearing once for an encore jam with Robert Plant when his *The Principle of Moments* tour hit

LED ZEPPELIN

Bristol at the end of 1983. The following year he stirred himself to score Michael Winner's film *Scream for Help*, a gig he got on the recommendation of Jimmy Page, who played guitar on two tracks. Elsewhere Jones played most of the instruments himself, with Yes's Jon Anderson and Madeline Bell helping out with the vocals and his daughter Jacinda contributing lyrics.

A brief appearance followed in Paul McCartney's film *Give My Regards to Broad Street* on the track 'Ballroom Dancing'. Donning his producer's hat, he then worked with Ben E King on his comeback album *Save the Last Dance for Me* (1987), The Mission's 1988 album *Children* and an album by his daughter Jacinda (1990).

In 1991 he built a new studio near Bath, where he worked on various commissioned pieces, including the renaissance-influenced *Amores Pasodas* (1991) and a composition called *Macanda* (1992), both of which were premiered at London's South Bank. Throwing himself a little more into the mainstream, he played on albums by Peter Gabriel and Brian Eno and contributed arrangements to R.E.M.'s blockbuster album, *Automatic for the People*. During the 1990s he also produced the Butthole Surfers, Heart and Diamanda Galás, with whom he subsequently toured.

By 1996 he had built yet another studio, this time in London, where he recorded his first proper solo album, *Zooma*, released in 1999. "I spent all my time producing, arranging, starting classical composition. I was just working on everything else I suppose. I never really got around to it," Jones said when asked why it had taken him 19 years since the demise of Led Zeppelin to make a solo record. The all-instrumental set was followed two years later by a second album, *The Thunderthief*, which found him singing and writing his own lyrics for the first time. He

also toured both albums – and performed a number of Zeppelin songs – before returning to production duties, working on albums by New Zealand rockers The Datsuns (2004) and American bluegrass act Uncle Earl (2007).

Jones became a regular attender and enthusiastic performer at the Mandolines de Lunel festival in France and joined up with Ben Harper and Questlove of The Roots for the late-night Superjam at the 2007 Bonnaroo Music and Arts Festival in Tennessee. Guest appearances on the Foo Fighters' album *In Your Honor* (2005) led to Jones forming a new rock supergroup, Them Crooked Vultures, with Foo Fighters frontman and former Nirvana drummer Dave Grohl and Queens of the Stone Age's Josh Homme. The group's live debut, at the Metro in Chicago, was followed by performances on the European summer festival circuit and the release of their self-titled debut album *Them Crooked Vultures*, in November 2009.

All involved were insistent that there would be a second album, but by the end of 2013 a window had still not been found in busy schedules to record the follow-up and Homme and Grohl were back working with their own bands.

Jones, meanwhile, turned up somewhat improbably at the Royal Opera House, Covent Garden, as part of the band for Mark-Anthony Turnage's 2011 opera *Anna Nicole*. More in type, he also played a handful of festival dates that same year backing the American blues revivalist Seasick Steve. The pair reunited in 2013 when Jones appeared with the bluesman at live shows and on the BBC TV Show *Later... with Jools Holland*.

There were also guest appearances with a diversity of other acts, including Robyn Hitchcock, the Norwegian avant-gardists Supersilent and the Malian singer Rokia Traoré, with whom he played at Glastonbury in 2013.

ALBUMS AND SOLO PROJECTS

9

"I'd love to meet a chick who could fuck like Led Zeppelin I, *but she'd wear me out in a week.*"

OZ REVIEW, QUOTED BY THE PROSECUTION IN THE INFAMOUS OBSCENITY TRIAL, 1971

ALBUMS AND SOLO PROJECTS

9

This section catalogues all albums released by Led Zeppelin, including solo work and other major side projects since the band's break-up in 1980, until the present day. All albums are available on CD unless indicated.

LED ZEPPELIN

UK, Atlantic, March 28, 1969; US, Atlantic, January 17, 1969

GOOD TIMES BAD TIMES
BABE I'M GONNA LEAVE YOU
YOU SHOOK ME
DAZED AND CONFUSED
YOUR TIME IS GONNA COME
BLACK MOUNTAIN SIDE
COMMUNICATION BREAKDOWN
I CAN'T QUIT YOU BABY
HOW MANY MORE TIMES

Recorded: **Olympic Studios, Barnes, London. September–October 1968**
Producer: **Jimmy Page**
Engineer: **Glyn Johns**
Cover design and photography: **George Hardie/Chris Dreja**
Highest chart position: **UK 6; US 10**

When Led Zeppelin went into Olympic Studios in September 1968, the album they recorded was essentially the live set they had worked up for and during their first tour of Scandinavia earlier that month. Some of the material had its roots in repertoire The Yardbirds had played on their final tour of America earlier in the year. The rest may have been somewhat hastily cobbled together, but it had all been well-rehearsed and fully arranged by a meticulous Page, who seems to have known exactly the sound he wanted. As a result, they were just 30 hours in the studio, only nine of which were actually spent laying down the tracks, all paid for out of Page's savings. The Plant–Page writing partnership that would serve them so well on later albums was not yet fully operational but that there was an energy and dynamism about the new group and a sense of drama that was something out of the ordinary was evident from every note.

LED ZEPPELIN

9

The album is often cited as 'the birth of heavy rock', a somewhat misleading description when Cream, The Jimi Hendrix Experience and The Jeff Beck Group had already preceded it. Yet what was undoubtedly fresh and exciting was Page's vision to use dynamic contrasts of light and shade, quiet and loud – an approach perhaps most evident on the stunning acoustic-electric arrangement of 'Babe I'm Gonna Leave You', Joan Baez's version of which Page had played to Plant during their bonding session at his Pangbourne home. The track was also the most notable example of what would become the trademark Plant vocal style, with its repeated "baby, baby, baby" mannerisms, which he now wishes he could remove from the record completely.

Now widely recognised as one of the great debut albums, 'Good Times Bad Times' kicks off proceedings and has a close affinity with the old Yardbirds, particularly in its catchy pop chorus. But it's given an astonishing kick by Bonham's drums, making his presence as the loudest, heaviest sticksman of them all felt from the outset. Plant gives us the first taste of his primeval scream and Page cuts loose with a soaring Telecaster solo before the show fades out after a terse two minutes 46 seconds like a jukebox hit that leaves you wanting to put a coin in the slot and play it all over again. After the staggering, hair-raising intensity of 'Babe I'm Gonna Leave You', the band's blues roots come to the fore on a version of Willie Dixon's 'You Shook Me'. The slow groove is never plodding and, according to Jones, was a *tour de force* for Bonham. "He kept a really straight groove on slow numbers and there aren't many that can," the bass player said. "To play slow and groove is one of the hardest things in the world, so it was a joy to sit back on a beat like 'You Shook Me' and just ride it." Page switches to a Gibson Les Paul to effect the blues-drenched sustain on his solo, Plant wails

away on harmonica and Jones's organ swirls around magnificently, before the track ends with guitar and vocal trading licks off each other in breathtaking fashion.

'Dazed and Confused' had its roots in The Yardbirds' repertoire when page had taken a folk song by Jake Holmes and rearranged it as 'I'm Confused'. Here it's transformed into the first Zeppelin epic with Plant moaning over some echoing Page guitar effects and a powerhouse rhythm provided by Jones and Bonham. Its power was sufficient to ensure its presence in every Led Zeppelin live show until 1975. Jones's childhood history as a church organist is evident on the intro of 'Your Time Is Gonna Come' and the track builds into a gospel-styled chorus with Page – who came up with a different guitar sound for almost every track on the album – this time adding pedal steel.

His acoustic guitar showcase 'Black Mountain Side' is in effect a homage to the folk fingerpickers he admired so much, such as Bert Jansch and Davey Graham, and recalls the similar 'White Summer' which had appeared on The Yardbirds' *Little Games* album. It cuts abruptly and dramatically straight into Jones's throbbing bass line to the album's other major epic, 'Communication Breakdown', a masterful fusion of heavy rock and a brutal Stooges-style stacatto riff that predated punk by some eight years. Listen to it and you can hear how Plant could keep a straight face many years later when he claimed Led Zeppelin had welcomed the mid-1970s punk revolution because it reminded him of early Zeppelin.

'I Can't Quit You Baby' is another slow Chicago blues work-out, written by Willie Dixon, with arguably Plant's finest vocal on the record, although the album's closer 'How Many More Times' also has a strong claim. The track was another that had its origins in the old Yardbirds repertoire, but Plant transforms it as he ad-libs wonderfully, borrowing freely from several other songs including 'Rosie' and 'The Hunter', while Page creates one of his most experimental Hendrix-style solos before getting out his violin bow to add some even more extraordinary sounds.

One of the most overlooked aspects of the album is the sheer brilliance of Page's production. If the album isn't intrinsically any heavier than Cream's *Wheels on Fire* or Jeff Beck's *Truth*, it sounds as if it is simply because of the stunning and dynamic contrasts between the quieter moments and the manic, dense quality of the louder passages, which his production deliberately sets out to emphasise. In particular, nobody had ever recorded drums like that before and he made it sound as if Bonham is setting off volleys of cannon fire. "I had been on so many sessions where the drummer was stuck in a little booth and he would be hitting the drums for all he was worth and it would just sound as though he was hitting a cardboard box," Page later recalled. "I knew that drums would have to breath to have that proper sound, that ambience. So consequently we were working on the ambience of everything, of the instruments, all the way through." The use of stereo-panning and other effects such as the backwards echo at the end of 'You Shook Me' is staggeringly sophisticated for its time, too, given the relatively rudimentary equipment on which the album was recorded.

As a template, Led Zeppelin's debut was raw and flawed and, in many ways, the next album would be a far superior effort. On the other hand, it is possible to make out a case for the first album as the purest expression of their art that the band ever made. "There was a naïvety," says Plant, who is highly critical of some of his own singing on the album, and with the benefit of hindsight has described

his vocal style as over-hysterical. "But that's what was splendid about it in a way. I was 19 or 20 when we started nuancing those songs, so I don't have a problem with any of it, really. I just prefer the way it grew later. But the spontaneity of the band was phenomenal. It's simply kicking through the grooves of *Led Zeppelin 1...*"

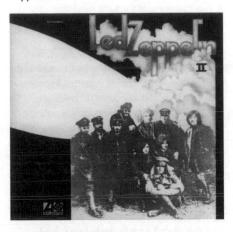

LED ZEPPELIN II
UK, Atlantic, October 22, 1969; US, Atlantic, October 31, 1969

WHOLE LOTTA LOVE
WHAT IS AND WHAT SHOULD NEVER BE
THE LEMON SONG
THANK YOU
HEARTBREAKER
LIVING LOVING MAID (SHE'S JUST A
  WOMAN)
RAMBLE ON
MOBY DICK
BRING IT ON HOME

Recorded: **Olympic Studios, Barnes, London; Mirror Sound, Los Angeles; Mystic Studios, Hollywood; Juggy Sound, New York; Morgan Studios, Willesden,**

LED ZEPPELIN

9

London; Atlantic Studios, New York; A&R
Studios, New York, April–August 1969
Producer: **Jimmy Page**
Engineers: **George Chkiantz; Chris Huston;
Andy Johns; Eddie Kramer**
Cover design: **David Juniper**
Highest chart position: **UK 1; US 1**

It was not unusual for hard-working
groups to record their albums in snatched
windows of opportunity while on the
road. The Rolling Stones, for example, had
regularly recorded in studios in Chicago and
Hollywood while touring America between
1964 and 1966. *Led Zeppelin II* , however,
was an extreme case by anyone's standards.
"It was crazy really," Plant remembers. "We
were writing the numbers in hotel rooms and
then we'd do a rhythm track in London, add
the vocal in New York, overdub harmonica
in Vancouver and then come back to finish
mixing in New York."

Road manager Richard Cole pointed out
that this placed a particularly heavy load
on Page, who again produced. "On several
occasions Jimmy and I would catch a plane
into New York from a gig in Minneapolis
or Chicago," he has written. "I would carry
the unfinished tapes on the plane with me,
wrapped in foil. We'd grab a taxi to A&R
Studios, spend half a day there and then fly
out to the next concert." Page, as Cole noted,
was also a hard task master in the studio:
"He would become much more nervous than
he ever did on stage. No matter how well
prepared he was, he rarely seemed completely
satisfied. He always wanted something a little
closer to perfection. It was long, exhausting
work and as much as he enjoyed the creative
process, it would sometimes overwhelm him."
Yet his attention to detail paid off for out of
such far from ideal circumstances, he crafted
a record that is regularly voted as one of the

greatest rock albums of all time.

By the time of its release in October 1969,
the band were already well on the way to
becoming rock gods, although the artwork
of the inside cover of the gatefold sleeve
is somewhat over the top: a huge zeppelin
picked out in spotlights above a Greek
temple topped with the band's logo and four
plinths in front of it bearing the names of
Page, Plant, Bonham and Jones, as if they
were Olympian deities. That the plinths were
empty was presumably meant to indicate that
they were at least hard-working gods, far too
busy to hang around on Mount Olympus and
rest on their laurels when there was a gig to
play. Yet if it was intended as a prediction of
Led Zeppelin's elevation to the very top of
the rock pile, it was unerringly accurate. By
the end of the year the album was sitting at
number one in America, having dislodged
The Beatles' *Abbey Road.* By February 1970 it
was also number one in Britain, where *Led
Zeppelin II* eventually spent 138 weeks on the
album chart.

Inside, the riffs were as monumental as
the cover's imagery. The album opens with
'Whole Lotta Love', which became not only
the band's signature but came to define heavy
metal, a phrase which, as Dave Lewis points
out in his excellent survey *Led Zeppelin:
A Celebration,* was not yet in usage. Page's
three-note riff was a killer and the descending
chord structure irresistible, while the middle
section was nothing short of apocalyptic, with
Plant squealing orgasmically over a palette of
extraordinary sound effects created by Page
and engineer Eddie Kramer at the mixing
desk. Inevitably, this section was edited out of
the shorter version, which became a top five
single in America. More problematic were the
lyrics. After Plant had failed to come up with
any new words, he simply started singing the
words from 'You Need Love', as recorded by

THE MUSIC: **ALBUMS AND SOLO PROJECTS**

Muddy Waters and written by Willie Dixon. That they then forgot to credit the bluesman caused the band no end of legal trouble in a dispute that was not settled until 1985 and earned Zeppelin an unwelcome reputation for plagiarisation.

That there was much more to Led Zeppelin than heavy rock was evident from the next track, 'What Is and What Should Never Be'. This time Plant did manage to come up with some words on the first song he wrote for the band. The track begins in mellow mood over an almost jazzy chord progression and Jones's arresting bass part, which is almost a counter-melody in its own right, before Bonham's drums explode and introduce another classic Page riff.

'The Lemon Song' is a part-rewrite of Howlin' Wolf's 'Killing Floor' with some dirty blues guitar from Page and with Plant sounding every inch like a gnarled old Delta bluesman rather than a 20-year-old ingenue as he pays homage to one of Robert Johnson's classic metaphors in the line 'squeeze my lemon 'til the juice runs down my leg'. 'Thank You' is a heartfelt tribute from the singer to his wife, Maureen, with some gorgeous swirling, psychedelic organ from Jones and delicate acoustic lead picking from Page, proving that Led Zeppelin were not merely a heavy rock monster but could make great and highly accessible pop music. Indeed in many ways, the arrangement brings to mind Rod Stewart's version of 'Handbags and Gladrags'.

In its original vinyl format the LP was cleverly sequenced to allow for a pause after 'Thank You', before the listener turned the record over for a return to the relentless riffing. On CD, the listener is abruptly bounced back into the heavy blues-rock of 'Heartbreaker', a track which seems to have divided authors of books about Zeppelin. The extended guitar solo which commences unaccompanied by the rest of the band is,

according to Dave Lewis, "a platform for Page to express his guitar virtuosity with a breathtaking exercise in string-bending technique". Keith Shadwick, on the other hand, reckons it's one of Page's poorest on any Led Zeppelin record, "repeating time-worn fingerboard patterns rather than attempting anything fresh". Most fans will surely side with Lewis's favourable assessment.

It's followed by 'Living Loving Maid (She's Just a Woman)', allegedly written about a lady of the night with whom the band had got acquainted in Los Angeles. Plant has identified it as one of the weakest songs in Zeppelin's canon and both lyrically and musically today it sounds distinctly clichéd, although the riff is sharp enough.

'Ramble on', by contrast, is one of the album's highlights, the quiet passages contrasting dramatically with the uplifting chorus and Plant singing his Tolkien-inspired lyrics with great expressiveness. With Bonham's extended drum solo already a highlight of Zeppelin's live show, it was inevitable that he would be given a similar showcase on the record and it comes on 'Moby Dick'. On stage the number could go on for half-an-hour but here is mercifully truncated at less than four-and-half minutes, and is introduced and closed by a potent Page riff that frankly seems to have little to do with the assortment of rolls and paradiddles in the middle. The album closes with 'Bring It on Home', another homage to Plant's blues roots which begins with his rather good Sonny Boy Williamson harp imitation and a slurred pastiche of a Jimmy Reed vocal over a repetitive 12-bar motif played on Jones's bass, but then drives into a storming heavy rocker with some great multi-layered guitar from Page.

More than three decades later, Barney Hoskyns described *Led Zeppelin II* as a

LED ZEPPELIN

9

"tour de force of pulverising riffs and febrile bluesology that stands at the gateway to the 1970s as a monstrously powerful record". All true, of course. Yet listening to it more than three decades on, one is also struck by the fact that the record has little in common with the sins subsequently committed by so many heavy metal bands in Zeppelin's name. Compare Led Zeppelin II, for example, to the first Black Sabbath album released only a few months later. Not only did Page, Plant, Jones and Bonham have the better riffs but they also boasted a subtlety, sophistication, eclecticism and musicality at which few of their imitators could ever even hint.

LED ZEPPELIN III
UK and US, Atlantic, October 5, 1970

IMMIGRANT SONG
FRIENDS
CELEBRATION DAY
SINCE I'VE BEEN LOVING YOU
OUT ON THE TILES
GALLOWS POLE
TANGERINE
THAT'S THE WAY

BRON-Y-AUR STOMP
HATS OFF TO (ROY) HARPER

Recorded: **Headley Grange, Hampshire;
Olympic Studios, Barnes, London;
Island Studios, London; Ardent Studios,
Memphis, May–August 1970**
Producer: **Jimmy Page**
Engineer: **Andy Johns**
Cover design: **Richard Drew**
Highest chart position: **UK 1; US 1**

Probably the most misunderstood album in the group's entire canon, Led Zeppelin III confused critics and fans alike on its release in October 1970 – although that did not stop the album topping the charts in both America and Britain, where two weeks before its release Led Zeppelin had been voted 'best group' in the Melody Maker poll, displacing The Beatles from number one for the first time since 1963.

Mostly conceived and written by Page and Plant at the cottage they rented in Snowdonia, Wales, in the spring of 1970, the material subsequently changed shape and character in the studio and yet retained strong elements of its acoustic guitar origins amidst the riffs to create the strongest expression yet of Page's vision of a new kind of rock music, rich in dynamic contrasts. Or, as the notes on the cover put it: "Credit must be given to Bron-Yr-Aur, a small derelict cottage in South Snowdonia for painting a somewhat forgotten picture of true completeness which acted as an incentive to some of these musical statements."

Yet although Page once again took the producer's chair and had the final say in most matters, his role was less dominant than it had been on the first two albums and there were comparably fewer set-piece Page guitar

9

solos. Led Zeppelin had hit its stride as a collective via its endless touring, particularly in America, and Plant had visibly grown in confidence. "It'll be acoustic as well as electric with the emphasis on everyone in the group," the singer told *NME* while they were still recording the album. To *Rolling Stone* he enthused about "the trip into the mountains" and the beginning of the new "ethereal Page and Plant".

Released in an elaborate gatefold sleeve designed by Richard Drew, a friend of Page's who was a lecturer in fine arts at Leeds Polytechnic, the CD reissue is a pale imitation of the packaging of the original vinyl LP, which contained a rotating inner wheel. Echoing the rural origins of the songs on the album, the wheel was based on crop rotation charts, although in the end it didn't come out quite as the band had planned or hoped. A crestfallen Page lamented that it looked "teeny-bopperish", but by the time the band saw the finished artwork, they were on top of a deadline and it was too late to change it.

The album kicks off with the galloping fury of 'Immigrant Song', a classic Zeppelin pile-driver telling of a Viking force of invaders raping and pillaging across the land ("We come from the land of the ice and snow, from the midnight sun where the hot springs blow/The hammer of the gods will drive our ships to new lands."). At two minutes 23 seconds its brevity is commendable but it packs an astonishing punch as Plant howls like a testosterone-doped Valkyrie. He later suggested that the lyric – which gave Zeppelin one of its enduring nicknames as 'the hammer of the gods' – was tongue-in-cheek, although this was probably lost on most of the band's fans, who did not expect humour from a heavy rock band.

'Friends' is in dramatic contrast, introduced by ringing Crosby, Stills, Nash and Young-style acoustic guitars, which are soon joined by Indian-influenced strings and an ethereal Plant vocal that owes more to his West Coast influences than his blues roots. It segues straight into the slashing slide guitar of 'Celebration Day', with a funk-blues riff that is reminiscent of Jimi Hendrix's 'Freedom'.

At seven-and-a-half minutes, 'Since I've Been Loving You' is the album's longest track by almost two minutes and it's also one of the highlights. A slow blues number on which Page's guitar in places sounds rather like Duane Allman, is complemented by Plant's most assured blues shouting to date, but it's also a superb ensemble piece, with Jones and Bonham making major contributions. 'Out on the Tiles' is the album's second signature Zeppelin riff after 'Immigrant Song'. Led by Bonham's drum pattern, it's not one of their most inventive riffs but the production is inspired and there were few technicians at the time who could match Page's ability to capture such raw energy in the studio. He later explained that the sound was based on a combination of close and distant miking: "That's ambient sound. Getting the distance of the time lag from one end of the room to the other and putting that in as well. The whole idea, the way I see recording, is to try and capture the sound of the room live and the emotion of the whole moment and try to convey that."

'Gallows Pole' is an extraordinary hybrid that confused fans as much as anything else on the album. Based on a traditional song popularised by Lead Belly in the 1930s, instead of the blues-rock riffing one might have expected from a Zeppelin transposition, it's delivered initially by just voice and acoustic guitar before Jones adds some mandolin and Page joins in on banjo and pedal steel. By the

LED ZEPPELIN

9

end, the whole thing sounds more like Traffic than Led Zeppelin. There's more pedal steel on 'Tangerine', an acoustic tune Page had first worked up with Keith Relf while he was still in The Yardbirds, when it went under the title 'Knowing that I'm Losing You'. Plant adds a new and simple romantic lyric which he sings with a double-tracked vocal, and in retrospect the song's more baroque elements can be seen as something of a dry run for 'Stairway to Heaven' on the next album.

'That's the Way' is the third consecutive track to feature Page's new toy, the pedal steel guitar, although this time he plays it in a spacier, more echoing style that owes more to Jerry Garcia's use of the instrument rather than the standard country style he had employed on 'Tangerine'. Perhaps the finest compostion to come out of the Bron-Yr-Aur experience, its wistful, bittersweet quality owes much to Plant's obsession with Neil Young's early solo albums. 'Bron-Y-Aur Stomp', as its name suggests, is another track that has its roots in the Welsh mountains as a fireside jam, although it was initially titled 'Jennings Farm Blues' after the farm Plant had just bought in Worcestershire. Jones plays a fretless bass and Bonham adds spoons and castanets. The album closes with 'Hats off to (Roy) Harper', dedicated to the maverick singer-songwriter who the band had befriended but actually based on an old blues tune called 'Shake 'Em On Down', first recorded by Bukka White in 1937. Plant's vocal is a highly convincing recreation of the style of a pre-war Mississippi country bluesman and Page's acoustic bottleneck guitar makes all the right noises but it sounds like little more than a demo. Page admitted it was taken from "a whole tape of us bashing out different blues things" and it's a low-key and slightly puzzling way to end an album by the biggest, loudest,

heaviest rock band in the world – which is, no doubt, exactly what Page and Plant intended.

Many of the reviews that greeted the album were dismissive. In some cases, it was the same critics who had attacked them for being too loud and bludgeoning who now pilloried them for 'going acoustic'. However, speaking in 2005 Page was magnanimous about the bad reviews. "With hindsight, I can see how if somebody got *Led Zeppelin III*, which was so different from what we'd done before, and they only had a short time to review it on the record player in the office, then they missed the content," he told *Uncut*. "They were in a rush and they were looking for the new 'Whole Lotta Love' and not actually listening to what was there. It was too fresh for them and they didn't get the plot. So in retrospect it doesn't surprise me that the diversity and breadth of what we were doing was overlooked or under-appreciated at the time."

Yet at the time the criticism undoubtedly hurt for the band regarded the 'cottage album' as an absolutely critical step in their development. Plant later described the LP as the band's "single most important statement" and noted that, "It wasn't until *Led Zeppelin III* that I was able to calm it down and have the confidence to sing in a different style."

Although it topped the charts, ultimately *III* was the poorest-selling of Led Zeppelin's first four albums. As Keith Shadwick noted, "its radicalism proving a long-term problem for the band's less adventurous fans", while on the other hand, fans of folk-rock groups, such as The Incredible String Band and Fairport Convention which had inspired much of the record, might have provided a new constituency but remained suspicious of Zeppelin's reputation as monsters of the all-conquering mighty riff.

LED ZEPPELIN IV

UK, Atlantic, November 11, 1971; US, Atlantic, November 8, 1971

BLACK DOG
ROCK AND ROLL
THE BATTLE OF EVERMORE
STAIRWAY TO HEAVEN
MISTY MOUNTAIN HOP
FOUR STICKS
GOING TO CALIFORNIA
WHEN THE LEVEE BREAKS

Recorded: **Headley Grange, Hampshire; Island Studios, London; Sunset Sound, Los Angeles; December 1970–February 1971**
Producer: **Jimmy Page**
Engineers: **Andy Johns; George Chkiantz**
Cover design/artwork: **Graphreaks/Barrington Colby MOM**
Highest chart position: **UK 1; US 2**

After the mixed reaction that had greeted their third album, Led Zeppelin took their time over the follow-up, although the delay was also exacerbated by horrendous technical problems with the mixing. At one time they considered releasing a double album and then toyed with the idea of issuing the material on four EPs. Once they had reverted to the concept of a standard LP, the band then sought other ways to make their fourth album distinctive and hit upon the idea of not giving it a title but presenting it under the banner of four symbols, each representing one of the group's members. This has led to considerable confusion, and over the years the album has variously been referred to as *Led Zeppelin IV*, The Fourth Album, Untitled, Four Symbols, ZoSo (an approximation of the non-existent word that Page's symbol resembled) and The Runes.

The front cover, with its depiction of a character from Britain's rural past, came from a print found by Plant in an antique shop in Reading and its use resembled the cover of Fairport Convention's *Liege & Lief*. However, it was then contrasted with a scene of 20th-century urban decay shot in Dudley in the West Midlands on the back cover while inside a drawing of a hermit was inspired by Page's interest in the mysteries of the tarot pack. For the first time, the band also allowed a lyric to be printed on the inside sleeve, with the words of 'Stairway to Heaven' singled out for the honour.

Faced with the problem of how to market a record that lacked a title, Atlantic placed a series of full-page ads in the music press featuring each of the four symbols, which generated a sense of mystery and intrigue around the album, which went straight to number one in Britain, where it remained in the chart for a total of 62 weeks. In America, its chart residency was even longer, although surprisingly it was kept from the top spot by Carole King's *Tapestry*.

Once again Page and Plant had begun writing the album by retiring in the autumn

9

LED ZEPPELIN

9

of 1970 to the cottage at Bron-Yr-Aur. Before Christmas they had enough material to go into Island Studios. In January they transferred to Headley Grange, using The Rolling Stones' mobile recording truck, although when the rambling old house proved a tad too cold in winter, they then moved back again to Island.

A screw-up in mixing the tapes in Los Angeles resulted in a delayed release when the band rejected the muddy sound and the tapes were remixed again in London. Then there was a prolonged fight with Atlantic over the band's insistence that neither their name nor that of the label should appear on the album's cover. "I remember being in an Atlantic office for two hours with a lawyer who was saying 'you've got to have this'," Page recalled. "It was a hard job but fortunately we were in a position to say 'this is what we want', because we had attained the status whereby that album was going to sell a lot anyway." At a concert at New York's Madison Square Garden in September 1971, Plant actually apologised to fans for the delay of the album, telling the audience, "We've got problems trying to get a record cover that looks how we want it." They won the battle by telling the label "they couldn't have the master tapes until they got the cover right", although the band climbed down in one small detail. They had originally not wanted the record to even have a catalogue number, but the point was conceded when Atlantic pointed out that it would mean stores would not be able to order the record. "The whole story of the fourth album reads like a nightmare," Plant later observed.

Yet as they would do so often in their career, out of the jaws of disaster Led Zeppelin fashioned a triumph. The album kicks off with the turbulent, supercharged groove of 'Black Dog', based on a bass riff that Jones developed from a track on Muddy Waters' experimental blues-rock album,

Electric Mud. Plant contributes one of his most swaggering, carnal vocals ("Hey, hey mama said the way you move, gonna make you sweat, gonna make you groove") and Page overdubs multiple guitars.

With the bassist having come up with the riff on the opening track, it was the drummer's turn on 'Rock and Roll', which came out of a jam inspired by Bonham playing the intro to Little Richard's 'Good Golly Miss Molly/ Keep a Knockin'. Page added a guitar riff, Plant improvised some suitable lyrics ("Been a long time since I rock and rolled") and within 15 minutes the band effectively had the song in place, a perfect example of Zeppelin at their most inspired and spontaneous. The song became the opening number or was used as an encore in their live set at every show for the next six years.

After two classic pile-driving Zeppelin anthems comes the ethereal, mandolin-driven 'Battle of Evermore'. One of Page and Plant's most haunting and understated songs, it has inevitably been overshadowed down the years by the iconic status of the track that follows it on the album, but unfairly so. The tune was composed by Page playing around on Jones's mandolin while Plant added a lyric inspired by a combination of *The Lord of the Rings* and a book of myths and legends about the Scottish border wars. It was also Plant's idea to invite Fairport Convention's Sandy Denny to duet with him. "Sandy and I were friends and it was the most obvious thing to ask her to sing on it," he recalled in 2005. "It's pretty and if it suffered from a naïvety and tweeness, it makes up for it in the cohesion of the voices and the playing."

Then comes 'Stairway to Heaven'. If anybody had said in 1971 that a song that opened with the pastoral sound of overdubbed school recorders would come to be regarded as one of the greatest rock track of all time

– "a mystical epic beloved of suburban metal-heads from sea to shining sea" as Barney Hoskyns memorably put it – the laughter would surely have been loud enough to drown out not only its initial gentle chord progression but the soaring electric guitar solo which closed it as well. 'Stairway to Heaven' is dealt with at length in the '50 Great Led Zeppelin Tracks' section and so suffice it to say here that however hackneyed it may now sound due to over-familiarity, it is a breathtaking piece of music and Page's internal construction of the song is inspired. It's more than four minutes before Bonham makes his entrance on drums and almost six minutes before Page's dramatic electric guitar solo cuts loose. Regardless of its commercial success, Jones is surely right to claim it as one of the band's proudest musical moments, in which pop music attained a previously unknown peak. "Everything built nicely," the bass player says. "Both Jimmy and I were quite aware of the way a track should unfold and the various levels that it would go through. I suppose we were both quite influenced by classical music and there's a lot of drama in the classical forms. It just seems natural for music to have that as opposed to everybody starting and just banging away and finishing. That's part of song structure. It's also part of pop music." At least, it was after 'Stairway to Heaven'.

Side two of the original vinyl release opened with 'Misty Mountain Hop', driven by a crashing riff played on guitar, bass and keyboards, over which Plant sings a salutary, of-its-time tale about a bunch of hippies smoking dope in a park and getting busted. It's followed by 'Four Sticks', another crunching riff but without much of a tune, other than in the rather pretty but slightly incongruous bridge. Featuring Jones on synthesiser, it's basically a studio exercise in playing in a 5/4 time signature with Bonham crashing around

not to the best effect. It's the album's weakest moment and, perhaps unsurprisingly, was only ever attempted once in concert and then swiftly dropped.

Far more successful is the wistful 'Going to California', all mandolin and acoustic finger-picking born of "a late night guitar twiddle" at Headley Grange. Plant's lyric pays tribute to Joni Mitchell ("There's a girl out there with love in her eyes and flowers in her hair") and is arguably the singer's most effective expression of his on-going romantic attachment to the ideals of 1967's 'Summer of Love'. Indeed, he has cited it as his favourite among Zeppelin's softer numbers, claiming: "It's a really nice song, so simple and the lyrics just fell out of my mouth." Several years later, the writer Cameron Crowe asked him how he felt about being criticised for writing such "dated flower-child gibberish". Plant was unrepentant. "The essence of the whole trip was the desire for peace and tranquility and an idyllic situation," he reasoned. "That's all anybody could ever want, so how could it be dated flower-child gibberish? If it is, then I'll just carry on being a dated flower child."

The album closes with the primeval blues of 'When the Levee Breaks', based on a song written by Memphis Minnie and her husband Kansas Joe McCoy about the flood that devastated Mississippi when the river burst its man-made banks or levees in 1927. Plant's vocal and the monolithic riff, with Page slide guitar to the fore, seem to echo the dread of the elemental forces the song is describing.

Although Led Zeppelin's fourth album went on to become the joint third best-selling of all time in the US (behind only the Eagles and Michael Jackson) with shipments of 23 million, once again many of the critics didn't initially appreciate either its power or its range. In Britain, the music weekly *Sounds* declared it a "much over-rated album", reckoned

LED ZEPPELIN

9

'Black Dog' had all "the grace and finesse of a farmyard chicken" and declared 'Stairway to Heaven' so dull that it's reviewer suffered "first boredom and then catatonia". *Melody Maker* sat on the fence and judged it "not their best or their worst". Ironically, *Rolling Stone*, for so long Zeppelin's leading press tormentor, actually for once liked the album and praised its "low-keyed and tasteful subtlety".

HOUSES OF THE HOLY
UK, Atlantic, March 26, 1973; US, Atlantic, March 18, 1973

THE SONG REMAINS THE SAME
THE RAIN SONG
OVER THE HILLS AND FAR AWAY
THE CRUNGE
DANCING DAYS
D'YER MAK'ER
NO QUARTER
THE OCEAN

Recorded: **Stargroves, Berkshire; Headley Grange, Hampshire; Island Studios, London; Olympic Studios, Barnes, London; Electric Lady, New York, April-August 1972**
Producer: **Jimmy Page**

Engineers: **Eddie Kramer; Andy Johns; George Chkiantz**
Cover design/artwork: **Hipgnosis**
Highest chart position: **UK 1; US 1**

How to follow *Led Zeppelin IV*? The answer is that they didn't – at least not for almost 18 months, by the standards of the time an astonishingly long gap. The long wait hadn't been planned and Page had originally hoped to release the album as early as June 1972 in time for the eighth American tour, on which they previewed much of the material. By then large chunks of the album had been recorded, after they had initially convened in the studio at Stargroves, Mick Jagger's country pile at Newbury, Berkshire. (They had initially planned to record *Led Zeppelin IV* there, but Page, living up to his 'Led Wallet' nickname, had balked at the cost.) Several other locations were also used and deadlines came and went as the band could now afford to work at its own pace and – in stark contrast to the rush of the first album – Page "demanded that the final product have decimal-point precision", in the words of Richard Cole.

In the event, by the time the tour started Page had concluded that there was still a lot of further overdubbing and re-recording necessary before the album was ready and the band was still some way off making the final track selection. They concluded that there was no point in rushing the album out to meet a tour deadline (particularly when *Led Zeppelin IV* was still camped out in the charts), and while in America they took the opportunity to go into a New York studio to carry out further work.

But it was the sleeve that once again caused the longest delays. This time they were not fighting with Atlantic, who were only too delighted that for the first time in five albums, the band had come up with a 'proper' title. The *Houses of the Holy* title wasn't printed on the sleeve because the band argued it would ruin the integrity of the artwork, but they allowed the label to put a paper wrapper around the record with the title printed on it, a compromise that was the brainchild of Peter Grant. The problem was a technical one of colour registration, and trying to match the exact hues of the original artwork with those that came off the printer's press took an age. When they got an acceptable match, quite what the sleeve was meant to signify was anyone's guess. The outside depicted a naked young girl in various poses climbing a mountain. Inside was an image that suggested some sort of sacrificial worship in a ruined castle. Despite Page's well-known interest in the occult, it seems certain the images were for effect rather than genuinely containing any deep esoteric message.

At first the album was to be called *Burn that Candle*, as Plant told audiences from the stage on several dates on the 1972 American tour. However, once it had changed to *Houses of the Holy*, the band ran up against a new problem: when they finally came to select the songs for the album in early 1973, the newly-anointed title track found itself unceremoniously dropped on the grounds that it was too similar to another song, 'Dancing Days'. Confusingly, the song titled 'Houses *of the* Holy' then turned up on the next album, *Physical Graffiti*.

After kicking off previous albums with such riff-heavy monsters as 'Whole Lotta Love', 'Immigrant Song' and 'Black Dog', 'The Song Remains the Same' is a disappointingly low-key opener. Not that it's a poor track: there are some fascinating rhythmic twists and turns and lovely shimmering guitar textures, which owe something to the old Yardbirds number 'Tinker, Tailor, Soldier, Sailor'. At

times the track has a jangling West Coast vibe and Jones plays a lovely, fluid bass part in the upper register, more in the style of Jack Casady or Phil Lesh than his usual bottom-end sound. At other times there's a vaguely Indian influence, presumably imbibed when Page and Plant had stopped in Bombay to do some recording on the way back from an Australian tour in 1972. The piece was originally intended as an instrumental, Page later explained. "It was going to be an overture that led into 'Rain Song', but I guess Robert had different ideas, You know: 'This is pretty good. Better get some lyrics, quick!'" This doesn't explain why Plant's vocal is irritatingly speeded up in places as he gabbles "all you gotta do now, all you gotta do now", sounding as if he's on helium.

'The Rain Song' is an under-rated Zeppelin classic. In some ways it echoes the band's earlier acoustic work. But although the arrangement is serene it's also considerably more complex than anything they had attempted before and marks Jones' first use of the mellotron, creating a one-man virtual orchestra which, as Keith Shadwick notes, almost sounds as if The Moody Blues have crashed the party. Plant's love lyric uses what Coleridge described as the 'pathetic fallacy', in which human emotions are seen as echoes of the natural elements and also echoes the Elizabethan poet Ben Jonson's famous line 'drink to me only with thine eyes'.

'Over the Hills and Far Away' opens with a jangling guitar part in the same key as 'The Rain Song', contributing strongly to the idea that the whole of the first side of the original vinyl LP was conceived as a suite of songs. Then the drums and bass and electric guitar kick in, but it's still clear this isn't the old carnal Led Zeppelin as Plant continues to sing about his wide-eyed wonder at the world ("Mellow is the man who knows what

LED ZEPPELIN

9

he's been missing, many men can't see the open road"). 'The Crunge' is Led Zeppelin having fun, a jokey number that came out of Bonham and Jones messing around with a Stax rhythm during a jam at Stargroves. Page adds a James Brown guitar riff, Jones contributes some Stevie Wonder-style synths and Plant joins in with a pastiche vocal and lyrics that check the titles of several classic soul songs, including Otis Redding's 'Mr Pitiful' and Aretha Franklin's 'Respect'. The final exchange between Plant and a studio engineer about looking for the song's bridge (a classic James Brown stunt) is mildly amusing the first time one hears it but swiftly palls. Is it a parody or an affectionate tribute to 1970s black music? Perhaps the problem is that it tries to be a bit of both at the same time and calling the non-existent 'dance' 'The Crunge' – the sort of gag Peter Cook and Dudley Moore might have come up with – was perhaps the wittiest aspect of the entire exercise. At one time, the band even considered putting a spoof diagram of how to dance 'the crunge' on the cover.

'Dancing Days' is one of the album's highlights, a mid-tempo rocker with a snarling guitar motif with its roots in Page and Plant's recent stopover in Bombay on the way back from Australia, while Plant's vocal shows admirable restraint on a lyric that combines sly lasciviousness ("I told your mamma I'd get you home but I didn't tell her I had no car") and hippie gibberish ("I got my flower, I got my power"). Engineer Eddie Kramer recalls the band literally dancing with delight on the lawn at Stargroves when they first heard the playback. However, 'D'yer Mak'er' is just awful, a piece of self-indulgence of the kind that all great bands probably come up with from time to time as a way of letting off steam but few are dumb enough to release. If they got away

with the joke on 'The Crunge', they were not capable of pulling it off twice, particularly when the jape was so witless. From its title to everything else about it, 'D'yer Mak'er' is crap: cod-reggae of the most banal kind, with a totally hopeless thrashing heavy rock rhythm from Bonham where a Jamaican one-drop rhythm is called for and a lyric from Plant so totally devoid of content that it sounds as if it was ad-libbed on the spot – which it probably was. "We had just laid down 'The Song Remains the Same' which is a real belter," he told *Zig Zag* shortly after the album's release. "It was about 5 am and I had been hoping for a long time to do something like 'D'yer Mak'er'. It was born then and there." Jones and Bonham both hated the song and the bass player candidly admitted that the track made him "cringe". Or was that "crunge"?

Fortunately, the album's final two tracks ensure *Houses of the Holy* ends strongly. 'No Quarter' is arguably the album's strongest track, a brooding, complex piece on which Jones unusually took the lead compositional credit. His grand piano and synthesiser lend the track a melancholic, jazzy majesty that resembles Emerson, Lake & Palmer (a band who it was rumoured at one point Peter Grant was going to add to his management stable) but without the bombast. Even Bonham for once plays with restraint (by his standards, at least) and the subdued effect only heightens the song's drama while Plant sings obscurely about some incident from Viking mythology, his voice treated by studio trickery to sound distant and almost disembodied.

'The Ocean' closes the album with a classically brutal Zeppelin riff as Plant's lyric both pays tribute to the band's 'ocean' of fans and tells of his love for his three-year-old daughter, Carmen. There's a memorable turn-around in the rhythm halfway through and the track ends on a doo-wop note as an excited Plant spontaneously – and accurately – shouts 'So good!'

The reviews that greeted *Houses of the Holy* were an even more mixed bunch than usual – but there was unanimity that the biggest band in the world had not come up with their masterpiece their status demanded. Even Page himself seemed to recognise the record's faults and failings. "I'm deaf to the album now because we made it such a long time ago," he told *NME* immediately after its release. He sounded almost apologetic in conceding that 'The Crunge' and 'D'yer Mak'er' were "just a giggle" and even more defensive when he added, "But I know there's some good stuff on there." It was hardly the stoutest defence on behalf of a disappointing album and it's impossible not to conclude that Page knew full well that they had failed to deliver an album that matched any of its four predecessors.

History has done nothing to salvage the album's reputation and today *Houses of the Holy* sounds not only like the oddest album in the Led Zeppelin canon but probably the least satisfying. Had they worked to a deadline and released the album as originally planned in June 1972, it would no doubt have sounded quite different and a lot sharper. For the first time in their career, Led Zeppelin sounded like they could have benefited from an outside producer who might have imposed a little order and discipline. Instead indecision and drift set in and Page – his growing cocaine consumption possibly clouding his previously impeccable judgement – clearly failed to exert the visionary leadership that had informed and inspired the first four albums.

Yet if *Houses of the Holy* is flawed, almost fatally so in places, its strongest asset is that it finds the band still creatively restless and not

content simply to repeat past glories. As Dave Lewis put it: "Though devoid of the electricity of *Led Zeppelin I* and *II* or the sheer diversity of *Led Zeppelin III* and lacking the classic status of some of the fourth album, *Houses of the Holy* took stock of their situation. In doing so, it laid several foundations on which they would expand their future collective musical aspirations."

PHYSICAL GRAFFITI

UK and US, Swan Song, February 24, 1975

CUSTARD PIE
THE ROVER
IN MY TIME OF DYING
HOUSES OF THE HOLY
TRAMPLED UNDERFOOT
IN THE LIGHT
BRON-YR-AUR
DOWN BY THE SEASIDE
TEN YEARS GONE
NIGHT FLIGHT
WANTON SONG
BOOGIE WITH STU
BLACK COUNTRY WOMAN
SICK AGAIN

LED ZEPPELIN

9

Recorded: **Stargroves, Berkshire; Headley Grange, Hampshire; Island Studios, London; Olympic Studios, Barnes, London, April-August 1971–74**
Producer: **Jimmy Page**
Engineers: **Ron Nevison; Keith Harwood; Eddie Kramer; Andy Johns; George Chkiantz**
Cover design/artwork and photography: **AGI; Dave Heffernan; Elliott Erwitt, BP Fallon and Roy Harper**
Highest chart position: **UK 1; US 1**

After failing to deliver the killer album everyone had expected with *Houses of the Holy*, Led Zeppelin knew that if they were to maintain their status as the greatest rock band in the world, their sixth LP needed to be a major statement. They had long talked about a double album and each time rejected the idea as too self-indulgent. The multi-disc excesses of the likes of Yes and ELP had given a bad name to the notion that an album could contain more than 40 minutes of music and retain a clarity of focus and so Zeppelin had preferred to eschew such company and cast itself as a lean, mean fighting machine. Yet the 'joke' tracks on *Houses of the Holy* had proved that it was perfectly possible to be just as flabby and wasteful on a single album. What mattered was not the quantity but the tightness of the quality control and so the decision was taken: the band's first release on its own label Swan Song would be a double. Plant even grandiosely told one interviewer: "What we talk about is creating something as notable as Beethoven's Fifth. Not just something that would still be remembered in 50 years but something so mammoth that it would last forever." Such hyperbole aside, they were helped by the fact that they had a backlog of already recorded material, some of which was actually superior

to several tracks that had made it on to previous albums. Plant recognised as much when in an interview in *Sounds* immediately after the release of *Houses of the Holy*, he observed: "Yesterday, actually, I was playing some tracks I hadn't heard in years and sometimes the tracks that haven't gone on are better than the ones that have."

The band reconvened at Headley Grange in November 1973 to see what material, both old and new, was around. After a Christmas break, they reconvened there again in February 1974, right in the middle of Britain's three-day week and compulsory power cuts forced by the OPEC oil price rise hike. Not that it worried Zeppelin, who had their own generator installed. It soon became clear that the band was back on a roll as they readied new pieces and resurrected old ones, emerging at the end of the process with a 50–50 split between previously recorded songs and fresh compositions. "At the time of *Physical Graffiti* we were right on top of it," Page recalled later. "There was such freedom and coherence between the players." Plant was similarly enthusiastic and in an interview in March 1974 dropped the first hint that a double album was in the making. "Our music is more of an excitement thing. It has to be impromptu," he went on. "It just drops out of your mind. It falls out of your head and on to the floor and you pick it up as it bounces. That's how we work. We hire this recording truck and head off to some cruddy old house in the country. The last thing you'd expect is the music to fall right into place. But it does. We even spent one night sitting around drinking ourselves under the table telling each other how good we were."

The cover art depicted a pair of New York brownstone houses (actually 96 & 98 St Mark's Place in the East Village, Manhattan).

THE MUSIC: **ALBUMS AND SOLO PROJECTS**

The inner sleeves for the discs were inserted in different orientations, so that various objects and people would appear in the windows of the building. They included not only the obligatory shots of the band (and Peter Grant) but a range of iconic images, including paintings by Leonardo da Vinci and Dante Gabriel Rossetti, Elizabeth II's coronation, Jean Harlow and Lee Harvey Oswald. The effect recalls both the cover of The Beatles' *Sgt Pepper's Lonely Hearts Club Band* and the artwork of The Rolling Stones' *Exile on Main St*, again reinforcing the message that in *Physical Graffiti*, Led Zeppelin were consciously setting out to make a major statement.

Disc one kicks off with 'Custard Pie', one of the new songs which Page described as appearing more or less spontaneously during the sessions at Headley Grange "as great little diamonds just sparkling". The muscular riff is a classic with a passing nod to Bo Diddley and a lyric that, like 'Hats off to (Roy) Harper' on *Led Zeppelin III*, owes much to Bukka White's 'Shake 'em on Down'. 'The Rover' is even better. The song had first emerged as an acoustic blues number in 1970 but was then worked up during the *Houses of the Holy* sessions and its inclusion would have immeasurably improved that album. Bonham and Jones lock into a remorseless groove and Page essays a perfectly constructed solo as Plant sings with some prescience, "I've all this wonder of earthly plunder; will it leave us anything to show?"

'In My Time of Dying' is one of the band's most intense blues adaptations, this time from a song recorded by Blind Willie Johnson in 1927 and then covered by Bob Dylan on his debut album 35 years later. At 11 minutes it's an epic, but the interest is sustained by Page's bottleneck invention, Plant's vocal improvisations and one of

Bonham's most monumental performances on the drums. *Houses of the Holy*, as its title suggests, was originally intended for the previous album and was recorded in 1972. Its jauntiness is appealing enough but it doesn't really go anywhere and after 'In My Time of Dyin'' sounds distinctly like Zeppelin-lite. The impression is reinforced by it being followed by 'Trampled Under Foot', with its irresistible funk rhythm, which unlike 'The Crunge' this time thankfully avoids any hint of parody. Jones contributes a fine clavinet solo and Page unleashes a barrage of effects including backwards echo and wah-wah as Plant sings a great lyric that is an extended, erotic metaphor about the similarities between a pneumatic woman and a souped-up car ("Trouble-free transmission, helps your oil's flow"). Although the lyric is recessed too far back in the mix, you can even dance to it.

More than 30 years on, 'Kashmir' remains one of the peaks of Zeppelin's career. Born of Plant's fascination with Indian and Arabic music, the use of scales not normally found in western music lends an eeriness and sense of mystery and yet Page's Moorish riff is also still utterly rock 'n' roll. The Pakistani string orchestra (who actually came from Southall in west London) are brilliantly arranged and conducted by Jones, who also joins in on the mellotron. In eight-and-a-half minutes there's actually very little development of the basic theme, yet it doesn't seem to matter. It's a staggering, even awesome achievement that represented new ground in 1970s rock music and it's the repetitive, hypnotic effect that gives the track its majestic power.

There's more eastern promise on 'In the Light', which opens with a long, two-minute Indian drone, over which Jones's keyboards imitate the sound of a shehnai. When Page's R&B-tinged guitar comes in

LED ZEPPELIN

9

the contrast is dramatic, although the riff was the invention of Jones, who gets the lead songwriting credit on the track. "You can always tell my riffs from Page's," he says. "Mine have got a lot more notes and are linear. His are chunkier and chordier." Some will find it overlong at almost nine minutes, but there are several changes of tempo, a lovely bridge and the fade-out is a *tour de force* of exquisitely overdubbed guitars and Bonham at his very best. After two such epics, Page's acoustic guitar instrumental 'Bron-Yr-Aur', originally written for the third album, offers a small oasis of tranquility and then gives way to another old track, 'Down by the Seaside', also written at Bron-Yr-Aur. It's essentially Plant's homage to the kind of songs Neil Young was writing around the time of *After the Gold Rush*, complete with Page on pedal steel and Plant's 1971 vocal finding him sounding appreciably younger than on the Headley Grange recordings from three years later. Its friendly, lazy ramble is lifted halfway through by a dynamic change of tempo into a thrilling instrumental passage in which aficionados of early-1970s British prog-rock might find echoes of Bronco, who were good friends of Plant's and whose line-up included his old Band of Joy colleague Kevyn Gammond and future Honeydripper Robbie Blunt.

'Ten Years Gone' is another highlight but hardly typical Zeppelin. Those who have detected echoes of The Beatles' 'Dear Prudence' and Wings' 'Band on the Run' in the song are surely right, but it's a brilliantly crafted and constructed piece with a touchingly melancholic vocal by Plant about an old love affair that climaxes dramatically as he pleads, "Did you ever really need somebody?" 'Night Flight' is another 1971 recording that failed to make *Led Zeppelin IV*. Plant is in exuberant form, there's a chugging

raunch that sounds like one of Dave Edmunds' rock 'n' roll pastiches, and if it sounds retro, then that's all part of its attraction.

The change in Plant's vocals over three years is again evident when 'Night Flight' is followed by 1974's 'The Wanton Song'. He sounds strained, although the effect is not necessarily a bad one, particularly as his voice seems to reflect the life of sexual exhaustion the lyric describes: shagged out is probably the vernacular phrase. The album takes something of a dip in intensity with 'Boogie with Stu', a 1971 jam based on Ritchie Valens' 'Ooh! My Head', with Rolling Stones *alumni* Ian Stewart on piano. For once, the band tried to do the right thing in the songwriting credit, adding the name of the late Valens' mother, although it seems the gesture was not appreciated. "What we tried to do was give Ritchie's mother credit because we heard she never received any royalties from any of her son's hits and Robert did lean on that lyric a bit," Page says. "So what happens? They tried to sue us for all of the song! We had to say bugger off!"

'Black Country Woman' is in similar vein, an acoustic guitar and mandolin country-blues stomp recorded in the garden at Stargroves in 1972 – the track even opens with the sound of an aricraft overhead and a snatch of conversation about whether to leave the intrusive sound in. Charming but disposable, the song was originally called 'Never Ending Doubting Woman Blues' and Plant's highly stylised vocal suggests he's having great fun in pretending he's singing on a Memphis street corner circa 1930.

Fortunately, the album ends on a more dynamic note with 'Sick Again', a classic Zeppelin pile-driver with a Plant lyric about the ever-willing ladies they met in Los Angeles while on the road ("Clutching pages from your teenage dream in the lobby of the Hotel

Paradise"), some suitably brutal drumming from Bonham and a Page solo of some considerable flair.

It is always a reasonable question, whenever confronted with a double album, to ask whether it would actually have made a better single disc with some judicious editing. *Physical Graffiti* isn't a perfect album but it would surely have been butchery to chop it down to a single LP. True, it is 10 or more minutes longer than several other classic double albums, including the Stones' *Exile on Main St*, The Beatles' *White Album* and Dylan's *Blonde on Blonde*, but it still isn't overlong: in this CD age, all but one of the album's 15 tracks could be fitted onto a single silvered four-and-a-half-inch compact disc. Had the format been available at the time, perhaps 'Boogie with Stu' or 'Black Country Woman', rather than both, might have made it onto the album and *Physical Graffiti* would then have been a superb single CD.

The first review to appear – an exclusive track-by-track preview by Nick Kent in *NME* some three months before the album's release – set the tone. "The album's tonal density is absolutely the toughest, most downright brutal I've heard on record in well over a year. It could easily end up in the same pantheon as the band's first and fourth works, a good country mile above the second and third. One thing's for sure – for sheer ferocity, *Physical Graffiti* can eat *Houses of the Holy* for breakfast."

At the time Page told *Rolling Stone*: "I look at it as a document of a band in a working environment. People might say it's sloppy but I think this album is really honest. (It's) a more personal album and I think it allows the listener to enter our world." Thirty years later he'd grown even prouder of *Physical Graffiti*, telling *Uncut* magazine that he regarded the album as the band's high watermark.

9

PRESENCE

UK, Swan Song, March 31, 1976; US, Swan Song, March 28, 1976

ACHILLES LAST STAND
FOR YOUR LIFE
ROYAL ORLEANS
NOBODY'S FAULT BUT MINE
CANDY STORE ROCK
HOTS ON FOR NOWHERE
TEA FOR ONE

Recorded: **Musicland Studios, Munich, Germany, November–December 1975**
Producer: **Jimmy Page**
Engineer: **Keith Harwood**
Cover art: **Hipgnosis**
Highest chart position: **UK 1; US 1**

After Robert Plant's car accident in Greece in August 1975, the band's autumn tour of America, due to start just three weeks later, was cancelled. Unable to receive treatment in Britain due to his tax exile status, the singer was moved first to Jersey and then to Malibu, where in September he met up with Jimmy Page. The two swiftly decided

LED ZEPPELIN

9

that necessity was the mother of invention: although Plant was too crocked to tour, he was fit enough to work in the studio and the enforced vacation became a working one as they set about preparing and recording the band's seventh studio album.

In fact, the writing process had already started during a trip Page and Plant had made to Morocco in June 1975. More work was done on the material in the adjacent beach houses at Malibu which the pair hired, and Plant was further encouraged by a get well telegram from Elvis Presley. By October the entire band had been assembled at Hollywood's SIR rehearsal studios to begin working up their initial song sketches into full-on Zeppelin epics. Perhaps struck by the same notion that rock 'n' roll was getting too overblown and fanciful and would soon inspire the punk movement, the band concluded that they wanted to make a no-frills back-to-the-roots album built around the basic guitar-bass-drums power trio format, while Plant mined his passion for the blues for inspiration.

The process was not without its problems. Plant was singing from a wheelchair, there was a blizzard of cocaine and heroin flying around certain band members and mounting friction between Page and Jones. The guitarist claimed the bass player was never around when he was needed, although the bassist told a different story. "Robert and I seemed to keep a different time sequence to Jimmy," Jones complained. "We couldn't find him... we drove to the studios every night and waited and waited until finally we were all in attendance, by which time it was two in the morning." Bonham, meanwhile, was not coping well with tax exile and being away from his family and sought solace in a one-man mission to drink L.A. dry, his frustrations coming out as he went on the

rampage, which got him into a series of unseemly fights in various bars around the Sunset Strip.

Despite these distractions, the rehearsals were dynamite. It seemed that adversity had once again brought the best out of Led Zeppelin. Within a couple of weeks they felt they had enough material for an album and – needing to get out of America in order not to pay US taxes – at the beginning of November they flew to Germany to record in the Musicland studio, located in the basement of the Arabella hotel, Munich. On the way they stopped off for a couple of days in New York where Plant, now out of his wheelchair and supporting himself unsteadily with a walking stick, enthused to Lisa Robinson about the new material. "I've had time to see," he told her. "Before I was always bowled over with the sheer impetuousness of everything we did, of what we are, and what was created around it. That was knocked off course. The fulcrum was tilted a little. I had to think everything anew, instead of just being allowed to get on with the rampaging. So it turns out that the new lyrics all come from the period of contemplation where I was wondering, 'Christ, is it all through? Is it ended?' And as such the album is full of energy, because of that primal fight within me to get back."

Staying conveniently in the hotel above the studio, things went equally well in Germany and despite the heroin that road manager Richard Cole was supplying Page and Bonham on a daily basis and a tumble in the studio that put Plant back to singing from a wheelchair, the band worked intensely, sometimes putting in 18 hours a day in the studio. Within less than two weeks, the album was finished. Working to a tight deadline (The Rolling Stones had an imminent booking on the studio to record *Black and Blue*), it was by far the quickest and smoothest recording since the group's debut six years and as many albums earlier. "We didn't go out one night. No riots," Plant later observed laconically.

Of course, being Led Zeppelin nothing could be quite that simple and a six-month delay ensued between finishing the record and its release, due, once again, in large part to problems with the sleeve design. The original plan had been to call the album *Thanksgiving*: it had been completed the day before the American holiday and Plant, who came up with the idea, also felt it reflected his gratitude that none of his family had died in the road accident and that such a strong album had been miraculously snatched from the jaws of disaster. Page and the designers Hipgnosis had different ideas and came up with a series of prints from *Life* magazine depicting middle-class American life, into which they dropped the image of a mysterious black obelisk. At one point the album was almost called *Obelisk*, but in the end *Presence* won the day, apparently chosen to reflect the 'aura' that Hipgnosis's designers felt surrounded the band.

The title also reflected the power of the music inside. The 10-minute opener 'Achilles Last Stand' is a glorious Zeppelin epic, even if in places it recalls Yes's 'Roundabout' with Page's multi-tracked guitars sounding uncannily like Steve Howe. Bonham's martial attack relentlessly drives the track forward and although recorded from a wheelchair there's nothing sedentary about Plant's vocal on a lyric that reflects on his recent visit to Morocco. 'For Your Life' has a grinding, stop-start riff that is not instantly catchy but buries itself in your brain with repeated listening while Page adds what he described as "a guitar

army". 'Royal Orleans' – at less than three minutes one of the shortest ever Zeppelin tracks – is the only song on the album to feature the names of all four band members in the songwriting credits (the other six tracks are listed as Page-Plant). Recounting on-the-road antics in the band's favourite hotel in New Orleans, its funky riff recalls 'The Crunge' and it's easily the album's most light-hearted moment.

Like 'In My Time of Dying' on *Physical Graffiti*, 'Nobody's Fault but Mine' was originally recorded in the 1920s by Blind Willie Johnson – not that he gets a credit. "The arrangement I came up with had nothing to do with the original," Page insisted defensively in 1998. However, the melody and lyrics certainly do and it's exactly the sort of piracy that gave Zeppelin a bad name. That said, there's no doubt the band take the song into dramatic new territory with Plant's intense, pleading vocal echoing the song's lyric about a man looking for deliverance from his sins. That doesn't stop him celebrating carnal debauchery on the next track, 'Candy Store Rock', an updated homage to the Sun Records sound *circa* 1954 with Page playing homage to one of his first guitar heroes, Scotty Moore.

'Hots on for Nowhere' is a light, frothy piece with another stop-start rhythm and a clever Plant lyric that seems to describe recent events before the album ends with 'Tea for One', the album's second longest track, opening with a typically frantic heavy riff from Page before cutting dramatically into a slow-burning blues track with an anguished vocal from Plant about time hanging heavy on his hands (presumably during his recovery). Ultimately, though, it's overlong and never quite matches the excitement of *Led Zeppelin III*'s 'Since

LED ZEPPELIN

I've Been Loving You', to which it's an obvious cousin.

Despite this slightly disappointing ending, for once the reviews were nearly all good. The band were delighted to have returned to a more spontaneous way of working and felt that the benefits of such an approach showed. "There's a lot of urgency about it. There's a lot of attack to the music," Page commented. "With this one it came straight up. There's a hell of a lot of spontaneity about it." He went on to call the album "pure anxiety and uninterrupted emotion". Plant was even more enthusiastic. "My only alternative was to turn around and stand against the storm with my teeth gritted and fists clenched and make an album," he told *Rolling Stone* in early 1976, while still hobbling around with a brace on his leg. "All the energy that was smouldering inside us getting ready for a lot of gigs came out in the writing and later in the studio. What we have is an album that is so Zeppelin. It sounds like the hammer of the gods." Thirty years later he had lost none of his enthusiasm for the album, telling Nigel Williamson in *Uncut*: "I think *Presence* has got some of the hottest moments Led Zeppelin ever had – agitated, uncomfortable, druggy, pained."

Yet despite this and the fact that it went straight to number one, *Presence* remains an under-rated album in the Zeppelin canon. One of the reasons was that as it was another year before they went back on the road, only two of the tracks ('Achilles Last Stand' and 'Nobody's Fault but Mine') were ever performed by the band live. The other factor that soon drowned out the success of *Presence* was the hullabaloo surrounding the imminent release of their full-length feature film and its accompanying soundtrack album, which gave the band its second number one of 1976.

SOUNDTRACK FROM THE FILM *THE SONG REMAINS THE SAME*

UK and US, Swan Song, October 22, 1976

ROCK AND ROLL
CELEBRATION DAY
THE SONG REMAINS THE SAME
THE RAIN SONG
DAZED AND CONFUSED
NO QUARTER
STAIRWAY TO HEAVEN
MOBY DICK
WHOLE LOTTA LOVE

Recorded: **Madison Square Garden, New York, July 27, 28 and 29, 1973; mixed at Electric Lady, New York; Trident, London**
Producer: **Jimmy Page**
Engineer: **Eddie Kramer**
Cover art: **Hipgnosis; Hardie**
Highest chart position: **UK 1; US 2**

The story of *The Song Remains the Same* film is told elsewhere in this book but the soundtrack album stands in its own right as a fine record of the awesome power Led Zeppelin were able to summonon their

9

1973 American tour. Recorded over three nights in New York at the end of a gruelling tour that had kicked off in Florida almost three months earlier, they weren't the best shows they played that year (Plant's voice in particular shows signs of wear and tear) but the music on the soundtrack obviously had to fit the footage in the movie, so they were restricted for choice – although the three filmed concerts totalled almost nine hours in length.

By the time the film and accompanying album appeared, two further Zeppelin studio albums had been written and recorded. Drawing on the first five albums, the material that made the soundtrack included one song apiece from *Led Zeppelin I* and *Led Zeppelin III*, two apiece from *Led Zeppelin II* and the fourth album and three from the then current *Houses of the Holy*. In the end, much of the material chose itself. 'Rock and Roll' opened every show on the 1973 tour and kicks off disc one with a suitable thump, although Plant, treating his semi-wrecked voice with caution, sings in an unusually low key. 'Celebration Day' follows, oddly edited out of the film. Why is not clear for it's one of the best performances on the soundtrack album. 'The Song Remains the Same' is another excellent take and segues into 'The Rain Song', the more delicate passages of which make one regret that they chose not to include any material from the acoustic portion of the set.

At almost 27 minutes, 'Dazed and Confused' is way too long, although there's a great moment when Plant starts singing a snatch of Scott McKenzie's 'Summer of Love' number one 'San Francisco (Be Sure to Wear Some Flowers in Your Hair)'. A 13-minute version of 'Moby Dick' also outstays its welcome. However, 'No Quarter' justifies its

12-and-a-half-minutes with the band judging the song's dynamics to perfection and Plant sounding less strained than elsewhere on the soundtrack.

Listening to 'Stairway to Heaven' is interesting, because although Plant's introduction in which he describes it as "a song of hope" is greeted with a loud cheer, it's clear that at this stage the song had not quite attained the legendary status it was later to attain. The crowd's reaction is subdued throughout, although that may because Plant also told them, "It's a very quiet song, so shut up!" The album closes strongly with a 14-minute 'Whole Lotta Love', which despite a few moments of dullness sustains interest by inserting such oddball elements as the funk chord sequence from 'The Crunge', some Page sorcery with the theramin (see box) and Plant's delightful burst of 'Let that Boy Boogie'.

A better live album might have been possible had it been recorded earlier in the tour and in at least a couple of instances the choice of material was puzzling – a great version of 'Since I've Been Loving You' was included in the film but not on the soundtrack and decent performances of 'Black Dog' and 'Heartbreaker' were similarly omitted from the album. Although it went to number one in Britain in November 1976 and number two in America (where it was kept from the top spot by Stevie Wonder's *Songs in the Key of Life*), over the years it has come to be disregarded by Zeppelin fans, who know only too well that much better live performances are available on various bootlegs. Interestingly, *The Song Remains the Same* wasn't even included in the 10-CD Led Zeppelin box set issued in 1993.

LED ZEPPELIN

IN THROUGH THE OUT DOOR

UK and US, Swan Song, August 15, 1979

IN THE EVENING
SOUTH BOUND SAUREZ
FOOL IN THE RAIN
HOT DOG
CAROUSELAMBRA
ALL MY LOVE
I'M GONNA CRAWL

Recorded: **Polar Studios, Stockholm, Sweden; Plumpton Place, Sussex, November–December 1978**
Producer: **Jimmy Page**
Engineer: **Leif Mases**
Cover art: **Hipgnosis**
Highest chart position: **UK 1; US 1**

Following the death of Robert Plant's five-year-old son Karac and the hiatus in all band activity that the tragedy caused, by the time Led Zeppelin finally reconvened for recording purposes at ABBA's Polar Studios in Stockholm at the end of 1978, it was three years since the dynamic sessions in Munich

that had produced *Presence*. In the world of the modern corporate music industry, that's a standard gap between albums by major acts such as U2, Coldplay or Radiohead. In the 1970s, such an absence was considered a career-destroying lifetime – indeed, Creedence Clearwater Revival, one of the biggest-selling bands of the decade, released seven albums and split up within virtually the same time span.

That Led Zeppelin could disappear for so long and then return with an album that went straight to number one was testimony to just how completely they had dominated 1970s rock, although the success of their comeback was by no means a foregone conclusion, for the punk revolution had dramatically altered the musical landscape by 1979. Yet the release of *In Through the out Door* generated such renewed interest in the band that in October that year Led Zeppelin's entire back catalogue re-entered the American chart.

Commendably, neither the band and its management nor Atlantic Records put any pressure on Plant to return and allowed him to take his own time. An exploratory get-together at Clearwell Castle in the Forest of Dean in May 1978 proved abortive when it became clear that the singer was still not in a fit state of mind to resume work and it was almost another six months before he finally agreed to begin serious album rehearsals in London in early November. The band then moved to Stockholm where they took over ABBA's studio for three weeks, commuting back to Britain each weekend. "ABBA came to us and offered it," Peter Grant revealed. "It was actually a real slog to do it. We used to get the noon flight out on a Monday and then return on the Friday. And it was cold and dark the whole time."

For the first time in eight studio albums, Page, hampered by his heroin addiction, was not the driving musical force. With his songwriting partner Plant so long out of contact, it seemed that he had fewer musical ideas to offer the band than ever before. Faced with this void, Jones stepped into the breach. "For much of the time at those Polar sessions only Robert and I were turning up," he later said. "There were two distinct camps by then and we were in the relatively clean one. We'd turn up first, Bonzo would turn up later and Page might turn up a couple of days after that. When that situation occurs, you either sit around waiting or get down to some playing. So that's what we did in the studio. We made it happen."

Most of the tracks began with Jones and Plant recording keyboards and guide vocals. Then the drums were added and the guitars – often not recorded by Page in Sweden at all, but overdubbed in his studio at Plumpton Place, Sussex, when he took the tapes home for the weekend. Jones enjoyed his enhanced role. "When I was playing keyboards I sort of had control of everything tonally," he noted. "If I wanted to change key, it would change key." As a result, most of the songs have a more conventional verse-chorus format than is evident on previous Zeppelin albums, and according to road manager Richard Cole, Page grew increasingly resentful, particularly of Jones's writing credit on almost every track. He also griped that Jones was "trying to take over as producer". In fact, Page takes all the production credits on the record but so chronic was his heroin addiction that however much he disliked Jones's enhanced role, he appeared incapable of imposing any better ideas of his own on the record.

The sessions were wrapped up before Christmas and Page, taking charge of the tapes, spent the early part of 1979 sifting the material and creating a running order. Three of the toughest-edged numbers recorded in Stockholm, 'Wearing and Tearing', 'Ozone

Baby' and 'Darlene', were left on one side for a planned souvenir EP intended to coincide with the band's return to the live stage. The EP never materialised but the absence of the three tracks (all of which eventually surfaced on *Coda*) considerably changed the character of the album that was eventually released and weakened it in the process.

At one time it was rumoured the album was going to be called *Look*. In the end they settled on *In Through the out Door* in recognition of their long absence because, as Page put it, "that's the hardest way to get back in". The sleeve was shot in a mock New Orleans bar built by Hipgnosis at Shepperton Studios in Middlesex and the album was released in six alternative sleeves, each depicting a different bar room scene. The LP was then released in shrink-wrapped brown paper so that the buyer did not know which of the six sleeves they were getting. Peter Grant had long joked that you could "stuff a Led Zeppelin album in a paper bag and it would still sell" and took great delight in proving the conceit. He was less pleased when the packaging contributed to missing the deadline to get the album in the shops before the band's comeback concerts at Knebworth in August 1979.

When the album appeared two weeks late, the music was certainly a mixed bag, reflecting, as Keith Shadwick puts it, "the disunity and confusion in which it was written and recorded". The opener, 'In the Evening', starts with plenty of droning Eastern mystery courtesy of Jones's keyboards before Page makes his most telling contribution to the entire album with a dramatically insistent riff, while Plant reflects on the hand that fate has dealt him: "All the pain that you go through, you can turn away from fortune, 'cause that's all that's left to you. It's lonely at the bottom, man, it's dizzy at the top." 'South Bound Saurez' is a lightweight piece pitched

LED ZEPPELIN

9

somewhere between Little Feat and the boozy pub-rock of the Faces. 'Fool in the Rain' is another departure from standard Zeppelin fare, with a Latin-tinged rhythm (inspired by the 1978 World Cup in Argentina) that in its final section ends up sounding rather like 'La Bamba', with Bonham showing an unexpected facility for Afro-Cuban rhythms.

'Hot Dog' – the only song on the album credited solely to the Page-Plant songwriting team – is a throwaway rockabilly number inspired by a girl from Texas called Audrey Hamilton, with whom Plant was acquainted. Page enjoys bringing out the Scotty Moore impression he had first perfected as a teenager back in the late 1950s but frankly the track would have been better left in the can. Things look up with the 10-minute epic 'Carouselambra', which is one of the album's high points. Like all of Zeppelin's best marathon pieces, it moves through different movements in almost symphonic fashion, although today Jones's stabbing keyboards sound somewhat dated and veer dangerously towards ELP territory in the opening and closing sections. The song also boasts one of Plant's most poetic lyrics and lines such as "Who cares to dry the cheeks of those who saddened stand adrift upon a sea of futile speech?" suggested he'd been mugging up on Percy Shelley and the Romantics. Unfortunately, the vocal is buried far too deep in the mix. As Plant himself puts it, "The whole story of Led Zeppelin in its latter years is in that song – and I can't hear the words!"

'All My Love' – the one message of hope and optimism on an album that is otherwise dark and ominous – was a particular bone of contention within the band. With none of the acoustic numbers that populated the early albums, Plant and Jones came up with a pretty mid-tempo ballad which is sung with great warmth and underpinned by a semi-classical arrangement of the kind popular at the time with the likes of Genesis and ELO. It's given a loping rhythm inspired by Plant's admiration for Crazy Horse and Page contributes a vaguely Neil Young-ish guitar part, but he has made no attempt to hide his distaste for the track, which conspicuously lacks his name on the writing credit. "Jonesy started working more closely with Robert and I wasn't that keen on 'All My Love'. It just didn't seem us," he says. He then extended his criticism to the entire record: "Bonzo and I both felt it was a little soft, that album. We wanted to make a more hard-driving rock album."

The closing track 'I'm Gonna Crawl' also opens with Jones playing a synthesised string arrangement but the song then becomes a classy blues ballad with one of Plant's finest vocals, some highly expressive and unusually sensitive drumming from Bonham and clever use of dynamics.

Predictably, the punk hordes who had taken over the British musical press set about trashing Led Zeppelin. "The manner in which old superfart Led Zeppelin have consistently presented themselves has made the band's name synonymous with gratuitous excess," *NME* thundered. Paul Simonon, bass player with The Clash, was more succinct in his judgement. "Led Zeppelin? I don't need to hear the music. All I have to do is look at one of their album covers and I feel like throwing up." In America, the reaction was far more favourable and most rock fans were simply delighted to have a major-selling album to rescue them from the endless diet of disco that by 1979 was swamping the *Billboard* charts.

Page has seldom talked about the period but when pressed on the album he is highly defensive. "I couldn't have been in that bad a shape," he protests. "I wouldn't have been able to play and I wouldn't have been able to keep my head together." Some say that he barely did.

A quarter of a century later, Plant offered *Uncut* a highly thoughtful analysis of what had gone wrong. "I think the four members had reached a maturity so the music didn't send the same signals of abandon any more," he said. "But it had gone somewhere else and there were some great moments like 'In the Evening'. I'd lost my virginity. My joy of life had been cudgelled and bashed so hard. I became a time and motion study man for my own destiny. I was saying 'If I go tomorrow, is this where I want to find myself, in a sex club in Stockholm being silly with Benny and Bjorn from ABBA, with Agnetha and Frida driving round trying to find out to which den of iniquity Led Zep had taken their husbands? There were some whimsical times. But it was very difficult for me then and I think the others felt it, too."

CODA

UK, Swan Song, November 19, 1982; US, November 22, 1982

WE'RE GONNA GROOVE
POOR TOM
I CAN'T QUIT YOU BABY
WALTER'S WALK
OZONE BABY

DARLENE
BONZO'S MONTREUX
WEARING AND TEARING

Recorded: **various locations between 1970 and 1978**
Producer: **Jimmy Page**
Engineers: **Vic Maile; Andy Johns; Eddie Kramer; Leif Mases; John Timperley**
Cover art: **Hipgnosis; Assorted Images**
Highest chart position: **UK 4; US 6**

Jimmy Page believed that despite the unsatisfactory circumstances of *In Through the out Door* he could see a way forward for Led Zeppelin – and in Bonham he found a natural ally. "I'd already discussed the next album with him and we said we were going to resort to some really intense riffing," the guitarist told Nigel Williamson in *Uncut* in 2005. "I don't want necessarily to call it heavy, but you know what I mean by that. That's the way I figured the next album should be because the music had started to lighten up on *In Through the out Door* and I wanted to get back to that sort of urgent intensity we managed to evoke."

Bonham's death, of course, meant that it never happened. In December 1980 the band was formally dissolved, but they were still contracted to deliver Atlantic a final album. There were also various large tax demands due on past recordings and so Page agreed to assemble a posthumous album that would represent the band's entire career by rounding up the best left-over tracks from its different phases. Page made the selection during the summer of 1981, working at his studio in Cookham, Berkshire, and then called in Plant and Jones to help mix and add a few overdubs to the eight tracks he had selected.

If Bonham had lived, the three tracks set aside from the *In Through the out Door*

LED ZEPPELIN

9

sessions for the EP that never was would probably have made it onto the next Zeppelin album anyway. That gave Page a head start, to which he added earlier material to create an enjoyable and respectful elegy to the loudest, heaviest, mightiest rock band of the 1970s. But that it was a new era with a different set of priorities was made symbolically evident when the release of the album was delayed until November 1982, so as not to clash with Plant's solo debut *Pictures at Eleven*, which appeared that summer.

There's some confusion over the provenance of the album's opening track, 'We're Gonna Groove'. The *Coda* sleeve notes claim it was recorded using a mobile truck at the Royal Albert Hall on January 9, 1970. Certainly the band opened its set that night with the Ben E King number, but there's nothing to suggest that it was recorded live and Zeppelin expert Dave Lewis is convinced it's the studio version recorded at Morgan Studios, London, in June 1969 for possible inclusion on *Led Zeppelin II*. The issue of the Led Zeppelin DVD in 2003 which includes a film of the Albert Hall performance suggests Lewis is right for the live filmed version is considerably longer and slightly different in several respects to the version on *Coda*. However, it's not easy to tell exactly how Page may have spliced or edited the tapes, particularly as he overdubbed fresh guitar parts using a sub-octivider while putting the album together in 1981–82. Either way, it's a brilliant track that holds its own with much of the best material from the same era that surfaced on *Led Zeppelin II*.

'Poor Tom' is a product of the Page-Plant writing sessions for *Led Zeppelin III* at Bron-Yr-Aur and recorded at Olympic in May 1970. A lovely acoustic country-blues played on 12-string with some highly effective harmonica from Plant, it could have easily replaced 'Bron-Yr-Aur Stomp' or 'Hats off to (Roy) Harper'

on that album. That it didn't may be down to the fact that its structure and melody owe something to 'That's No Way to Get Along', a 1929 recording by Rev Robert Wilkins which The Rolling Stones had covered as 'Prodigal Son' on *Beggars Banquet*. 'I Can't Quit You Baby' is a reprise of a Willie Dixon blues song that appeared on *Led Zeppelin I*, again recorded at the Albert Hall. The unreliability of the *Coda* sleeve notes is once more evident for the date of the recording is given as September 1, 1970. In fact the band was playing several thousand miles way in Seattle that night, and it actually comes from the Albert Hall concert on January 9, 1970. The sleeve further claims it was recorded at an afternoon sound check but once again this may be further misinformation, for it sounds uncannily like the in-concert version featured on the *Led Zeppelin* DVD. It's followed by 'Walter's Walk', a 1972-recorded left-over from *Houses of the Holy*, dense and slightly ominous and arguably superior to several of the cuts that actually made that album.

Side two of the original 1982 vinyl release consists of the three out-takes from *In Through the out Door*, punctuated only by 'Bonzo's Montreux', a percussion showcase recorded during tax exile in Switzerland in September 1976 and included as a tribute to the late drummer. It's surprisingly inventive, sounding not unlike some of the ethno-percussion initiatives of the Grateful Dead's drummer Mickey Hart and with a definite African vibe that in parts sounds like the heavily distorted rhythms pedalled by the Congolese band Konono N° 1, who burst onto the world music scene in 2005.

That leaves the three *In Through the out Door* tracks. 'Ozone Baby' is a delight, a classic back-to-basics but tightly arranged guitar-bass-drums riff without the keyboards that dominated the album that it failed to make. 'Darlene' is a straightforward, rip-this-joint boogie rocker with Jones on piano that tends towards pastiche. But the masterpiece is 'Wearing and Tearing', conceived by the band as its response to punk. "That was our contribution to the whole thing, saying 'yes, you've got it right,'" Plant said many years later. Played at a frantic pace over a simple four-chord structure with a yelping Plant vocal, this is surely the direction that Page and Bonham had wanted the next, never-to-be-recorded album to pursue. Led Zeppelin the punk album? Sadly we will never know, but 'Wearing and Tearing' suggests that it could have been a killer.

COMPILATIONS

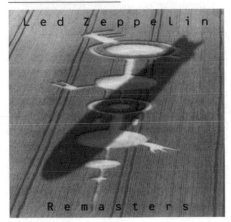

REMASTERS
UK, Atlantic, October 15, 1990; US, Atlantic, March 4, 1992

COMMUNICATION BREAKDOWN
BABE I'M GONNA LEAVE YOU
GOOD TIMES BAD TIMES
DAZED AND CONFUSED
WHOLE LOTTA LOVE

HEARTBREAKER
RAMBLE ON
IMMIGRANT SONG
CELEBRATION DAY
SINCE I'VE BEEN LOVING YOU
BLACK DOG
ROCK AND ROLL
THE BATTLE OF EVERMORE
MISTY MOUNTAIN HOP
STAIRWAY TO HEAVEN
THE SONG REMAINS THE SAME
THE RAIN SONG
D'YER MAK'ER
NO QUARTER
HOUSES OF THE HOLY
KASHMIR / TRAMPLED UNDER FOOT
NOBODY'S FAULT BUT MINE
ACHILLES LAST STAND
ALL MY LOVE
IN THE EVENING

Producer: **Jimmy Page**
Engineer: **George Marino**
Highest chart position: **UK 10; US 47**

Unhappy with the quality of sound transfer from vinyl to CD engineered by Atlantic Records, in 1990 Jimmy Page and engineer George Marino digitally restored Zeppelin's entire catalogue from the original two-track master tapes. All of the albums were subsequently reissued in sonically upgraded form. Page also compiled a track list for a two-CD 'best of' which he submitted to Plant and Jones for their approval. Although fans will argue about individual selections (and four tracks from *Houses of the Holy* and only three from *Physical Graffiti* surely seems the wrong way round), overall it is a decent introduction. Once again, the surviving band members vetoed proposals to release 'Stairway to Heaven' as a single.

LED ZEPPELIN

9

HOW THE WEST WAS WON

UK, Atlantic, May 27, 2003; US, May 28, 2003

LA DRONE
IMMIGRANT SONG
HEARTBREAKER
BLACK DOG
OVER THE HILLS AND FAR AWAY
SINCE I'VE BEEN LOVING YOU
STAIRWAY TO HEAVEN
GOING TO CALIFORNIA
THAT'S THE WAY
BRON-YR-AUR STOMP
DAZED AND CONFUSED
WHAT IS AND WHAT SHOULD NEVER BE
DANCING DAYS
MOBY DICK
WHOLE LOTTA LOVE (MEDLEY)
ROCK AND ROLL
THE OCEAN
BRING IT ON HOME

Recorded: **LA Forum, June 25, 1972; Long Beach Arena, June 27, 1972**
Producer: **Jimmy Page**
Engineers: **Eddie Kramer; Kevin Shirley**
Cover art design: **Phil Lemon**
Highest chart position: **UK 5; US 1**

Searching through the archives for visual and audio material for the *Led Zeppelin* DVD, Jimmy Page came across the master tapes of two concerts from the band's 1972 US tour and merged both shows to create a brilliant two-and-a-half-hour, three-CD set that gave Zeppelin fans the official live album they had always craved.

That they were spectacular shows is beyond doubt. "Playing the West Coast was always fantastic and each member of the band was playing at their best during those 1972 performances," Page said when the live album was released. "When the four of us were playing like that we combined to make it a fifth element. That was the magic – the intangible."

Most of the stage chatter has been cut to leave the music to speak for itself – and probably just as well: to have left in Plant's introduction of 'Black Dog' as "nothing to do with a chick in Detroit" would have won him few friends in these politically correct times. 'Immigrant Song' is a brutal opener with Bonham sounding like he's got six arms never mind four sticks, while Plant wails at his most primeval. The energy doesn't let up through 'Heartbreaker' and 'Black Dog' but an elegantly graceful 'Stairway to Heaven' is greeted in near silence, not yet having attained its status as lighter-waving anthem. It is followed by a lovely acoustic set that includes 'That's the Way' and 'Going to California', on which after the line about "a girl with love in her eyes and flowers in her hair", Plant ad-libs, "I didn't see too many this time."

The second and third discs offer more scope for the band to stretch out. 'Dazed and Confused' from the Forum show lasts more than 25 minutes, a showcase for Page to produce some astonishing guitar effects with the violin bow while Plant moans and screams in the Arabic semi-tones he'd learned to imitate on his trips to Morocco. The track also incorporates the funk riff from the still-to-be-released 'The

Crunge'. After a fantastic 'Dancing Days', which the crowd are also hearing for the first time, Plant announces: "John Henry Bonham – Moby Dick." Almost 20 minutes later, Bonzo is still thrashing about, but while you have to admire his energy, and from the reaction of the crowd it sounds like one of the best-received pieces of the night, you also wonder why Page imagined that three decades on anybody would actually want to listen to it.

A 23-minute 'Whole Lotta Love' is far more excusable, for it also inventively takes in John Lee Hooker's 'Boogie Chillun', the Elvis Presley/Wanda Jackson standard 'Let's Have a Party', Ricky Nelson's 'Hello Mary Lou' and almost nine minutes of the blues classic 'Goin' Down Slow' before returning thrillingly to the original riff. The oddest thing is that apart from *The Song Remains the Same* soundtrack, Led Zeppelin never released a live album when they were in their pomp. Had *When the West Was Won* been released in 1972 between *Led Zeppelin IV* and *Houses of the Holy*, it would surely be revered alongside The Who *Live At Leeds*, The Allman Brothers' *Live At Fillmore East* and the Stones' *Get Yer Ya-Ya's Out!* as one of the great live albums of all time.

BBC SESSIONS

UK, Atlantic, November 18, 1997; US, November 19 ,1997

YOU SHOOK ME
I CAN'T QUIT YOU BABY
COMMUNICATION BREAKDOWN
DAZED AND CONFUSED
THE GIRL I LOVE SHE GOT LONG BLACK
  WAVY HAIR
WHAT IS AND WHAT SHOULD NEVER BE
COMMUNICATION BREAKDOWN
TRAVELLING RIVERSIDE BLUES
WHOLE LOTTA LOVE
SOMETHIN' ELSE

COMMUNICATION BREAKDOWN
I CAN'T QUIT YOU BABY
YOU SHOOK ME
HOW MANY MORE TIMES
IMMIGRANT SONG
HEARTBREAKER
SINCE I'VE BEEN LOVING YOU
BLACK DOG
DAZED AND CONFUSED
STAIRWAY TO HEAVEN
GOING TO CALIFORNIA
THAT'S THE WAY
WHOLE LOTTA LOVE (MEDLEY)
THANK YOU

Recorded: **1969–71**
Highest chart position: **UK 23; US 12**

Led Zeppelin's early BBC Radio 1 broadcasts had long circulated among collectors on bootleg but surprisingly did not receive an official release until 1997. The two-disc set makes an essential companion piece to the band's first four albums. The first session recorded for John Peel's *Top Gear* programme on March 1, 1969, just two weeks after their return from their first US tour, finds them in rip-roaringly earthy

LED ZEPPELIN

9

form on four songs featured on their debut album. 'You Shook Me' features Jones on organ and a quite different Page guitar solo from the album version. 'I Can't Quit You Baby' is notably different for Plant slipping into Muddy Waters' 'Shes 19 Years Old' halfway through the track, although 'Dazed and Confused' is presented in very similar style to the way it's heard on *Led Zeppelin I.* A storming 'Communication Breakdown' from the same session is not included here. The session was broadcast on March 23, 1969, a week before Zeppelin's debut album was released in the UK, and so represented the first chance many British listeners had to hear the band. Sessions by The Moody Blues, Free and Deep Purple were also all broadcast on the same programme.

Three months later after a second American tour, they were back at the Beeb for three more sessions in the space of 11 days. The first, recorded on June 16, 1969 for the long-forgotten *Tasty Pop Sundae* show and broadcast six days later at a rather inappropriate 10am on a Sunday morning, found presenter Chris Grant introducing them by saying, "Alright boys, let's go underground!" (although unfortunately this wonderfully time-warped piece of crassness is not included on the official CD release). What we do get from the session is a powerful 'Communication Breakdown' deemed superior to the version broadcast in March and with a Page solo played at breakneck speed, plus two songs that never featured on an official Zeppelin studio album. The first, 'The Girl I Love She Got Long Black Wavy Hair' is based on a Sleepy John Estes song and its main riff would soon mutate into the intro for Bonham's drum showcase, 'Moby Dick', on the second album. The second is Eddie Cochran's

'Somethin' Else', which was a stage favourite at the time and features Jones on some rollicking Jerry Lee Lewis-style piano and a super-confident Plant ridiculously hamming it up. The fourth track recorded but not included here was a preview of 'What Is and What Should Never Be' from the forthcoming second album.

Just eight days later they were back at the BBC recording their second *Top Gear* session. All four tracks are featured here, including 'What Is and What Should Never Be' and a slightly shorter and crisper 'Communication Breakdown'. Of most interest, however, is the first airing of the song that was to become the band's early anthem, 'Whole Lotta Love'. It already sounds majestic with some great wah-wah effects from Page and Plant ad-libbing at the end about having "those West Bromwich blues". The set is completed by an equally magnificent version of Robert Johnson's 'Travelling Riverside Blues', with some terrific slide guitar from Page and Page delivering some more Midlands blues. Although a section of the blues lyric was subsequently lifted for 'The Lemon Song' on *Led Zeppelin II*, it's the only known recording by the band of the original Johnson song. The session was broadcast on Sunday June 29, 1969, more or less as the band was taking the stage at the Royal Albert Hall for its biggest London appearance to date.

Two days earlier on June 27, 1969, Zeppelin had recorded their third BBC session of the month when they played a six-song set at London's Playhouse Theatre in a pilot show for what was to become Radio 1's long-running *In Concert* series, which the band would return to play two years later. They opened with 'Communication Breakdown', included for the third time in this collection, but the inclusion by Plant of lines from The Isley Brothers' 'It's Your Thing' makes it sufficiently different from the previous versions to warrant its presence. They followed with 'I Can't Quit You Baby' and then 10-minute-plus versions of 'You Shook Me' (with a long and moody organ solo from Jones) and 'How Many More Times', which includes band introductions and excursions into 'The Hunter' and 'The Lemon Song'. It was the first time the band had been allowed to stretch out on the radio as they did in their live shows, and the session was eventually broadcast on Peel's *Top Gear* on August 10, 1969. Not featured here, the session also included Page's acoustic guitar showcase 'White Summer'/'Black Mountain Side' (which turned up in 1990 on the *Led Zeppelin* box set) and a 10 minute 'Dazed and Confused'.

The second disc is taken up with the band's recording for Radio 1's *In Concert* programme, recorded at the BBC's Paris Theatre on April 1, 1971, some six months before the release of *Led Zeppelin IV* and capturing them in the middle of their British 'return to the clubs' tour. They played a dozen tracks, eight of which were broadcast on April 4 and 10 of which are included here, the only omissions being 'What Is and What Should Never Be' and 'Communication Breakdown', sensibly not included for what would have been a fourth time. After a Peel introduction in which he notes "this is something we've waited for a long time", the band crash into 'Immigrant Song'. Plant initially sounds uncertain as if he's testing his voice (the recording had been postponed from the week before because he had throat problems), but by the time they're into 'Heartbreaker' his confidence has returned.

Highlights include a great 'Black Dog' from the forthcoming album (surprisingly not included in the original radio broadcast), a 19-minute version of 'Dazed and Confused' that finds Page deploying his full range of effects, including violin bow, and the radio premiere of 'Stairway to Heaven', which sounds slightly tentative but builds nicely as Page gives an early try-out to the double-neck guitar.

After the recording, Peel hung out with the band and was impressed enough to record in his diary: "Zeppelin played for 100 minutes. Nice people, too."

MOTHERSHIP
UK, Atlantic, November 12, 2007; US, Atlantic, November 13, 2007

GOOD TIMES BAD TIMES
COMMUNICATION BREAKDOWN
DAZED AND CONFUSED
BABE I'M GONNA LEAVE YOU
WHOLE LOTTA LOVE
RAMBLE ON
HEARTBREAKER
IMMIGRANT SONG

LED ZEPPELIN

9

SINCE I'VE BEEN LOVING YOU
ROCK AND ROLL
BLACK DOG
WHEN THE LEVEE BREAKS
STAIRWAY TO HEAVEN
THE SONG REMAINS THE SAME
OVER THE HILLS AND FAR AWAY
D'YER MAK'ER
NO QUARTER
TRAMPLED UNDER FOOT
HOUSES OF THE HOLY
KASHMIR
NOBODY'S FAULT BUT MINE
ACHILLES LAST STAND
IN THE EVENING
ALL MY LOVE

Producer: **Jimmy Page**
Cover art: **Shepard Fairey**
Highest chart position: **UK 4; US 7**

Did the world really need another Zep
compilation? Released on the eve of the band's
reunion concert at London's O2, the answer was
a resounding 'yes', with more than two million
copies shifted in America alone and another
650,000 in the UK. Attractively packaged and
containing liner notes by *Rolling Stone*'s David
Fricke, the two-dozen tracks contained few
surprises and no rarities and *Mothership*'s main
selling point was that the material was said to
have been "personally selected" by Zep's three
surviving members. Drawing on the band's
eight studio albums (with nothing from the
posthumous *Coda*), the result was a somewhat
lop-sided collection. For example, there were
more tracks from *Houses of the Holy* than from
any of the first three albums and more than half
of the songs selected carried a John Paul Jones
co-writing credit. A deluxe edition also included
a third disc containing excerpts from *Led
Zeppelin the DVD*.

CELEBRATION DAY

UK Atlantic 19 November 2012; US, Atlantic 20
November 2012

GOOD TIMES BAD TIMES
RAMBLE ON
BLACK DOG
IN MY TIME OF DYING
FOR YOUR LIFE
TRAMPLED UNDER FOOT
NOBODY'S FAULT BUT MINE
NO QUARTER
SINCE I'VE BEEN LOVING YOU
DAZED AND CONFUSED
STAIRWAY TO HEAVEN
THE SONG REMAINS THE SAME
MISTY MOUNTAIN HOP
KASHMIR
WHOLE LOTTA LOVE
ROCK AND ROLL

Producer: **Jimmy Page**
Cover art: **Shepard Fairey**
Highest chart position: **UK 4; US 9**

It took almost five years for Zeppelin's
reunion at the Ahmet Ertegün Tribute
Concert on December 10, 2007 at London's
O2 Arena to appear on album – and when

it did, the package included not just CDs of the performance but a DVD of the show, too. Why it took so long is not entirely clear. Page announced in 2008 that it was a "massive job to embark on" and the release of the audio had to await director Dick Carruthers to finish work on the film to enable simultaneous release. In the event, despite Page's misgivings about the amount of work involved in mixing the multi-track tapes, only minimal overdubbing and "correction" was required, an indication of how well rehearsed and executed the performance had been. "If I say there might have been a handful of fixes, what I'm really saying is the minimum to what other people would do," Page told a London press conference to launch *Celebration Day*. "The concert was what it was. There was very little that needed to be messed about with, because we'd already done it well in the first place."

The audio reveals that despite his years of relative inactivity, the standard of Page's playing remains outstanding. Some of his solos are overlong but there are breathtaking moments, such as his ferocious slide on 'In My Time of Dying'. Plant's voice also retains much of its primal power, although he avoids some of the screaming high notes heard on the original studio versions. One of the tweaks involved tuning his vocals at the end of 'Kashmir' because, as he explained, "I'd run out of steam. There's only so many long notes that you can do."

At one point during the show Plant tells the audience, "There are certain songs that have to be played" – and against the odds even 'Stairway to Heaven' overcomes hackneyed over-familiarity to sound curiously affecting. But if most of the 16 songs constitute a 'greatest hits' set, the collector's item here is 'For Your Life' from *Presence*, the first – and we must presume last – time the band ever played the song in concert. At another point,

Plant good-naturedly introduces 'Nobody's Fault but Mine' by saying the band first heard Blind Willie Johnson perform the song "in a church in Mississippi about 1932". It's a neat way of belatedly apologising for the fact that when the song appeared on *Physical Graffiti* in 1975 the writing credit had read 'Page/Plant'.

John Paul Jones is a discreet and solid presence for the most part, but contributes one of the set's more thrilling moments on 'Trampled Under Foot' when he switches to piano and engages in an explosive duel with Page's lead guitar. Jason Bonham also acquits himself well, powering the songs with a muscular force that would have made his father proud.

LED ZEPPELIN I–IV AND HOUSES OF THE HOLY EXPANDED REISSUES

Swansong 2014

Disc one of each album features the original album. Details of the 'bonus' material on the second discs as follows:

LED ZEPPELIN

Disc two:
Live At The Olympia – Paris, France, October 10, 1969:
GOOD TIMES BAD TIMES/COMMUNICATION
  BREAKDOWN
I CAN'T QUIT YOU BABY
HEARTBREAKER
DAZED AND CONFUSED
WHITE SUMMER/BLACK MOUNTAIN SIDE
YOU SHOOK ME
MOBY DICK
HOW MANY MORE TIMES

LED ZEPPELIN II

WHOLE LOTTA LOVE (alternate mix)
WHAT IS AND WHAT SHOULD NEVER BE
  (alternate mix)

LED ZEPPELIN

9

THANK YOU (backing track)
HEARTBREAKER (alternate mix)
LIVING LOVING MAID (SHE'S JUST A
    WOMAN) (backing track)
RAMBLE ON (alternate mix)
MOBY DICK (alternate mix)
LA LA (previously unreleased)

LED ZEPPELIN III

THE IMMIGRANT SONG (studio outtake)
FRIENDS (studio outtake)
CELEBRATION DAY (studio outtake)
SINCE I'VE BEEN LOVING YOU (studio
    outtake)
BATHROOM SOUND (previously unreleased
    instrumental version of "Out on the Tiles")
GALLOWS POLE (studio outtake)
THAT'S THE WAY (studio outtake)
JENNINGS FARM BLUES (previously
    unreleased instrumental forerunner to
    "Bron-Y-Aur Stomp")
KEYS TO THE HIGHWAY/TROUBLE IN MIND
    (previously unreleased)

PAGE AND PLANT

NO QUARTER: UNLEDDED

UK, Fontana, October 14, 1994; US, Atlantic

NOBODY'S FAULT BUT MINE
NO QUARTER
FRIENDS
THE TRUTH EXPLODES
THE RAIN SONG
CITY DON'T CRY
SINCE I'VE BEEN LOVING YOU
THE BATTLE OF EVERMORE
WONDERFUL ONE
WAH WAH
THAT'S THE WAY
GALLOWS POLE
FOUR STICKS
KASHMIR

Recorded: **South Bank Television Studios,
London, August 25 & 26, 1994; Marrakesh,
Morocco, August 9–10, 1994**
Producers: **Jimmy Page and Robert Plant**
Engineer: **Mike Gregovich**
Highest chart position: **UK 7; US 4**

After resisting huge amounts of money to reform Led Zeppelin for almost a decade-and-a-half, Robert Plant finally agreed to team up again with Jimmy Page in February 1994 for a programme in MTV's popular *Unplugged* series. Rather than simply do straightforward acoustic versions of the band's best-known songs, the pair used the show to reinterpret favourites from the band's classic repertoire in completely fresh and new ways. John Paul Jones was miffed at not being told let alone invited, but Plant insisted that it was nothing personal: he simply wanted to present the show as a new Page and Plant project rather than risk the project being presented as a new incarnation of Led Zeppelin.

Backed by Charlie Jones (bass), Porl Thompson (guitar/banjo), Michael Lee (drums), Nigel Eaton (hurdy-gurdy), an Egyptian ensemble and the London Metropolitan Orchestra, two shows were eventually recorded in August 1994 and the resulting film aired on MTV in Europe and America that October. It was followed by a soundtrack album which included 13 Zeppelin classics, many of them quite brilliantly reinvented. Highlights included 'The Battle of Evermore', with Najma Akhtar singing the Sandy Denny part, and a string-laden 'Since I've Been Loving You'. 'Kashmir' was given a dramatic new twist as the Eastern and Western orchestras inter-twined thrillingly. The performance also included 'Wonderful One', the first joint Page-Plant composition in 15 years. Drawing on folk, blues and ethnic or world music influences, there's a diversity and richness to the arrangements that may not have been what diehard Led Zeppelin fans wanted to hear, but was far more rewarding than the usual reunion of middle-aged men trying to recreate past glories.

Two further tracks, 'Yallah' (subsequently retitled 'The Truth Explodes') and 'City Don't Cry', were recorded on location in Morocco. Collectors should note that several different versions of the album exist. 'The Rain Song' replaces 'Thank You' on some editions and 'Wah Wah' was not included on the original release, but added later as a bonus.

WALKING INTO CLARKSDALE

UK, Mercury, April 20, 1998; US, Atlantic, April 21, 1998

SHINING IN THE LIGHT
WHEN THE WORLD WAS YOUNG
UPON A GOLDEN HORSE
BLUE TRAIN
PLEASE READ THE LETTER
MOST HIGH
HEART IN YOUR HAND
WALKING INTO CLARKSDALE
BURNING UP
WHEN I WAS A CHILD
HOUSE OF LOVE
SONS OF FREEDOM
Recorded: **Abbey Road Studios, London, autumn 1997**

LED ZEPPELIN

9

Producers: **Jimmy Page and Robert Plant**
Engineer: **Steve Albini**
Highest chart position: **UK 3; US 8**

Recorded in 35 days and named after a
town in Mississippi soaked in blues history,
there's a dry and sombre sound to the
first (and to date only) full-length studio
collaboration by Page and Plant since
Zeppelin split up in 1980. Backed by bassist
Charlie Jones (no relation) and drummer
Michael Lee, highlights include the epic
'Most High', which vaguely hints at the
majesty of 'Kashmir', and 'When the World
was Young', which might also have made a
decent Led Zeppelin song. But Page seems
unusually restrained and hesitant to cut
loose on electric guitar. The solo on 'Sons
of Freedom' offers the best example of his
lead work, while his acoustic dexterity can
be heard to good effect on 'Shining in the
Light'. Few of the other songs really stand
out, sounding solid and at times even stolid,
disappointingly one-dimensional and bereft
of the dynamics that Zeppelin always prided
themselves on.

Ironically, the album won a Grammy
for best hard rock performance in 1999 –
something Led Zeppelin never achieved
during the band's existence. Despite this
recognition, overall it's a dispiriting affair
that offers incontrovertible evidence that
you can't turn back the clock. With the
benefit of hindsight, there was no more
chance of the pair of them repeating their
triumphs of the 1970s together than there
was of John Bonham returning from the
grave to join them, and Plant's reluctance
since to team up with Page again suggests
that he's all too aware that *Walking into
Clarksdale* did nothing to enhance either
of their reputations.

JIMMY PAGE

DEATH WISH II OST

UK and US, Swan Song, February 15, 1982

WHO'S TO BLAME
THE CHASE
CITY SIRENS
JAM SANDWICH
CAROLE'S THEME
THE RELEASE
HOTEL RATS AND PHOTOSTATS
SHADOW IN THE CITY
JILL'S THEME
PRELUDE
BIG BAND, SAX, AND VIOLENCE
HYPNOTIZING WAYS (OH MAMMA)

Producer: **Jimmy Page**
Highest chart position: **UK 40; US 50**

For his first post-Zeppelin project, Page
improbably agreed to score Michael Winner's
nasty, sleazy, exploitative junk film *Death
Wish II*, starring Charles Bronson. Some of the
music was rescued and remodelled from his
aborted soundtrack for Kenneth Anger's *Lucifer
Rising*, and in parts the soundtrack is highly

listenable. Much of it is standard blues-rock but there's a creepy, chilling and at times genuinely menacing atmosphere to much of it that fitted the film's purpose well. The 1980s synth sounds inevitably lend a somewhat dated quality in places, but Page's guitar-playing on the funky 'Jam Sandwich' and 'Big Band, Sax, and Violence' are particularly fine. Much of the album is instrumental and frankly it might have worked better if all of it was for the vocals by Chris Farlowe and others are uninspiring.

THE FIRM (WITH THE FIRM)

UK and US, Atlantic, February 11, 1985

CLOSER
MAKE OR BREAK
SOMEONE TO LOVE
TOGETHER
RADIOACTIVE
YOU'VE LOST THAT LOVIN' FEELING
MONEY CAN'T BUY
SATISFACTION GUARANTEED
MIDNIGHT MOONLIGHT

Producers: **Jimmy Page and Paul Rodgers**
Highest chart position: **UK 15; US 17**

By the mid-1980s, Page's lack of action since the break-up of Led Zeppelin suggested that he badly needed someone to provide the creative foil that Plant had offered so effectively. On the surface, former Free/Bad Company singer Paul Rodgers seemed an inspired choice after the two had collaborated on the ARMS benefit tour for Ronnie Lane in 1983. However, joined by veteran drummer Chris Slade and bassist Tony Franklin, The Firm's album received a critical drubbing and sold disappointingly – and it's easy enough to hear why. Slade batters the skins in a decent imitation of Bonham, Rodgers' voice is still in fine shape and Page's layered guitar textures are reminiscent of some of his overdubs on *Coda* – but there's an almost total lack of memorable songs. The opener 'Closer' has a half-decent riff but goes nowhere and the horn section is ineffective. The cover of The Righteous Brothers' 'You've Lost that Lovin' Feeling' was a bad idea in the first place and the execution is even more horrible. 'Radioactive', which was a minor hit single, today sounds risibly gimmick-ridden. 'Midnight Moonlight' attempts to recreate the Zeppelin acoustic/electric dynamic but collapses under the banality of the arrangement. 'Someone to Love' is a decent rocker that could almost have been late-period Zeppelin were it not for a plodding rhythm section that makes you realise just how good Jones and Bonham were. The mid-tempo 'Satisfaction Guaranteed' chugs along nicely enough on the back of an insistent Page riff and a snaking solo but the track that is of greatest interest to Zeppelin fans is the album closer, 'Midnight Moonlight', based on an unfinished cut entitled 'Swan Song' left over from the *Physical Graffiti* sessions. It's the finest moment on a disappointing set and the fact that the best song on the album was a decade old says it all.

9

MEAN BUSINESS (WITH THE FIRM)

UK and US, Atlantic, February 3, 1986

FORTUNE HUNTER
CADILLAC
ALL THE KING'S HORSES
LIVE IN PEACE
TEAR DOWN THE WALLS
DREAMING
FREE TO LIVE
SPIRIT OF LOVE

Producers: **Jimmy Page, Paul Rodgers and Julian Mendelsohn**
Highest chart position: **UK 46; US 22**

If The Firm's debut album was a disappointment, the follow-up was no better. That said, it kicks off in dramatic fashion on 'Fortune Hunter', an urgent, turbulent track that for the first time actually sounds exactly as you might imagine a mix of Zeppelin and Free should sound. It ranks as one of Page's better post-Zeppelin moments, but sadly and predictably from there it's mostly down hill all the way.

'Cadillac' finds Page's guitar growling with menace but the song itself is a droning non-entity. 'All the King's Horses' is a keyboard-driven song that sounds like something John Paul Jones might have come up with for *Presence* but then rejected, and 'Tear Down the Walls' has a Page riff that Zeppelin might have turned into a killer but which is here thrown away. 'Live in Peace', 'Free to Live' and 'Spirit of Love' are tedious, mid-1980s corporate stadium rockers depressingly free of inspiration and as hollow as their banal song titles would suggest.

WHATEVER HAPPENED TO... JUGULA (WITH ROY HARPER)

UK and US, Beggars' Banquet, March 1985

NINETEEN-FORTY-EIGHTISH
BAD SPEECH
HOPE
HANGMAN
ELIZABETH
FROZEN MOMENT
TWENTIETH CENTURY MAN
ADVERTISEMENT (ANOTHER
   INTENTIONAL IRRELEVANT SUICIDE)

Producer: **Roy Harper**
Highest chart position: **UK 44; US 60**

With its cover designed to resemble an orange-coloured packet of Rizla cigarette rolling papers, it's not entirely clear why Page's name gets co-billing on what is essentially a Roy Harper solo album, other than it raised the maverick singer-songwriter's profile and enabled him to make a rare foray into the lower reaches of the album charts. In fact, it was the fifth Harper album that Page had played on and the idea of promoting it as a 'joint' album (a pun which presumably inspired the cover art work) came out of an appearance they made as a duo at the Cambridge Folk Festival in 1984, followed by a 15-minute televised slot on *The Old Grey Whistle Test* which featured Harper and Page playing their acoustic guitars and being interviewed on the side of Scafell Pike in the English Lake District.

Harper produced and wrote all eight of the songs, the only co-writing credit on 'Hope' going not to Page but to Pink Floyd guitarist David Gilmour. Page is credited on the sleeve with "electric and/or acoustic guitar on everything including the snooker table". The interplay of their two acoustic guitars is often quite lovely but it's really an album whose appeal is restricted to Harper's cult following rather than mainstream Led Zeppelin fans.

OUTRIDER
UK and US, Geffen, June 19, 1988

WASTING MY TIME
WANNA MAKE LOVE
WRITES OF WINTER
THE ONLY ONE
LIQUID MERCURY

HUMMINGBIRD
EMERALD EYES
PRISON BLUES
BLUES ANTHEM

Producer: **Jimmy Page**
Highest chart position: **UK 27; US 26**

And finally – 20 years after forming Led Zeppelin, Jimmy Page gets around to recording his first real solo album. As you would expect, it's a guitar-heavy set of blues-rock tempered with 1980s influences and featuring a variety of sidemen, including John Bonham's son Jason on drums and Robert Plant, who co-wrote and sings on 'The Only One'. The other featured vocalists and co-writers are John Miles and Chris Farlowe, whose bludgeoning efforts did little to enhance the *Death Wish II* soundtrack but whose voice here complements Page's guitar rather well on the blistering slow blues of 'Prison Blues', arguably the album's most impressive track. Of the three instrumentals, 'Emerald Eyes' stands out as the most inventive.

There's an impressive diversity to Page's guitar sounds as he switches between a Les

LED ZEPPELIN

9

Paul, Telecaster, Stratocaster, Roland synth and Martin and Washburn acoustics, but although some respected Zeppelin watchers such as Dave Lewis have heralded the set as representing "an almost phoenix-like rebirth", the reality is that *Outrider* merely proved that Page was never really cut out to be a solo artist. It seems that Page himself knew it, too. Despite no end of hints and promises of a new studio album in countless interviews since, to date *Outrider* remains his only solo album.

COVERDALE/PAGE

UK and US, Geffen, March 15, 1993

SHAKE MY TREE
WAITING ON YOU
TAKE ME FOR A LITTLE WHILE
PRIDE AND JOY
OVER NOW
FEELING HOT
EASY DOES IT
TAKE A LOOK AT YOURSELF
DON'T LEAVE ME THIS WAY
ABSOLUTION BLUES
WHISPER A PRAYER FOR THE DYING

Recorded: **Little Mountain Studios,**

Vancouver; Criteria, Miami, Florida; Abbey Road, London; Highbrow Productions, Hook City, Nevada, autumn 1992
Producers: **Jimmy Page and David Coverdale**
Highest chart position: **UK 4; US 5**

It is widely held that Page teamed up with David Coverdale merely to annoy Robert Plant, who believed that the bouffant-haired Whitesnake singer had ripped off his vocal style and was possessed of little or no original talent. If so, it worked. After rumours that the Plant–Coverdale pairing would be joined by John Paul Jones and Jason Bonham in a reformed Led Zeppelin, Plant was sufficiently irked to agree to team up with Page a year later for *No Quarter*. Plant may also have been spurred into action by the fact that the sole Page-Coverdale album proved to be the guitarist's most commercially successful project since Zeppelin. Listening to the album today, it's hard to understand why for it's difficult to disagree with the judgement expressed on *Amazon.com* that the record represents "the worst kind of Led Zep mimicry". Page's guitar rocks out with abandon on 'Shake My Tree' and 'Feeling Hot', while 'Take Me for a Little While' and 'Over Now' find him in slower, bluesier mode. But the songs are poor, and if Coverdale is a third-rate Plant copyist as a singer, his lyrics are even more woeful. Ultimately, it's an album of karaoke sub-Zeppelin heavy-metal posturing and unworthy of Page's talents. A further six tracks recorded at the time of the album remain unreleased and should probably remain that way.

LIVE AT THE GREEK (JIMMY PAGE & THE BLACK CROWES)

UK and US, TVT, July 4, 2000

CELEBRATION DAY
CUSTARD PIE
SICK AGAIN
WHAT IS AND WHAT SHOULD NEVER BE
WOKE UP THIS MORNING
SHAPES OF THINGS TO COME
SLOPPY DRUNK
TEN YEARS GONE
IN MY TIME OF DYING
YOUR TIME IS GONNA COME
THE LEMON SONG
NOBODY'S FAULT BUT MINE
HEARTBREAKER
HEY HEY WHAT CAN I DO
MELLOW DOWN EASY
OH WELL
SHAKE YOUR MONEY MAKER
YOU SHOOK ME
OUT ON THE TILES
WHOLE LOTTA LOVE

Recorded: **Greek Theatre, Los Angeles,
October 18 & 19, 1999**
Producer: **Jimmy Page**
Highest chart position: **UK 39; US 64**

Following the 1998 tour with Plant around the
Walking into Clarksdale album, Page seemed
to rediscover his taste for live appearances.
With Plant unprepared to countenance any
further projects ("I've been trying to propose
scenarios whereby we could do this or that,
but Robert didn't want to do anything, and
kept postponing and cancelling, so in the
end I just lost patience," Page reported at
the time), in 1999 the guitarist teamed up
with The Black Crowes. After joining the
Atlanta rockers at a one-off London charity
concert in June, four American dates were
then announced for October that year,
under the banner "A Rock 'n' Roll Evening".
Following two shows at New York City's
Roseland Ballroom, the remaining two
performances at the Greek Theatre, Los
Angeles, were recorded for a double album.
Due to contractual problems with their
record company, none of The Black Crowes'
own repertoire from the shows (on which
Plant did not play, in any case) was available
for inclusion, leaving an album of classics
drawn from Led Zeppelin's illustrious back
catalogue and half-a-dozen other blues and
rock standards.

There's nothing adventurous or innovative
about the set and Page and the band stick closely
to the original arrangements. But unlike David
Coverdale, Black Crowes singer Chris Robinson
doesn't try to imitate Plant but allows his
own personality to shine, lending his soulful,
southern swagger to the Zeppelin covers, which
account for no less than 14 of the 20 tracks.
Pleasingly, the choices are not always the most
obvious, and include 'Out on the Tiles' from
Led Zeppelin III and 'Sick Again' and 'Ten Years
Gone' from *Physical Graffiti*. The Black Crowes
excel on the more blues-based material. Standouts include 'In My Time of Dying', sung with
aplomb by Robinson, a magisterial 'Nobody's
Fault but Mine', a delightfully shuffling take
on BB King's 'Woke up this Morning' and a
stomping version of the blues standard 'Sloppy
Drunk'. The non-Zeppelin covers include songs

LED ZEPPELIN

9

by Fleetwood Mac and The Yardbirds.

Page was said to have been paid one million dollars for the album, which was initially released only via the internet. When online sales proved disappointing (reportedly less than 50,000 copies), the album was released to record stores in July 2000. The Crowes were also allegedly paid a million dollars, in which case the record company made a heavy loss. Accusations that the record was a cynical money-making exercise were strongly rebutted by Robinson, who insisted: "Jimmy Page is a musician who happened to be in a band called Led Zeppelin that we all love. We're musicians who have a band called The Black Crowes, and we got together 'cause we wanted to play music together. You know, it's not really that difficult a concept. There's no marketing strategy."

An enjoyable enough live album that found Page playing with some of his old fire, it was, however, soon eclipsed by the belated release in 2003 of the 1972-recorded live Led Zeppelin set, *How the West was Won*.

LUCIFER RISING AND OTHER SOUND TRACKS

Spring Equinox, 2012 (vinyl only)
LUCIFER RISING – MAIN TRACK
INCUBUS
DAMASK
UNHARMONICS
DAMASK – AMBIENT
LUCIFER RISING – PERCUSSIVE RETURN
Recorded: **1971–72**
Producer: **Jimmy Page**

Page started to compose his music for Kenneth Anger's film *Lucifer Rising* while Led Zeppelin were recording their fourth album. Page and Anger had become friends through a mutual interest in the magician Aleister Crowley. After Page had bought Crowley's old home near Loch Ness, he invited Anger to the house to help exorcise a 'headless ghost' he believed was haunting the place. It was during the visit that Page agreed to write the soundtrack for Anger's next film. By 1972, with deadlines looming, Page had delivered only 23 minutes of music and the pair fell out irrevocably, their mutual animosity further exacerbated by a feud between Anger and the guitarist's wife, Charlotte. The director subsequently denounced Page with unhinged viciousness in the media: "He's a multi-millionaire miser. He and Charlotte, that horrible vampire girl – the druggie that got him on heroin – they're both junkies… I put the curse of King Midas on them. If you're greedy and just amass gold you'll get an illness. So I did turn her and Jimmy Page into statues of gold because they've both lost their minds. He can't write songs anymore."

Amid this insanity, the music was dropped from the film but eventually appeared as a bootleg around 1981, and became much sought-after by collectors. But an official release had to wait until 2012, when Page released the music via his website on limited edition red vinyl that sold out instantly.

As befitting the diabolic subject of the film for which it was composed, the music is weird, perverse, mysterious and, in occasional flashes, rather compelling – an ambient, *avant garde* tableaux of middle eastern drones, sinister chanting, tabla, mellotron and shimmering 12-string guitar.

ROBERT PLANT

robert plant

pictures at eleven

PICTURES AT ELEVEN

Es Paranza, June 28, 1982

BURNING DOWN ONE SIDE
MOONLIGHT IN SAMOSA
PLEDGE PIN
SLOW DANCER
WORSE THAN DETROIT
FAT LIP
LIKE I'VE NEVER BEEN GONE
MYSTERY TITLE

Recorded: **Rockfield Studios, Monmouth, September 1981–spring, 1982**
Producer: **Robert Plant**
Engineer: **Pat Moran**
Highest chart position: **UK 2; US 5**

Plant's debut album found him trying hard – possibly too hard – not to sound like Led Zeppelin. Accompanied by guitarist Robbie Blunt (who also co-wrote the songs),

Paul Martinez on bass, Jezz Woodroffe on keyboards and Phil Collins and Cozy Powell on drums, the rhythms are lighter, the tunes more melodic and his vocals contain few of the "mmm baby, baby" mannerisms he patented with the group. Critics have suggested that where Plant used to rock, here he is content to noodle. Others regard it as his finest solo album. Overall, it's an engaging collection of mature, polished adult-oriented rock with progressive influences. That is has stood the test of time better than some of his 1980s solo work is down to the fact that the synths heard on some of his later albums are mercifully absent and his clean and crisp production – on the only set he ever produced entirely on his own – sounds remarkably fresh.

Highlights invclude the lovely 'Like I've Never Been Gone', which owes much to his early West Coast influences, 'Moonlight In Samosa' with its brooding strings and minor keys and the jazz-rock 'Pledge Pin' with a great sax solo by Raphael Ravenscroft. But he hasn't quite sloughed off his old skin and the bluesy 'Worse Than Detroit' owes something to his Zeppelin past, as does the melodramatic blues-rock ballad 'Slow Dancer' with its eastern Kashmir-style semi-tones and a riff from Blunt that is almost worthy of Page himself. Somewhat surprisingly, Plant did not include anything from *Pictures at Eleven on Sixty Six to Timbuktu*, the only solo album not represented on the 37 track, two disc career retrospective.

THE PRINCIPLE OF MOMENTS

UK and US, Es Paranza, July 11, 1983

OTHER ARMS
IN THE MOOD
MESSIN' WITH THE MEKON
WRECKLESS LOVE

LED ZEPPELIN

THRU' WITH THE TWO STEP
HORIZONTAL DEPARTURE
STRANGER HERE... THAN OVER THERE
BIG LOG

Recorded: **Rockfield Studios, Monmouth, December 1982–April 1983**
Producers: **Robert Plant, Pat Moran and Benji Lefeure**
Engineer: **Pat Moran**
Highest chart position: **UK 7; US 8**

Using the same group of musicians who had performed so well on *Pictures at Eleven*, except for the arrival of Jethro Tull's Barriemore Barlow on drums, Plant went back into the Rockfield studio in Wales to record the follow-up less than six months after the release of his solo debut. The style is broadly similar, although certain 1980s techniques have started to creep into the production, particularly in the drum sound and the widespread use of synths as Plant seems even more determined to offer as few echoes of Led Zeppelin as possible. When he supported the album with his first solo US tour, he refused to sing any songs by the band at all. "The times had changed. I was determined to go my own way and start again with no reference to the Zeppelin songbook," he subsequently

explained. "I am sure I frustrated many people in so doing. However, that's the way it worked." Indeed, Blunt's smooth, crystaline guitar work could not be further removed from Page's pyrotechnics and Plant is clearly enjoying the opportunity to sing rather than wail and shout, his voice roaming impressively and at times experimentally across the spectrum.

The album opens with 'Other Arms' and Plant screaming 'lay down your arms!' on a mid-tempo rocker that might have done service on *In Through the out Door*. Yet that's as close to Zeppelin as it gets. For the rest it's clever, inventive soft-rock and cool atmospherics, climaxing with the closer 'Big Log', with its meandering but brooding sense of mystery enhanced by a mercifully subtle synth arrangement. The song gave Plant his biggest solo hit single, when the track made the top twenty on both sides of the Atlantic in July 1983.

THE HONEYDRIPPERS: VOLUME ONE

UK and US, Es Paranza, November 12, 1984
I GET A THRILL
SEA OF LOVE
I GOT A WOMAN

YOUNG BOY BLUES
ROCKIN' AT MIDNIGHT

Recorded: **Atlantic Studios, New York;**
London, March–April 1984
Producers: **Fabulous Brill Brothers; Ahmet**
Ertegün (credited as Nugetre)
Highest chart position: **UK 56; US 4**

Named after the 1945 instrumental 'The
Honeydripper', recorded by Joe Liggins
and the blues pianist Roosevelt Sykes, who
revelled in the sexually charged nickname,
Plant first played with an *ad hoc* group he
dubbed The Honeydrippers at a Stourbridge
wine bar in March 1981. The notion of a
semi-anonymous bar band playing old
R&B, rockabilly and even doo-wop hits
remained with him, and during his 1983 tour
of America he took advantage of a day off in
Memphis to record a version of Charlie Rich's
'Philadelphia Baby' at the Sun Studio with
Phil Collins on drums. Encouraged by Atlantic
Records boss Ahmet Ertegün, once the tour
was completed, he went back into the label's
New York studio in March 1984 with a bunch
of top players including Chic's Nile Rodgers,
Jeff Beck, keyboardist Paul Shaffer, bassist
Wayne Pedziwiatr and drummer Dave Weckl
to record a bunch of vintage numbers under
Ertegün's supervision. Back in London,
Jimmy Page then added guitar to a cover
of Phil Phillips and The Twilights' 1959 hit
'Sea of Love' and 'I Get a Thrill'. Also on
the five-track EP are an explosive version
of Roy Brown's jump blues tune 'Rockin'
at Midnight', a string-laden, Spector-esque
'Young Boy Blues' and a lightweight but
enjoyable cover of Ray Charles's 'I Got a
Woman'.

Although the record sold poorly in Britain,
in America it was a major success, providing
Plant with a number three hit single with

'Sea of Love' – one place better than Led
Zeppelin's highest-charting single, 'Whole
Lotta Love'. The expanded version of the EP
included in the *Nine Lives* box set includes
a superlative live version of 'Rockin' at
Midnight' with a spirited vocal from Plant
that actually betters the studio version. To
date, a *Honeydrippers Volume Two* has never
appeared, Plant apparently reluctant to align
himself too heavily with the Shakin' Stevens
rock 'n' roll pastiche market.

SHAKEN 'N' STIRRED
UK and US, Es Paranza, May 20, 1985

HIP TO HOO
KALLALOU KALLALOU
TOO LOUD
TROUBLE YOUR MONEY
PINK AND BLACK
LITTLE BY LITTLE
DOO DOO A DO DO
EASILY LEAD
SIXES AND SEVENS

Recorded: **Swanyard Studios, London,**
and Rockfield, Monmouth, autumn
1984–spring 1985

LED ZEPPELIN

9

Producers: **Robert Plant, Benji Lefeure and Tim Palmer**
Engineer: **Benji Lefuere and Tim Palmer**
Highest chart position: **Uk 19; US 20**

When Plant was asked about his 1980s output in an interview in *Uncut* magazine in 2005 and replied "Will sorry do?", *Shaken 'n' Stirred* is probably the album he had foremost in his mind. Today it sounds horribly dated with its brash 1980s production having more in common with a Phil Collins solo album than Led Zeppelin.

The Genesis drummer isn't actually on the album and Richie Hayward fills the drum stool, but his playing seldom recaptures the effortless funk he once lent to Little Feat. Elsewhere Robbie Blunt, after his sterling work on Plant's first two solo albums, struggles to come to terms with his Roland synth guitar, the backing vocals of former Eurythmics singer Toni Halliday are hopelessly inappropriate and Jezz Woodroffe's synthesised keyboards just sound plain nasty. Even Plant's own vocals seem to have fallen prey to the 1980s emphasis on trickery rather than emotion.

'Little by Little' and 'Sixes and Sevens' emerge as the most interesting compositions, yet even they are virtually ruined by the dated arrangements and production. It's no wonder that when Plant came to compile his career retrospective *Sixty Six to Timbuktu*, only 'Little by Little' made the cut – and that only by dint of having been a hit single in America and therefore hard to omit.

NOW AND ZEN
UK and US, Es Paranza, February 29, 1988

HEAVEN KNOWS
DANCE ON MY OWN
TALL COOL ONE
THE WAY I FEEL
HELEN OF TROY

BILLY'S REVENGE
SHIP OF FOOLS
WHY
WHITE, CLEAN AND NEAT
WALKING TOWARDS PARADISE

Recorded: **Swanyard Studios and Marcus Studios, London, spring–autumn 1987**
Producers: **Robert Plant, Tim Palmer and Phil Johnstone**
Engineers: **Rob Bozas, Martin Russell, Dave Barratt, Michael Gregovich, Tim Burrell and Jonathan Dee**
Highest chart position: **UK 10; US 6**

After a two-and-a-half-year break, Plant eventually returned in 1988 with a new band and apparently more at ease with his past than at any time since Led Zeppelin had broken up. At the heart of the new project were Dave Barratt and Phil Johnstone, who worked as the production team Act of War and were dubbed by Plant "The Dangerous Brothers". Impressed by a demo tape by the pair that included their songs 'Heaven Knows' and 'Upside Down', he began working with them in early 1987 on an album that was originally given the working title *Wolves*, a reference to Plant's new tour logo. With additional support from drummer Chris Blackwell (no relation to the Island Records founder), bassist Phil Scragg and guitarist Doug Boyle, this line-up was responsible for eight of the album's 10 tracks. The other two were the result of an earlier alliance with Robert Crash from the New York post punk band The Psychotic Tanks, who had been recommended to Plant by Dave Stewart.

Despite some heavily programmed keyboards that today sound a little dated (particularly on 'Why' and 'Dance on My Own', the two electro-pop tracks recorded with Crash), *Now and Zen* was a major improvement after the disappointments of *Shaken 'n' Stirred*. No longer running from the shadow of Led Zeppelin, he even sampled several of the band's greatest moments on 'Tall Cool One', which also features Page in the studio on guitar, as does 'Heaven Knows'.

For the most part it's mid-tempo, radio-friendly adult rock of the highest quality, although it's the album's sole ballad, the lovely 'Ship of Fools', that is the undoubted stand-out with a wonderfully subtle vocal and lyric. The rockabilly tones of 'Tall Cool One' and 'Billy's Revenge' echo The Honeydrippers, but there's nothing retro about their entirely contemporary treatment.

MANIC NIRVANA
UK and US, Es Paranza, March 19, 1990

*HURTING KIND (I'VE GOT MY EYES ON
    YOU)*
BIG LOVE
SSS & Q
I CRIED
SHE SAID
NIRVANA

9

TIE DYE ON THE HIGHWAY
*YOUR MA SAID YOU CRIED IN YOUR
    SLEEP LAST NIGHT*
ANNIVERSARY
LIARS DANCE
WATCHING YOU

Recorded: **Olympic Studios, autumn 1989**
Producers: **Robert Plant and Phil Johnstone**
Engineer: **Mark 'Spike' Stent**
Highest chart position: **UK 15; US 13**

Using the same band that recorded *Now and Zen* but with Charlie Jones replacing Phil Scragg on bass, on its release in 1990 *Manic Nirvana* was the hardest rocking album Plant had made since the demise of Led Zeppelin. With guitars rather than keyboards taking the front seat again, it's clear this was a conscious decision from the outset as 'Hurting Kind (I've Got My Eyes on You)' and 'Big Love' kick and stomp with more venom than almost anything from the singer's 1980s output. 'S S S & Q' opens with a snarling guitar solo that owes as much to Hendrix as Page. 'Tie Dye on the Highway', with its sampled voices from the Woodstock

LED ZEPPELIN

festival, is a high-energy tribute to the hippie era, while the slashing guitar riffs of 'She Said' and 'Nirvana' also conjure the ghost of Zeppelin's 1970s pomp, revealing Doug Boyle as a highly under-rated axeman.

The more reflective material is impressive, too, particularly the gorgeous 'I Cried', 'Liars Dance', which recalls the acousting outings on *Led Zeppelin III*, and the haunting 'Anniversary', which refers to his divorce from his wife Maureen but which many fans also believe to be a tribute to John Bonham, occasioned by Plant's feelings upon reforming Led Zeppelin for a day without the late drummer for Atlantic Records' 40th birthday party in 1988.

FATE OF NATIONS
UK and US, Fontana, May 25, 1993

CALLING TO YOU
DOWN TO THE SEA
COME INTO MY LIFE
I BELIEVE
29 PALMS
MEMORY SONG (HELLO HELLO)
IF I WERE A CARPENTER

COLOURS OF A SHADE
PROMISED LAND
THE GREATEST GIFT
GREAT SPIRIT
NETWORK NEWS

Recorded: **RAK Studios, London, autumn 1992–spring 1993**
Producers: **Robert Plant and Chris Hughes**
Engineer: **Michael Gregovich**
Highest chart position: **UK 6; US 34**

More line-up changes saw the introduction of Kevin Scott MacMichael on guitar and Chris Hughes on drums, and a host of guests who helped to make *Fate of Nations* the most adventurous album of Plant's solo career to this point and sign-posted the way to some of his later work with The Strange Sensation. 'Calling to You' kicks the album off in crunching fashion with a 'Kashmir'-like riff before Nigel Kennedy's thrilling violin coda takes the track to new heights. The slow-burning 'Come into My Life' features Nigel Eaton on hurdy gurdy, Clannad's Márie Brennan on ethereal backing vocals and the unmistakable guitar of Richard Thompson on a track that recalls the mysterious moods of 'The Battle of Evermore', while 'Colours of a Shade' is another Celtic folk excursion. 'The Greatest Gift' and 'Great Spirit' are finely crafted ballads, the Tom Petty-ish '29 Palms' and the lovely, jangling 'I Believe' are object lessons in pop perfection and the tenderly sung cover of Tim Hardin's 'If I Were a Carpenter' is given a lovely arrangement with mandolin and strings by Lynton Naiff. After such gentle, melodic interludes, the album closes on a tougher-edged note with 'Network News', a protest song about the first Iraq war that makes an alarming companion piece to 'Freedom Fries' on *Mighty Rearranger* more than a decade later.

DREAMLAND

UK, Mercury, June 24, 2002; US, Universal,
July 16, 2002

FUNNY IN MY MIND (I BELIEVE I'M FIXIN'
*   TO DIE)*
MORNING DEW
ONE MORE CUP OF COFFEE
LAST TIME I SAW HER
SONG TO THE SIREN
WIN MY TRAIN FARE HOME (IF I EVER   GET
*   LUCKY)*
DARKNESS, DARKNESS
RED DRESS
HEY JOE
SKIP'S SONG
DIRT IN A HOLE
Recorded: **RAK Recording Studios, early**
2002
Producers: **Robert Plant and Phill Brown**
Engineer: **Phill Brown**
Highest chart position: **UK 20; US 40**

After the 1990s reunion with Page on *No
Quarter* and *Walking into Clarksdale*, Plant
retreated into semi-anonymity with his pub
band, Priory of Brion. He eventually re-emerged

in 2002, nine years after his last solo album,
with *Dreamland*, a collection which mined the
covers that formed the repertoire he'd been
playing with Priory of Brion. In interviews at
the time, he went out of his way to stress that
he saw the album very much as a band effort
by The Strange Sensation, comprising Justin
Adams and Porl Thompson on guitars, John
Baggott on keyboards, Charlie Jones on bass and
Clive Deamer on drums. The brace of original
group compositions, 'Last Time I Saw Her' and
'Dirt in a Hole', are lightweight but there's no
doubting the passion of Plant's interpretive skills
on some of his favourite songs by West Coast
troubadours Tim Buckley and Jesse Colin Young
('Song to the Siren' and 'Darkness, Darkness'),
Bob Dylan ('One More Cup of Coffee') and
some of his old blues heroes, including Bukka
White on 'Fixin' to Die' and Arthur 'Big Boy'
Crudup, John Lee Hooker and Robert Johnson,
all of whom crop up in the course of the
medley 'Win My Train Fare Home'.

MIGHTY REARRANGER

UK, Sanctuary, May 2, 2005; US, May 10, 2005

ANOTHER TRIBE
SHINE IT ALL AROUND

LED ZEPPELIN

9

FREEDOM FRIES
TIN PAN VALLEY
ALL THE KING'S HORSES
THE ENCHANTER
TAKAMBA
DANCING IN HEAVEN
SOMEBODY KNOCKING
LET THE FOUR WINDS BLOW
MIGHTY REARRANGER
BROTHER RAY

Recorded: **The Lodge, Bathford, autumn 2004–spring 2005**
Producers: **Robert Plant and The Strange Sensation**
Engineer: **Steve Evans**
Highest chart position: **UK 4; US 22**

There's always a temptation when a significant artist returns with a decent album after a period of low-key activity to talk in over-excited terms of a 'comeback'. But after easing himself into the new millennium with Priory of Brion and an enjoyable but unchallenging cover album, 2005's *Mighty ReArranger* sounded like an important statement by a man with much to get off his chest. 'Another Tribe', 'Takamba' and the brilliant 'Freedom Fries' ("and burns and scars") seemed to provide a sharp and concerned commentary on the post 9/11 world. 'Tin Pan Valley' was a candid analysis of the dangers of living on former glories and a fairly uncoded attack on those who "flirt with cabaret" (take a tuxedoed bow, Rod Stewart) and continue in old age to "fake the rebel yell" (arise Sir Mick). Forays into mysticism ('The Enchanter' and 'Dancing in Heaven'), lyrical nods to old heroes ('Somebody Knocking' and 'Let the Four Winds Blow'), rock riffing ('Shine It All Around'), blues wailing (the title track), burnished West Coast filigree ('Dancing in Heaven'), *Zep III*-style acoustics ('All the King's Horses') and Arabic and North African influences ('Another Tribe' and 'Takamba') all collide in unexpected and often thrilling fashion. Backed again by The Strange Sensation, with guitarists Justin Adams and 'Skin' Tyson making a particularly outstanding contribution, Plant reckoned it was the best he'd ever sung, with plenty of subtle shading and nuance and that open-throated, leonine roar unleashed only when strictly necessary.

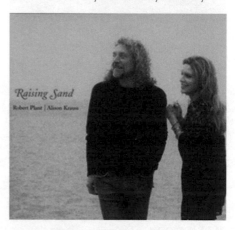

RAISING SAND (WITH ALISON KRAUSS)

UK, Rounder Records, October 22, 2007; US, Rounder Records, October 23, 2007

RICH WOMAN
KILLING THE BLUES
SISTER ROSETTA GOES BEFORE US
POLLY COME HOME
GONE GONE GONE (DONE MOVED ON)
*THROUGH THE MORNING, THROUGH   THE
   NIGHT*
PLEASE READ THE LETTER
TRAMPLED ROSE
FORTUNE TELLER
STICK WITH ME BABY
NOTHIN'
LET YOUR LOSS BE YOUR LESSON
YOUR LONG JOURNEY

Q&A WITH ROBERT PLANT ON MIGHTY REARRANGER

Who is the Mighty ReArranger?

"He's an abstract character. He's around all of us. He's fate. He's everything we want and everything we don't want. We're all governed by the Mighty ReArranger. He's right there and he's a pretty powerful dude."

There's a lot of imagery in the lyrics on the record drawn from the blues...

"Dylan has been a beacon to me as a writer all through my life. He judiciously borrows blues terms and I decided to write an entire song like that, which is 'Somebody Knocking'. There's stuff in there from Blind Willie McTell and Son House and all those references that are buried inside my brain."

Should we see this album as a great comeback?

"If people will think I've returned and say 'he's regaining his crown', that's very nice of them. But I don't know who had it last. It's a bit like pass the parcel, isn't it?"

Recorded: **Nashville, Tennessee, and Los Angeles, California**
Producer: **T Bone Burnett**
Highest chart position: **UK 2; US 2**

After duetting with Sandy Denny on 1971's 'The Battle of Evermore' (later reprised on *No Quarter* with Najma Akhtar), some 36 years later Plant finally got around to making a full album of duets when he teamed up with the American bluegrass singer Alison Krauss on a rootsy set of country, folk, blues and R&B songs by such writers as Townes Van Zandt, Gene Clark, Tom Waits, Doc Watson and The Everly Brothers. Only on 'Please Read the Letter', previously recorded somewhat unsatisfactorily with Jimmy Page on *Walking*

into Clarksdale, did he dip into his own songbook. Yet the result was the most critically and commercially successful album by any former Zep member since the band's break-up. Accompanied by Krauss's fiddle plus banjo, dobro and pedal steel, and with T Bone Burnett's production lending a suitably raw and rootsy feel, the dynamic contrast between Plant's wailing voice and Krauss's ethereal tones is both charming and goose-bump thrilling. The album went on to win a clutch of Grammy awards and swiftly came to be regarded as the finest work of Plant's mature solo career.

BAND OF JOY

UK, Decca, September 13, 2010; US Rounder, September 14, 2010

ANGEL DANCE
HOUSE OF CARDS
CENTRAL TWO-O-NINE
SILVER RIDER
YOU CAN'T BUY MY LOVE
FALLING IN LOVE AGAIN
THE ONLY SOUND THAT MATTERS
MONKEY
CINDY, I'LL MARRY YOU SOMEDAY

9

LED ZEPPELIN

HARM'S SWIFT WAY
SATAN YOUR KINGDOM MUST COME
*   DOWN*
EVEN THIS SHALL PASS AWAY

Recorded: **Woodland Sound Studios,**
Nashville, December 2009–February 2010
Producers: **Robert Plant and Buddy Miller**
Engineer: **Mike Poole**
Highest chart position: **UK 3; US 5**
Billed as "a timeless plunge into authentic
Americana", for once the record company
publicity hype hit the musical nail pretty
much on the head. The follow-up to *Raising
Sand* found Plant again working with a female
vocalist, although unlike his duets with Alison
Krauss his new partner, Patty Griffin, was
confined mostly to backing harmonies on a
rootsy set that combines country, gospel and
honky-tonk oldies ('Satan Your Kingdom Must
Come Down', 'Even this Shall Pass Away' and
'Cindy, I'll Marry You Some Day"), deep soul
classics ('You Can't Buy My Love' and 'Falling
in Love Again') and more contemporary
songs by Los Lobos ('Angel Dance'), Richard
Thompson ('House of Cards'), Townes
Van Zandt ('Harm's Swift Way') and two
compositions by the Minnesota 'slowcore'
band Low ('Silver Rider' and 'Monkey').
There's only one Plant original, the stomping
country-blues 'Central Two-O-Nine',
co-written with Buddy Miller. Overall the
sound is more freewheeling sonically than its
predecessor, bolder and messier, built around
the old-fashioned communal notion of
musicians playing together live in a room, but
with the roots flavour laced with more than a
hint of Plant's lifelong passion for 1960s West
Coast psychedelia. The results are spirited
and full of *joie de vivre*, the fire and fury of
old diminished but not extinguished, and
any diminution compensated by the relaxed
intimacy of the performances.

LULLABY...AND THE CEASELESS ROAR

UK/US Nonesuch September 8, 2014

LITTLE MAGGIE
RAINBOW
POCKETFUL OF GOLDEN
EMBRACE ANOTHER FALL
TURN IT UP
A STOLEN KISS
SOMEBODY THERE
POOR HOWARD
HOUSE OF LOVE
UP ON THE HOLLOW HILL
*   (UNDERSTANDING ARTHUR)*
ARBADEN (MAGGIE'S BABBY)

With the blood-curdling, screech-and-wail
he perfected in his Zeppelin pomp now
largely banished, Plant sings here in a more
reflective and nuanced style than ever; in
places, as on "Rainbow" and the moody ballad
"A Stolen Kiss", he almost croons like Elvis.
You can dismiss this subtle and more subdued
approach as "Arkle pulling a milk cart" (the
description his former manager Bill Curbishley
once applied to his low-key approach of later
years) or you can celebrate the ripe maturity

of a singer who has learnt a new vocal vocabulary with a richer palette of emotional expression and who has acceptedthat at 66 years old there is no point in trying to sound as he did in youthful virility - years ago. Most reviewers took the latter view and Plant's tenth solo album was greeted by a swathe of five star reviews. Musically the album represented a masterful and, in places, daring blend of his on-going musical obsessions from gritty southern r&b and jangling West Coast pyschedelia to sinuous African blues and Middle Eastern beats. But although billed as a solo release, in a very real sense, lullaby and... The Ceaseless Roar is a genuine band album, too, and Plant was anxious in interviews to give full credit to the Sensational Space Shifters. "There's no real boundary to where we can and cannot go," he remarked. "It's not like a band where there's a guitarist and a bass player and a drummer and a singer. The give and take and exchange is magnificent." Particularly notable are the contributions of guitarist Justin Adams and Juldeh Camara, playing a one string West African fiddle known as a ritti which adds an eerie, haunting sound to many of the tracks. The Welsh folk singer Julie Murphy contributes vocals to "Embrace Another Fall" and the production – by Plant himself – favours raw and earthy over gloss and artifice, yet still sparkles and perfectly suits the rootsy potency of the music.

COMPILATIONS

SIXTY SIX TO TIMBUKTU

UK, Mercury, November 4, 2003; US, Atlantic

TIE DYE ON THE HIGHWAY
UPSIDE DOWN
PROMISED LAND
TALL COOL ONE

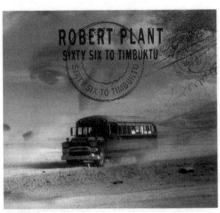

DIRT IN A HOLE
CALLING TO YOU
29 PALMS
IF I WERE A CARPENTER
SEA OF LOVE
DARKNESS, DARKNESS
BIG LOG
SHIP OF FOOLS
I BELIEVE
LITTLE BY LITTLE
HEAVEN KNOWS
SONG TO THE SIREN
DARKNESS, DARKNESS (VIDEO)
YOU'D BETTER RUN
OUR SONG
HEY JOE
FOR WHAT IT'S WORTH
OPERATOR
ROAD TO THE SUN
PHILADELPHIA BABY
RED FOR DANGER
LET'S HAVE A PARTY
HEY JAYNE
LOUIE, LOUIE
NAKED IF I WANT TO
21 YEARS
IF IT'S REALLY GOT TO BE THIS WAY
RUDE WORLD
LITTLE HANDS

LED ZEPPELIN

LIFE BEGIN AGAIN
LET THE BOOGIE WOOGIE ROLL
WIN MY TRAIN FARE HOME (LIVE IN
TIMBUKTU)
CALLING TO YOU (VIDEO)

Recorded: **1966–2002**
Highest chart position: **UK 27; US 134**

A well-chosen two-disc representation of
Plant's entire solo career, with tracks from
seven of his first eight albums (nothing from
his debut *Pictures at Eleven*) plus a generous
handful of rarities and previously unreleased
tracks. Disc one contains the highlights of his
solo albums plus one out-take, 'Upside Down',
which dates from the *Now and Zen* sessions.
The buried treasure, however, is to be found
on disc two. 'You'd Better Run' is his 1966
debut single with the ill-fated Listen and 'Our
Song' his own debut single on CBS a year later.
'Hey Joe' and a frankly awful version of Buffalo
Springfield's 'For What It's Worth' come
from Band of Joy's 1967 demo, recorded at
London's Regent Sound. 'Operator' is a rolling
acoustic blues song that represents his brief
pre-Zeppelin tie-up with Alexis Korner. The
rockabilly cover of Charlie Rich's 'Philadelphia
Baby' appeared in the 1985 film *Porky's
Revenge!* and 'Louie Louie' was recorded for
1993's *Wayne's World 2* and finds Plant playing
lead guitar on a highly creditable solo. A
rollicking cover of Elvis Presley's 'Let's Have a
Party', complete with weeping pedal steel was
recorded for *NME* in 1990. Other rare covers
include Moby Grape's 'Naked If I Want to',
only ever released as a B-side on a 1993 single,
and 'Little Hands', from 1999's *More Oar – A
Tribute to the Skip Spence Album*. 'Hey Jayne'
is another 1993 B-side, chiefly notable for the
fact that it finds plant playing sitar. 'Red for
Danger' is a techno-sounding oddity recorded
in 1988 with multi-instrumentalist Robin

George, a mate of Plant's from the Midlands.
'21 Years' features the Tucson, Arizona-based
guitarist Rainer Ptacek and appeared as the
B-side of Plant's 1993 single, '29 Palms'. 'Rude
World', another Ptacek song, is of particular
interest to Zeppelin fans as it teams Page and
Plant together again on a song from around
the time of 1997's *Walking into Clarksdale*
sessions which appeared on the US-only
tribute album to Ptacek, *The Inner Flame*. The
country-ish 'If It's Really Got to be this Way'
was recorded for the little-heard 1994 album
Adios Amigo: A Tribute to Arthur Alexander.
'Life Begin Again' finds Plant singing with
Welsh folk singer Julie Murphy on a track
recorded with Afro Celt Sound System in 2001
and 'Let the Boogie Woogie Roll' is a 2003
collaboration with Jools Holland.

NINE LIVES (BOX SET)
UK and US, Rhino, November21, 2006

Recorded: **1982–2005**

Coming just two years after *Sixty Six to
Timbuktu*, *Nine Lives* brought together all
nine of Plant's post-Zeppelin solo albums in
a splendidly packaged box set, but although

each album was offered in an 'expanded' version, in truth they contained little that was new. A total of 26 previously unreleased tracks consisted mostly of live versions of album cuts and remixes, with a handful of out-takes of varying interest.

JOHN PAUL JONES

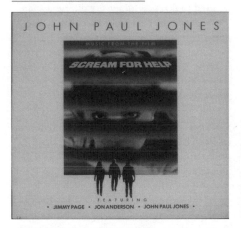

SCREAM FOR HELP (OST)

UK and US, Atlantic, March 22, 1985

SPAGHETTI JUNCTION
BAD CHILD
SILVER TRAIN
CRACKBACK
CHILLI SAUCE
TAKE IT OR LEAVE IT
CHRISTIE
WHEN YOU FALL IN LOVE
HERE I AM

Producer: **John Paul Jones**

A recommendation from Jimmy Page to the film director Michael Winner led to Jones's name appearing on a record as a solo artist for the first time in 20 years and Led Zeppelin fans have long sought out this hard-to-find soundtrack for the opening and closing instrumentals, both of which feature the guitar pyrotechnics of Jimmy Page. 'Spaghetti Junction' has a Booker T-inspired funky, Stax feel and 'Crackback' crunches hard and fast in true Zeppelin style with a bass part from Jones that recalls the riff on 'Black Dog'. In addition to playing a variety of instruments, Jones's vocals can be heard on 'Bad Child' and 'When You Fall in Love', backed on the latter by the folk guitar of John Renbourn. Other vocalists include Yes's Jon Anderson and Madeline Bell, while his daughter Jacinda Jones helped out with the lyrics. The film flopped badly, which accounts for the fact that the album is hard to find, but with the exception of the splendid 'Crackback' it's probably one for completists only.

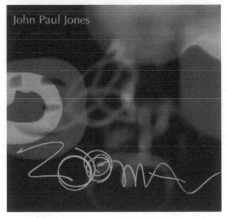

ZOOMA

UK and US, Discipline, September 1999

ZOOMA
GRIND
THE SMILE OF YOUR SHADOW
GOOSE

LED ZEPPELIN

9

BASS 'N' DRUMS
B. FINGERS
SNAKE EYES
NOSUMI BLUES
TIDAL

Producer: **John Paul Jones**

Appearing out of the blue in 1999, Jones's first genuine solo album was an all-instrumental affair that found him playing four-, eight- and ten-string bass guitars as well as synthesiser and organ. Standouts on the diverse collection include the title track with its torrents of guitar noise from Paul Leary of Butthole Surfers (whom Jones had produced), and the epic blues-rocker 'Snake Eyes'.

THE THUNDERTHIEF
UK and US, Discipline, February 2001

LEAFY MEADOWS
THE THUNDERTHIEF
HOEDIDDLE
ICE FISHING AT NIGHT
DAPHNE
ANGRY ANGRY
DOWN TO THE RIVER TO PRAY

SHIBUYA BOP
FREEDOM SONG

Producer: **John Paul Jones**

The follow-up to the all-instrumental *Zooma* found Jones adding vocals to his prowess on bass, keyboards, guitar, mandolin, autoharp, koto and ukulele. "I knew I wanted to do something very different than *Zooma*, and my first inclination was to use some computer voices to add a little bit of personality," he explained at the time. "After a while, I thought 'This is silly', and I decided to use my own voice." The results are not unpleasing, ranging from 'Angry Angry', which finds Jones adopting the persona of a Cockney-voiced punk, to the haunting tones of 'Ice Fishing at Night'. "It ain't Pavarotti and it ain't Plant, but I think it's all right," the reluctant singer modestly observed. Peter Blegvad contributed to the lyrics, but it is still as an inventive musical arranger that Jones's skills are best displayed. King Crimson's Robert Fripp – owner of the Discipline label – adds some imaginative guitar to the driving opener 'Leafy Meadows', the seven-minute 'Hoediddle' is an instrumental cornucopia of arresting eclecticism, 'Daphne' and 'Shibuya Bop' riff and rock with some force and 'Freedom Song' incorporates traditional Japanese influences.

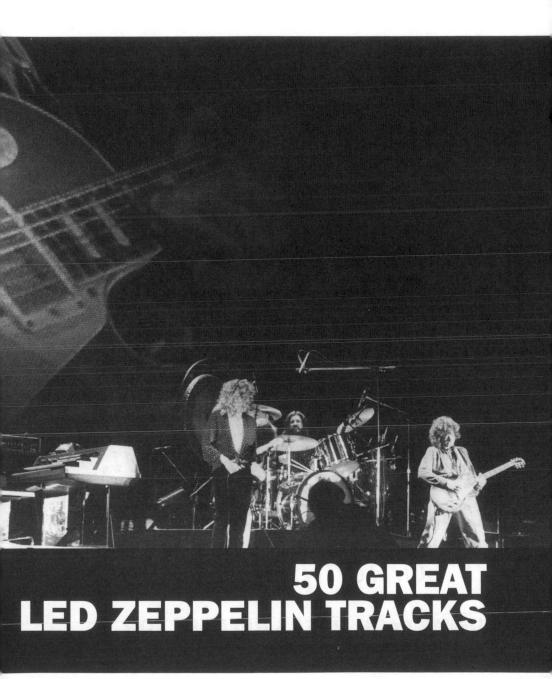

50 GREAT
LED ZEPPELIN TRACKS

10

"I can't put a tag to our music. Every one of us has been influenced by the blues, but it's one's interpretation of it and how you utilise it. I wish someone would invent an expression, but the closest I can get is contemporary blues."

JIMMY PAGE, PRESS RELEASE FOR *LED ZEPPELIN I*

50 GREAT LED ZEPPELIN TRACKS

Although Page described Plant as a tentative songwriter in the early days, their collaboration rapidly bore remarkable fruit. A shared interest in blues imagery helped, which in addition to Plant's ability to skilfully improvise within the idiom, meant that by *Led Zeppelin II* there was a distinct originality to their approach, which would only grow over the next decade.

1. BABE I'M GONNA LEAVE YOU

RECORDED OCTOBER 1968;
ALBUM: LED ZEPPELIN

Page and Plant first bonded over a 1962 recording of this folk song on the album *Joan Baez in Concert* during their initial get-together at the guitarist's home on the River Thames in August 1968. It then provided the perfect vehicle for Page's vision of a new kind of rock music built around dynamic contrasts of quiet and loud passages. The version Led Zeppelin recorded for their debut album shifts dramatically from folky verses accompanied by acoustic guitar to pummelling choruses driven by a wonderful descending riff and some unrestrained cymbal-crashing from Bonham. Keith Shadwick, whose book *Led Zeppelin: The Story of a Band and their Music* is particularly perceptive in its musicological analysis, suggests that a model for Zeppelin's arrangement was Big Brother & The Holding

Company's 1968 version of George Gershwin's 'Summertime' with its quiet, semi-whispered passages and interludes of screaming guitars and pounding drums. This has the ring of truth, for there are also obvious similarities between Janis Joplin's bravura vocal on the Big Brother track and Plant's performance, right down to the "baby, baby, baby" mannerisms.

The song was initially credited as "traditional, arranged by Jimmy Page". Rumours persist that there is an earlier unreleased version of the song recorded by the guitarist with Steve Winwood on vocals. In the 1980s, the song was re-credited to the American folk singer Anne Bredon, who, it transpired, had composed the song in the late 1950s. For once the failure to credit was not Zeppelin's fault: they genuinely didn't know who had written the song, for Baez's recording contained no composer credit and the liner note which described it as "a white blues, a form which was created in

LED ZEPPELIN

10

our century by the meeting of the Southern lyrical lament and the Negro blues" further suggested a composition in the public domain.

2. DAZED AND CONFUSED
RECORDED OCTOBER 1968;
AVAILABLE ON LED ZEPPELIN

Jimmy Page first heard this song one night in the autumn of 1967 at a folk club in New York's Greenwich Village while on tour with The Yardbirds. He and other members of the band had turned up at the Cafe Au Go Go to see Janis Ian, whose song 'Society's Child (Baby, I've Been Thinking)' was a big hit at the time, but arrived early and caught the support act, Jake Holmes, singing a song called 'Dazed and Confused', in which he described a bad acid trip to the accompaniment of droning guitar and a sinister-sounding descending bass scale. Page was impressed enough to seek out the album from which it came, *The Above Ground Sound of Jake Holmes*, and adapted the song for The Yardbirds, with Keith Relf reworking the lyrics. The band called their version 'I'm Confused' and worked it into their live set but never recorded the song. Page then put it forward for inclusion on the first Zeppelin album.

The arrangement opens with a superb walking bass line from Jones, Page rings some tortured and menacing effects out of his guitar by attacking it with a violin bow, and Plant turns in an open-throated falsetto vocal that perfectly suits the song's anguished lyrics. The performance can now be recognized as a key milestone in the development of so-called "heavy rock" and became a cornerstone of their live show.

3. COMMUNICATION BREAKDOWN
RECORDED OCTOBER 1968;
AVAILABLE ON LED ZEPPELIN

One of the all-time great Zeppelin anthems, 'Communication Breakdown' was first developed by the band while touring Scandinavia in September 1968. Like 'Dazed and Confused', the song deals with themes of disorientation and alienation, but in contrast to that six-minute-plus epic, everything here is done and dusted inside two-and-a-half minutes. The inspiration for the song may owe something to Eddie Cochran's 'Nervous Breakdown' and it has a simple pop structure built around three chords. The track is driven by the insistent, repeated guitar riff from Page and reaches its climax around Plant's cry of "suck it!" as the guitar screeches from one speaker to the other. An example of how brevity could suit Led Zeppelin, 'Communication Breakdown' was the number the band chose to play on their only ever live UK television appearance, in March 1969. The song remained a near constant in their set until the final 1980 tour and was often used over the years as a rabble-rousing encore.

4. BLACK MOUNTAIN SIDE
RECORDED OCTOBER 1968;
AVAILABLE ON LED ZEPPELIN

Away from the bludgeoning riffs and screaming electric guitar lines, Jimmy Page was a subtle and sophisticated exponent of acoustic guitar finger-picking, much influenced by the likes of Bert Jansch and Davy Graham. 'Black Mountain Side' was his take on a tune called 'Blackwater Side', which he learned from Jansch's 1966 album, *Jack Orion*, although the tune's origins were more complicated. In fact, Jansch had learned the song from the folk singer Anne

Briggs, adapting her vocal performance into a virtuoso guitar piece. Briggs in turn had got it from the noted folk song collector AL Lloyd, and when she discovered Led Zeppelin had adapted the piece she suggested that some of the royalties should be given not to her, but to Lloyd's widow.

Using a 12-string Gibson guitar, Page adds some frenetic improvisation with an almost sitar-like sound, and the Eastern feel is emphasised by the tabla playing of Viram Jasani, who today runs the Asian Music Circuit, the main body promoting Asian music in the UK. Oddly, Page and Jansch only got to meet for the first time in 1996. "He's a very good acoustic player." Jansch says. "He's always liked the folk thing but he leans a lot on other players apart from me. I don't think there was anything schizophrenic about Led Zeppelin playing acoustic music or using traditional tunes. In those days, everybody was trying to put different sounds together. Davy Graham probably started those fusions. He was very into Eastern music and then he crossed it with the blues. Jimmy Page was doing a similar thing."

5. HOW MANY MORE TIMES
RECORDED OCTOBER 1968;
AVAILABLE ON LED ZEPPELIN

The final track on Led Zeppelin's debut album was also the closing number of the band's early live shows. The song's archetypal, pile-driving blues riff owes something to Albert King's 'The Hunter' and the track also has antecedents in The Yardbirds' version of 'Smokestack Lightning'' and in the rhythm used in 'Beck's Bolero', written by Page and recorded with Jeff Beck in 1966. It later featured on The Jeff Beck Group's 1968 album *Truth*, a record which rivals Led Zeppelin's

debut as one of the foundation stones of heavy rock. 'How Many More Times' is one of Page's finest constructions on the first album, from the dramatic opening and the clever use of wah-wah to the manically eerie effects created by the use of the violin bow. Each change in the tempo and dynamics of the song is driven not by the rhythm section but primarily by the guitar, although this is done with impressive subtlety as Page cleverly avoids the usual axe-hero histrionics. Plant's vocal embellishments, which find him dropping in lines from 'Rosie' and 'The Hunter', were apparently ad-libbed in the studio during the session, as was his "Little Robert Anthony wants to come and play" line – although it's hard to imagine him today getting away with "I got a little schoolgirl and she's all mine."

6. WHOLE LOTTA LOVE
RECORDED SUMMER 1969;
AVAILABLE ON LED ZEPPELIN II

The signature tune that even 'Stairway to Heaven' never wholly displaced. The distinctive three-note opening blues riff played on bass and guitar must be one of the most memorable intros in rock – even if it was closely modelled on Muddy Waters' recording of Willie Dixon's 'You Need Love'. The late Steve Marriott went to his grave believing that Zeppelin had taken the idea from a number he sung with The Small Faces called 'You Need Loving', and which was also derived from Dixon's song. Yet whatever the antecedents and the rights and wrongs over songwriting credits, there's no doubt that Page and Plant take the track into previously uncharted territory. From the opening "you need coolin', baby I ain't foolin'", it's evident this is a supercharged, self-confident Plant who is rapidly overcoming any nerves

LED ZEPPELIN

10

he may have displayed on the debut album. Bonham plays his part too, with a staggering syncopated pattern that ricochets between snares, tom-toms, hi-hat and bass drum. It's also his hi-hat and cymbals that introduce the track's famously experimental middle section on which Page used a theremin, an early electronic instrument first patented in the 1920s by the Russian inventor after whom it is named and which was used to great effect by The Beach Boys on 'Good Vibrations'. Its spiralling, high-pitched tone careers from speaker to speaker as Plant overlays an orgasmic vocal, which then develops into a dialogue with Page's guitar. Many of the effects of the middle section Page later credited to engineer Eddie Kramer: "I told him exactly what I wanted to achieve and he absolutely helped me to get it," he said. "We already had a lot of the sound on tape, including the theremin and slide with backwards echo but his knowledge of low-frequency oscillation helped complete the effect. If he hadn't known how to do that I would have had to try for something else." The track's enduring power is evinced in the fact that 11 years after it was recorded, it was the last track Led Zeppelin ever performed live, when it was given a 17-minute work-out at their final gig in Berlin on July 7, 1980.

7. WHAT IS AND WHAT SHOULD NEVER BE

RECORDED SUMMER 1969;
AVAILABLE ON LED ZEPPELIN II

One of Plant's very first efforts as a lyricist, according to Richard Cole, the song was about a romance the singer apparently had behind his wife's back. He'd like to give up his present life and start a new one ("sail away, leave today"), but in his married state that's impossible ("the wind won't blow, you

really shouldn't go") – hence 'What Is and What Should Never Be'.

Whatever the inspiration, the lovely, dreamy, semi-whispered verses, which owe a debt to Julie Driscoll's version of Donovan's 'Seasons of the Witch', are driven by an inventive counter-melody played on the bass by Jones, and are dynamically contrasted with some kicking drums and a crashing guitar riff. However, Page's main solo (which found him using for the first time the Gibson Les Paul with which he would become so associated) has a pleasingly gentle and understated late-night quality. In another production triumph for the Page-Kramer team, the guitars pan thrillingly back and forth between the two channels and Plant's vocals are also impressively phased in places.

8. THE LEMON SONG

RECORDED JUNE 1969;
AVAILABLE ON LED ZEPPELIN II

One of the most notorious songs in Zeppelin's canon due to its blatant sexual innuendo, 'The Lemon Song' has its roots in Howlin' Wolf's 'Killing Floor' and, following legal action for breach of copyright, the bluesman's name later had to be added to the writing credit. The name of Robert Johnson also comes to mind, for the infamous line "squeeze my lemon 'til the juice runs down my leg" was taken from his 'Travelling Riverside Blues', which Zeppelin performed in a BBC Radio 1 session in 1969. There's also a debt to Albert King's 'Crosscut Saw', all of which help to make it one of the band's dirtiest and rawest-sounding blues outings. The song is given a contemporary flavour by Jones' funk-influenced bass line, although some have accused him of over-playing. The track was recorded more or less live in the studio, with Plant once again indulging in some considerable ad-libbing.

9. **THANK YOU**

RECORDED SUMMER 1969;
AVAILABLE ON LED ZEPPELIN II

Another of Plant's early lyric-writing efforts, if 'What Is and What Should Never Be' was about an illicit extra-marital love affair, 'Thank You' represents the other side of the coin – a heartfelt love song to wedded bliss and his wife Maureen, which finds him emotionally claiming "you to me are the only one". Movingly sung, and with Plant sounding surprisingly like Rod Stewart in places, it's one of the loveliest moments on the album, with Page's delicate picking on a Rickenbacker acoustic 12-string strongly underpinned by Jones' haunting Hammond part, which seems to owe something to Chris Stainton's organ-playing on Joe Cocker's 'With a Little Help from My Friends'. Often used live in the early days as a showcase for Jones' organ-playing, it was regularly used as an encore on the 1972-73 tours and was revived by Page and Plant when they were on tour together in the mid-1990s.

10. **HEARTBREAKER**

RECORDED SUMMER 1969;
AVAILABLE ON LED ZEPPELIN II

Opening with another blues-influenced riff, 'Heartbreaker' contains a typical Plant lyric about an "evil" woman well versed in "the wicked ways of love" but is primarily a platform for Page's guitar virtuosity. The unaccompanied solo he plays some two minutes in is a piece of blatant but glorious showing-off, although critics are divided about its merit. According to Dave Lewis, it's "a breathtaking exercise in string-bending",

but Keith Shadwick reckons that it's one of Page's poorest solos, concluding that, "He frequently stumbles in execution at speed and repeats time-worn fingerboard patterns rather than attempting anything fresh." It's an excessively harsh critique of a track that is an established and long-standing favourite with most fans. The track also became a live staple, with Page at different times adventurously incorporating into the song's basic structure snippets of everything from Bach's 'Lute Suite in E minor' to Simon & Garfunkel's 'The 59th Street Bridge Song'. At different times it was a show opener and an encore and it was still part of the set in 1980. It had the honour of being one of the five songs chosen for their reunion at Atlantic's 40th birthday gig in New York in 1988.

11. **RAMBLE ON**

RECORDED SUMMER 1969;
AVAILABLE ON LED ZEPPELIN II

Even more than 'What Is and What Should Never Be' or 'Thank You', 'Ramble On' sign-posted the way to the more ethereal sound that would come to the fore on *Led Zeppelin III*. The folk-rock combination of acoustic and electric guitars is much in the vein of something Fairport Convention might have recorded at the time, while the unusual bongo-like sound of Bonham's drums was reportedly obtained by him hitting a plastic garbage pail. Plant's vocals move effortlessly up the gears as the softly delivered narrative of the verses gives way to the high-octane punch of the chorus on a set of lyrics that are a jumble of images and characters from *The Lord of the Rings*. The track also features a wonderful double-tracked guitar solo from Page, with a tone quite unlike anything else on the album. Oddly, the song was never performed live.

LED ZEPPELIN

10

12. MOBY DICK

RECORDED SUMMER 1969;
AVAILABLE ON LED ZEPPELIN II

Drum solos have a bad name in rock music and will be forever associated with Spinal Tap banality and macho rock-boorishness. John Bonham's contribution to the genre was 'Moby Dick', on record a relatively crisp four minutes twenty-one seconds of inventive percussion, book-ended by a killer Page guitar riff that he didn't have any other use for (although it became the theme tune of the BBC2 music show *Disco 2*) and which was allegedly adapted from a blues tune by Sleepy John Estes. Bonham's percussive storm in the middle was assembled by Page and Kramer from a series of edits. "I didn't actually sit there and play a solo especially for the record," the drummer explained. "They just pieced it together."

Live, 'Moby Dick' was a different and far longer story. Originally known in early set lists as 'Pat's Delight' in honour of Bonham's wife, the drum showcase was retitled 'Moby Dick' in mid-1969 and stayed in the set until 1977, when it was renamed 'Over the Top' and reconfigured using the riff of 'Out on the Tiles', rather than the *Disco 2* theme. According to the writer and broadcaster Andrew Collins, the birth of punk in 1976 was "fanned by discontent at rising unemployment, industrial unrest and a 30-minute Led Zeppelin drum solo at Earls Court". Bonham performed 'Moby Dick' at every one of their five nights at the venue the previous year, and although the average length was probably nearer 20 minutes than half-an-hour, you know what Collins means.

13. IMMIGRANT SONG

RECORDED SUMMER 1970;
AVAILABLE ON LED ZEPPELIN III

A classic up-tempo rocker to kick off an album that included so many gentler, semi-acoustic flavours, 'Immigrant Song' is one of Zeppelin's most brutal assaults, from Plant's banshee war cry to the sonic assault of Page's martial riff. Keith Shadwick reckons Plant's wail is a repetition of the opening notes of 'Bali Hai' from Rodgers and Hammerstein's *South Pacific* and that the galloping guitar-drums rhythm is a cousin to Jimi Hendrix's 'Little Miss Lover'. The latter seems more probable than the former.

The lyrics were in part inspired by the band's visit in June 1970 to Iceland ("the land of the ice and snow") as part of a cultural exchange sponsored by the British government. They were apparently written by Plant with tongue somewhat in cheek, but few got the humour and the line "The hammer of the gods will drive our ships to new lands" was picked up by fans to give the band an Olympian nickname, which was used many years later by the writer Stephen Davis as the title of his salacious biography. Elsewhere, the imagery of Viking war and invasion dominates, although as an inveterate old hippie, Plant cannot resist ending the song by insisting that after all the rape and pillage, "peace and trust" will win the day. The song opened every Zeppelin concert from 1970 to 1972 and was released as a single in America, where it rose to number 16 on the *Billboard* chart.

14. GALLOWS POLE

RECORDED SUMMER 1970;
AVAILABLE ON LED ZEPPELIN III

The American folk-blues singer Huddie Ledbetter – better known as Lead Belly – popularized the traditional folk song 'Gallows Pole' in the 1930s, but the recording that inspired Jimmy Page to record it with Led Zeppelin was a later version by the 12-string guitarist Fred Gerlach on the Folkways label.

"We have completely rearranged it and changed the verse," Plant said at the time of the release of *Led Zeppelin III*. "That's John Paul Jones on mandolin and bass and I'm playing the banjo, six-string acoustic, 12-string, and that's Robert doing the harmonies as well as the lead."

One of the songs worked up by Page and Plant during their stay at the cottage in Bron-Yr-Aur, the rewrite is less comprehensive than the guitarist has suggested, for the song is still instantly recognizable as the one sung by Lead Belly, and most of the details of the narrative are still in place. Nevertheless, it's a wonderful reinterpretation, brilliantly executed as the tension builds powerfully as the different instruments come in, and Page caps it with a fine, understated electric guitar solo towards the end which cleverly mimics the phrasing of a saxophone. Rhythmically, the final section bears a strong resemblance to Traffic's 'You Can All Join In'.

15. **TANGERINE**
RECORDED SUMMER 1970;
AVAILABLE ON LED ZEPPELIN III
On one level, 'Tangerine' is one of the slighter pieces on *Led Zeppelin III* but it's a lovely song and occupies an interesting place in the band's history. When it began life as a joint Jimmy Page and Keith Relf composition in The Yardbirds, it was called 'Knowing that I'm Losing You'. The song was recorded by the band in New York in early 1968 but never released. When Zeppelin recorded the song as 'Tangerine' two years later it appeared with a sole Jimmy Page writing credit, although according to Yardbirds historian Greg Russo the lyrics were little changed from those which Relf had written. The song also points the way to the future, for the

mock-Renaissance style acoustic guitar intro can be seen as an early template for 'Stairway to Heaven'. Plant's double-tracked vocal is highly effective and the track is lifted out of its mid-1960s pop feel by the addition of some lovely pedal steel from Page. The song was often performed as part of the band's acoustic set, and at Earls Court in 1975 was unveiled in a revamped version with harmony vocals and Page on the famous double-necked Gibson.

16. **THAT'S THE WAY**
RECORDED SUMMER 1970;
AVAILABLE ON LED ZEPPELIN III
First known when it was written at the cottage in Bron-Yr-Aur as 'The Boy Next Door', 'That's the Way' is arguably the loveliest of all the gentler numbers on *Led Zeppelin III*. Opening with a simple acoustic guitar, Page soon introduces his newest toy, the pedal steel, while Plant abandons his usual high-energy delivery for a simple, conversational style, augmented by Crosby, Stills and Nash-style harmonies at one point. The lyrics, which Dave Lewis rates as among the best Plant ever penned, concern a pair of star-crossed lovers with the singer at one point philosophically noting that "all that lives is born to die". Page again makes his instrument sound horn-like on a wistful track notable for the total absence of drums. Unsurprisingly, it became a highlight of their acoustic set in the early 1970s.

17. **BRON-Y-AUR STOMP**
RECORDED SUMMER 1970;
AVAILABLE ON LED ZEPPELIN III
As its title suggests, no song on *Led Zeppelin III* evokes the folky, fireside jamming that Page and

LED ZEPPELIN

10

Plant enjoyed in their Welsh cottage better than this piece of light-hearted acoustic fun. There's an irresistible jubilation to this recording that makes it easy to understand why the band chose to include it on the album rather than 'Jennings Farm Blues', an electric take of the same song recorded around the same time. Page's virtuoso finger-picking at the song's commencement is borrowed from Bert Jansch's arrangement of the traditional 'The Waggoner's Lad' and it fits perfectly with Plant's lyric about the joys of rural life and walking the country lanes with his dog, Strider. Jones plays a fretless acoustic bass and Bonham joins in the fun on spoons and castanets. Perhaps very few fans would list 'Bron-Y-Aur Stomp' in their top ten Zeppelin tracks and, on its release, those who had hoped for an entire album of head-banging riffs like 'Immigrant Song' must have shaken their bonces in bafflement. Nevertheless, its spirit, humour and *joie de vivre* are unstoppable.

Incidentally, the band consistently misspelt the name of their Welsh bolt-hole, which is correctly called Bron-Yr-Aur.

18. SINCE I'VE BEEN LOVING YOU
RECORDED SUMMER 1970;
AVAILABLE ON LED ZEPPELIN III
Amid all the mighty riffs, it's often overlooked that Led Zeppelin were also a magnificent straight blues band, particularly in their element on the slower, moodier material. Nowhere is this more evident than on 'Since I've Been Loving You'. Each of the four members is at a peak here, and the interplay between them is extraordinary, with Plant's voice effectively operating as the fourth instrument. Jones' Hammond organ is unbelievably atmospheric (with the bass part played on the organ pedals) and Bonham locks down deep into the groove.

Page unleashes one of his most inventive solos, rooted in Chicago blues but elongated and expanded in a fashion that perhaps only Hendrix and Duane Allman were similarly capable of at the time (and prefaced by an entirely justifiable shout of "watch out!" from Plant, whose vocals scream and plead with awesome power). When it comes to British blues, you can forget about John Mayall, Chicken Shack, Savoy Brown and the rest: this is how it should be done.

19. BLACK DOG
RECORDED JANUARY–FEBRUARY 1971;
AVAILABLE ON LED ZEPPELIN IV
It was obligatory to kick off Zeppelin albums with a mighty surge of power and 'Black Dog' is up there with the best of them. The initial idea for the riff came to John Paul Jones one day after he and Jimmy Page had been listening to Muddy Waters' 1968 album, *Electric Mud*. A complicated series of changing patterns and time signatures were then added by Page so that the only way Plant can fit in one of his most carnal vocals is as a call-and-response with the bass and guitar riff, an idea that he later admitted was copied from Fleetwood Mac's 'Oh Well'. The fact that this means most of his vocals are sung unaccompanied between the instrumental fills only adds to the track's drama. Page layers up to four guitars and Bonham plays a remarkable rhythm that turns around and sounds as if it's likely to implode at any minute under its complexity, but instead explodes out of the speakers with bludgeoning force. In the face of all this musical mayhem and a classic Plant lyric about a mean, mistreating woman, it seems almost banal to add that the beast in the title with the "eyes that shine burning red" belonged to a dog that followed Plant around

10

when they were recording at Headley Grange.

20. ROCK AND ROLL
RECORDED JANUARY-FEBRUARY 1971;
AVAILABLE ON LED ZEPPELIN IV

A simple title for one of the most frenzied, swashbuckling tracks Zeppelin ever recorded, the genesis of 'Rock and Roll' lay in Bonham fooling around with the riff played by drummer Earl Palmer on Little Richard's hits 'Good Golly Miss Molly' and 'Keep a-Knockin'' during a jam at Headley Grange that included Rolling Stones alumnus Ian Stewart on piano. Page added the Chuck Berry-influenced guitar riff and within 15 minutes the track was delivered at full tilt. Plant hastily concocted a lyric and 'Rock and Roll' was used either as a set opener or an encore at almost every live show the band played until the end.

21. THE BATTLE OF EVERMORE
RECORDED JANUARY–FEBRUARY 1971;
AVAILABLE ON LED ZEPPELIN IV

Originally conceived by Page as an instrumental after he picked up Jones' mandolin late one night at Headley Grange, the ultimate realization of 'The Battle of Evermore' owes much to Plant and his admiration for folk-tinged groups such as Pentangle, The Incredible String Band and, of course, Fairport Convention, whose Sandy Denny duets on the track. The mandolin lends an ethereal quality and the combined voices of Plant and Denny work so well together that one regrets it is the only Zeppelin track to feature an outside voice. The lyric reflects Plant's fascination with the history of the ancient border wars fought between the English and their Scottish neighbours, although his ongoing fascination with *The Lord of the Rings* is also evident. The only downside is the malign influence the song has exerted on lesser bands; Andy Fyfe, in his book *When the Levee Breaks: The Making of Led Zeppelin IV*, blames 'The Battle of Evermore' for "much of the wizards and demons nonsense that many metal bands felt compelled to record in its wake".

The song was only ever played live by Led Zeppelin on a handful of dates on the 1977 tour, when John Paul Jones sang the Sandy Denny part, but it was revived in radically different form in 1994 by Page and Plant for *No Quarter*, with the British-Asian singer Najma Akhtar on vocals.

22. STAIRWAY TO HEAVEN
RECORDED JANUARY–FEBRUARY
1971; AVAILABLE ON LED ZEPPELIN IV

They say familiarity breeds contempt and Robert Plant is among those who have grown to hate 'Stairway to Heaven', damning it with faint praise as a "nice, pleasant, well-meaning, naïve little song". Yet overexposure cannot cloud the fact that 'Stairway to Heaven' is not only a benchmark in rock history but a staggering piece of music. Page had been working on the chord progression for some time and, according to Jones, the music was one of only two pieces brought to the Headley Grange sessions in early 1971 in anything like complete form – indeed, an instrumental version had first been essayed at Island Studios in December 1970. The song was swiftly developed: one night sitting around the fire at Headley Grange with Page (Jones and Bonham had taken the night off to attend a party at The Speakeasy in London), Plant found the lyrics pouring out. "I was holding a pencil and paper and for some reason I was in a very bad mood,"

10

he recalls. "Then all of a sudden my hand was writing out the words, 'There's a lady who's sure all that glitters is gold and she's buying a stairway to heaven'. I just sat there and looked at the words and then I almost leapt out of my seat." Within a couple of days Jones had added his multi-tracked recorders and the song was lifted to another level with the much-delayed entry of Bonham's drums. Although all of these elements came together very quickly, Page took the track away to add his guitar solo later at Island Studios.

Atlantic were desperate to put out the track as a single, but Grant and the band dug in their heels and refused to sanction its release. Plant may today be embarrassed by the fey mysticism and inchoate hippie fairy-tale of the lyric, but at the time he was proud enough to have the words printed on the album's inner sleeve, the first time Zeppelin had taken such a step. Since the band's demise, he has consistently refused to sing the song, although Page has been happy to celebrate its legacy in concert as an instrumental piece. Jones has also professed his continued affection for the song. "Everything built nicely," he says. "Both Jimmy and I were quite aware of the way a track should unfold and the various levels that it would go through."

23. MISTY MOUNTAIN HOP
RECORDED JANUARY–FEBRUARY 1971; AVAILABLE ON LED ZEPPELIN IV

At the time of *Led Zeppelin IV's* release, 'Misty Mountain Hop' tended to get overshadowed by some of the more obviously attention-grabbing songs such as 'Black Dog' and 'Stairway to Heaven'. Over the years, however, it has emerged as a much-loved classic, revived at band reunions and regularly performed by Plant in his solo

career. Driven by a bouncing electric piano part from Jones and a swinging drum beat from Bonham, the title again references *The Lord of the Rings*, although the subject matter is located elsewhere. One of the very few Zeppelin lyrics specifically to mention drugs, the song finds the singer walking through the park and being offered some pot by a bunch of hippies, whereupon the police show up and bust them. Plant once introduced the song on stage in America as "being caught in the park with wrong stuff in your cigarette papers". There has been much speculation that the inspiration came from a pro-cannabis rally in London's Hyde Park in July 1968 and/or an incident in Golden Gate Park, San Francisco.

24. GOING TO CALIFORNIA
RECORDED JANUARY–FEBRUARY 1971; AVAILABLE ON LED ZEPPELIN IV

Robert Plant's admiration for Joni Mitchell knew no bounds, and it all flowed out on 'Going to California'. With Page contributing some deft acoustic guitar and Jones on mandolin, Plant sings about "a girl out there with love in her eyes and flowers in her hair" and there's no doubt who he had in mind. "When you're in love with Joni Mitchell, you've really got to write about it now and again," he noted. However, the song also references the darker side of West Coast existence, living on a fault line with the constant threat of earthquakes – indeed Page and Peter Grant experienced a minor tremor when mixing the album in L.A. Stranded in the drab surroundings of the West Midlands, for Plant the hippie tribes who took over Haight-Ashbury in San Francisco in 1967 were "the children of the sun", and his wistful longing to join them received lyrical recognition here. His romantic attachment to the time never really left him, and four years after the so-called "Summer of Love" he introduced the song at a concert in Berkeley, California, in 1971 by saying: "Here's to the days when things were really nice and simple and everything was far out, all the time."

25. WHEN THE LEVEE BREAKS

RECORDED JANUARY–FEBRUARY 1971;
AVAILABLE ON LED ZEPPELIN IV

In 1927, the Mississippi River burst its banks and flooded an area of 27,000 square miles. It was the worst flood disaster in American history, and in some places the flood waters were 30 feet deep and the swollen river was 60 miles wide. Two years later, the blues singer Memphis Minnie and her husband Kansas Joe McCoy recorded 'When the Levee Breaks', which described the events in graphic terms. Led Zeppelin's version is one of their most towering achievements. The performance is driven by Bonham's remorseless, bone-crunching backbeat, recorded in the hall at Headley Grange with a single microphone. Page contributes some slashing slide guitar, Plant blows a mean harp and the mixing desk adds phasing, backward loops and echo to create a terrifying maelstrom of sound.

Andy Fyfe, author of a fine book about the making of *Led Zeppelin IV*, credits the track with helping "to give rise to an entire genre of music" when rap DJs began cutting up Bonham's sledgehammer beat and grafting it on to endless hip-hop tracks. One of the most prominent was its use by producer Rick Rubin on 'Rhymin' & Stealin'', the opening track of the Beastie Boys' landmark 1986 album *Licensed to Ill*. 'When the Levee Breaks' has since become one of the two most sampled drum beats in musical history, alongside James Brown's 'Funky Drummer'. According to Fyfe, "The simple

fact is that without Bonham and 'When the Levee Breaks', there would be no hip-hop as we know it." Plant was amused by the track's use, noting: "When Jimmy and I talked about it, we figured nothing was sacred as we'd been nicking old blues stuff since the beginning of time." Certainly, there is a delicious irony that a group so often accused of stealing from the blues should years later be credited with having indirectly helped to toughen up a new genre of black American music.

26. THE SONG REMAINS THE SAME

RECORDED SUMMER 1972;
AVAILABLE ON HOUSES OF THE HOLY

Originally conceived by Jimmy Page as an instrumental piece called simply 'The Overture', after Plant had added a lyric the song was given the working title 'The Campaign' before it eventually emerged as 'The Song Remains the Same'. The instrumental origins of the piece are evident in the fact that it's a minute-and-a-half before Plant's vocal enters, more than a quarter of the way through the track. When his voice does arrive, his singing has been slightly speeded up. The overall effect is rather Beatlesesque, with Page's shimmering, multi-tracked guitars displaying a strong Eastern flavour, of the kind often favoured by George Harrison. The lyric also makes the connection between East and West, from "California sunlight" to "sweet Calcutta rain" and from Hare Krishna to the Hoochie Coo.

27. THE RAIN SONG

RECORDED SUMMER 1972;
AVAILABLE ON HOUSES OF THE HOLY

Despite the acoustic tracks on previous albums, the opening moments of 'The Rain Song' hardly

10

sound like a Led Zeppelin song at all. There's a sweet, minor-key melody that might almost have come from the pen of Burt Bacharach, while the string arrangement (coaxed by Jones out of a mellotron) sounds, as Shadwick puts it, "as if The Moody Blues had crashed the party". Some of Page's guitar work sounds tropical-Hawaiian, further emphasising the easy-listening vibe. Yet at the same time, 'The Rain Song' is also extraordinarily beautiful, and evidence that Led Zeppelin still retained the capacity to surprise.

Whenever 'The Rain Song' was played by the band live, it invariably segued out of 'The Song Remains the Same', the song that also preceded it on the album, reinforcing the notion that side one of *Houses of the Holy* was conceived as a suite of songs rather than a series of unconnected individual compositions.

28. OVER THE HILLS AND FAR AWAY
RECORDED SUMMER 1972;
AVAILABLE ON HOUSES OF THE HOLY

The third track on *Houses of the Holy* also has musical themes and motifs in common with the tracks which precede it. The acoustic guitar opening recalls 'White Summer', the showcase that Page had worked up in The Yardbirds. Then the song changes direction with a potent guitar and bass riff and Bonham is allowed to unleash his full battery for the first time on the album. The title offers the perfect vehicle for Plant to indulge his romantic fancies and there's a touch of Donovan about his lyrics as he sings of his wanderlust and a quest of discovery. Some fans have taken the line a "pocketful of gold" to refer to Acapulco gold, a particularly fine strain of cannabis grown in Mexico which the

band enjoyed smoking while on tour in America. Pot heads are prone to finding unintended references to their drug of choice in all sorts of unintended places, but for once they may be right. Certainly the suggestion that Plant was simply talking about a love of money doesn't quite fit with the romantic yearnings expressed in the rest of the song.

29. DANCING DAYS
RECORDED SUMMER 1972;
AVAILABLE ON HOUSES OF THE HOLY

When Zeppelin listened to the playback of this song, recorded at Mick Jagger's country home Stargroves, according to engineer Eddie Kramer they danced on the lawn in delight. It's easy to hear why with a joyous, summery tune that may have been inspired by something Page and Plant heard while in Bombay several months earlier. Its high spirits are blissfully unselfconscious with one of Plant's wittiest, most playful lyrics: "I told your mama I'd get you home but I didn't tell her I had no car" might have come from the pen of Chuck Berry himself. Keith Shadwick reckons the melody line is "disappointing" and the piece sounds "uneasy" but is surely in a minority of one as the rest of us are out there on the grass gleefully dancing with the band to the most enjoyable track on the entire album.

30. NO QUARTER
RECORDED SUMMER 1972;
AVAILABLE ON HOUSES OF THE HOLY

John Paul Jones gets a rare, and deserved, lead namecheck in the credits for this atmospheric, keyboard-led, piece which had first been tried at Headley Grange while the band were recording *Led Zeppelin IV*. With the tempo slowed down and the addition of synthesised bass, it took on a far more mysterious feel, emphasised by a heavily treated Plant vocal. Jones' piano is stark almost to the point of austere, but it fits the mood perfectly and leads into a superb, jazzy solo from Page – or rather two solos which offer answering phrases from different channels. The lyrics find Plant at his most oblique. The references to the "winds of Thor" hark back to 'Immigrant Song', while "walking side by side with death, the devil mocks their every step" might have come from some ghastly death metal band. No matter, for it's still one of the album's highlights, and the track became a live favourite and was featured as a marathon Jones showcase at every show from 1973 through to Knebworth in 1979.

You can understand why it rankled with Jones when Page and Plant used the title of one of his finest compositional moments in the band for their 1994 reunion album *Unledded*, without even telling him they were getting back together, let alone inviting him to join them.

31. **THE OCEAN**
RECORDED SUMMER 1972;
AVAILABLE ON HOUSES OF THE HOLY

One of Page's most virile riffs opens the final song on *Houses of the Holy* after Bonham's voice has introduced the track by saying: "We've done four already but now we're steady, and then they went...one, two, three, four." However, overall the kick feels oddly restrained, as did much of the material recorded at Stargroves, leading some to suggest that Jagger's house was simply not suited to record the band to best effect. Towards the end of the track, the mood and tempo changes completely, with a doo-wop chorus as Plant declares "so good!" Elsewhere, the track alternates effectively between vocal

and non-vocal passages, with a lyric that makes an analogy between the ocean and the sea of faces in the audience at a Zeppelin concert. He ends up, however, singing not to the band's fans but to his three-year-old daughter Carmen, "the girl who won my heart". It was another riff that the Beastie Boys chose to sample, this time on 'She's Crafty' on their *Licensed to Ill* album.

32. **CUSTARD PIE**
RECORDED SUMMER 1974;
AVAILABLE ON PHYSICAL GRAFFITI

The title suggests more knockabout nonsense in the vein of 'D'yer Mak'er' and 'The Crunge', but the opening track on *Physical Graffiti* might almost have come from Zeppelin's debut album, and after the underachievement of *Houses of the Holy* the band could hardly have devised a more forceful way of announcing that it was business as usual once again. A killer Page riff warped and twisted out of a Bo Diddley beat is swiftly joined by some brutal Bonham drumming and it hardly seems mere coincidence that, as soon as they were back at Headley Grange, Zeppelin suddenly sounded heavier and more like their old selves again. A more contemporary mid-1970s feel comes from Jones' use of a clavinet, as popularised by Stevie Wonder, and Page's delivery of a piercing solo through an ARP synthesiser, while Plant delves back to Bukka White's 'Shake 'Em on Down' for his lyrical inspiration, although his vocals sound more strained than back in '68–'69 and clearly display the wearing and tearing of endless touring and screaming. Yet the effect is not entirely detrimental, adding a more mature, world-weary tone in keeping with Zeppelin's new-found status as elder statesmen of rock – Plant was now 27 years old, after all.

LED ZEPPELIN

10

33. IN MY TIME OF DYING
RECORDED SUMMER 1974;
AVAILABLE ON PHYSICAL GRAFFITI
Standing alongside 'When the Levee Breaks'
as one of Zeppelin's most monumental
transformations of a pre-war acoustic blues
song into an electric tumult, 'In My Time
of Dying' was first recorded by Blind
Willie Johnson in 1927 as 'Jesus Make Up
My Dying Bed' and was later popularized by
Bob Dylan on his debut album under the title
used on *Physical Graffiti*. The performance
is Zeppelin at their most intense, Bonham
creating a train-like backbeat, Page riffing
furiously and articulating some glorious
slide guitar and Plant delivering one of his
best, beseeching blues vocals with plenty
of spontaneous improvisation. At 11 minutes
plus, it is arguably overlong and yet it
doesn't feel so while listening. When it does
finally conclude, Bonham is heard coughing
and saying, "That's got to be the one, hasn't
it?" The reason for including the studio
chatter, according to Page, was to show the
world that Zeppelin weren't remote rock
gods but a working band.

34. TRAMPLED UNDER FOOT
RECORDED SUMMER 1974;
AVAILABLE ON PHYSICAL GRAFFITI
Most agree that Zeppelin's first attempt
at a James Brown-style funk riff on 'The
Crunge' was a failure, not least because it was
conceived as a joke and ended up sounding
like a pastiche or, even worse, a piss-take
of black music. 'Trampled Under Foot' is a
much more serious and successful visitation
of similar territory. Jones opens proceedings
with the clavinet and Page's guitar riff makes
innovative use of backwards echo and wah-
wah. Jones returns halfway through with a
thrillingly funky keyboard solo that paints

Zeppelin as disco dance-floor kings. Plant's
vocal is slightly too far back in the mix on
a lyric that makes a connection familiar in
blues poetry between a motor car and the
sexual act and for which Robert Johnson's
'Terraplane Blues' may have been the model.
Zeppelin at their most urgent and irresistible.

35. KASHMIR
RECORDED SUMMER 1974;
AVAILABLE ON PHYSICAL GRAFFITI
In addition to their attempt at recording in
India in 1972, Page and Plant were regular
visitors to Morocco and their fascination
with Arabic and Asian music reached its
apogee on the mighty 'Kashmir'. "Kashmir
from my angle was written on the road to
Tan-Tan in southern Morocco, just off the
Atlantic coast." Plant revealed almost 30 years
later. "It's a place where your mind can really
dance and where your imagination is way
open. After a while all the stuff you've ever
thought about has gone and you've got this
whole different view."
   Originally titled 'Driving to Kashmir',
the music came out of a jam between Page
and Bonham in late 1973 which, according
to Peter Grant, the band didn't like because
it was "a bit of a dirge". As a result, they
decided to add the Eastern strings and
found the players in a Pakistani orchestra
in Southall, West London. With its use of
Byzantine signatures and motifs not normally
found in standard Western scales, there's a
sense of mystery and ominous tension that
is sustained throughout its eight-and-a-half
minutes. That there is little variety in its
orchestration or dynamics is exactly what
makes it work, the repetition allowing it to
build almost imperceptibly. It's an approach
common in Eastern music but quite radical in
rock 'n' roll, and the result is one of the most

startling and majestic tracks Led Zeppelin ever recorded. Unsurprisingly, it was a highlight of every Led Zeppelin live show from 1975 until the band's demise in 1980 and was an obvious candidate for reinvention on 1994's *No Quarter*, the *Unledded* album. In 1998, Sean "Puff Daddy" Combs sampled the track on 'Come with Me' and performed it on *Saturday Night Live* with Page on guitar via satellite link. "It was a real privilege working with him. He has incredible energy and a great imagination," he reported.

36. **IN THE LIGHT**

RECORDED SUMMER 1974;
AVAILABLE ON PHYSICAL GRAFFITI

Originally called 'In the Morning', Page at one time cited this as his favourite track on *Physical Graffiti*, which is some accolade as he has also said that the album is his favourite in the entire Led Zeppelin canon. Jones takes much of the credit and his drone-like keyboards summon up a similar Eastern vibe to 'Kashmir'. This time, though, the mood of the intro is gentler and more specifically Indian, evoking echoes of some of George Harrison's similarly styled compositions for The Beatles, such as 'Within You Without You' and 'The Inner Light'. After three minutes, however, the tempo changes and Page's guitar introduces a blues-tinged riff, for which Jones also takes much of the credit. "You can always tell my riffs from Page's because mine have got a lot more notes and are linear," he reckons. "His are chunkier and chordier. Anything with chromatic movement would be mine." Plant's lyrics also draw inspiration from Harrison's portfolio of Indian mysticism ("in the light you will find the road") and Page essays a ringing, melodic guitar solo over a lovely descending bass line. The entire piece is marginally longer than 'Kashmir', but never outstays its welcome.

37. **THE WANTON SONG**

RECORDED EARLY 1974;
AVAILABLE ON PHYSICAL GRAFFITI

The Oxford English Dictionary defines wanton as: "licentious; lewd; sexually promiscuous" – all qualities associated in abundance with Led Zeppelin's on-the-road behaviour. Robert Plant has often protested that such stories have been overcooked, but in this lyric he blatantly celebrates wanton sex and the ability to lose one's senses in pure carnality. Musically the track thrusts and grinds suitably with another dynamite Page riff with a machine-gun repeat. The bridge then takes off in another direction completely with a set of unusual chords on which Page's guitar sounds slightly out of tune – an effect that is presumably deliberate.

Oddly, although it was played live on a handful of opening dates on their 1975 American tour, it was swiftly dropped. Was the song not working or had Plant had an earful from his wife for singing lyrics about ladies of the night taking the seed from his shaking frame? Only the singer himself knows.

38. **BLACK COUNTRY WOMAN**

RECORDED SUMMER 1972;
AVAILABLE ON PHYSICAL GRAFFITI

The "Black Country" is defined as the industrial region to the west of Birmingham in the British Midlands, so named in the mid-nineteenth century for the smoke from its foundries and forges and abundance of coal. Its environs were well known to both Plant and Bonham as the place where they had grown up and, although they moved to its more green and pleasant parts, both continued to live in the region.

Originally, the song was subtitled 'Never Ending Doubting Woman Blues', after a line

LED ZEPPELIN

at the end which was eventually left off the released version. Plant's lyric uses classic Delta blues phraseology ("hey hey mama, why you treat me mean") and transfers them to the West Midlands. Is he addressing his wife, Maureen? If so the line "I know your sisters, too" is playing with fire, given that the singer was also said to be sweet on his wife's younger sibling, Shirley.

The song itself is an enjoyable acoustic stomp in the style of 1930s Delta stars The Mississippi Sheikhs and was recorded in the garden of Mick Jagger's Stargroves home in 1972 during the *Houses of the Holy* sessions. At the commencement of the track an aircraft flies overhead and the band can be heard debating whether to leave the sound in or not.

39. SICK AGAIN
RECORDED SUMMER 1974;
AVAILABLE ON PHYSICAL GRAFFITI

Physical Graffiti ends as it began – with a swagger. 'Sick Again' finds Plant revisiting the subject matter of 'The Wanton Song' but with palpable distaste as he sings about the increasingly juvenile groupies who flung themselves at the band, particularly in Los Angeles, derided here as "the city of lies". That the girls are underage is made clear when Plant sings: "One day soon you're gonna reach 16." The singer elaborated in an interview in *Rolling Stone*: "If you listen to 'Sick Again' the words show I feel a bit sorry for them – 'clutching pages from your teenage dream in the lobby of the Hotel Paradise, through the circus of the L.A. queens, how fast you learn the downhill slide'. One minute she's 12, and the next minute she's 13 and over the top. Such a shame."

The track is given a heavy blues-rock muscularity with some battering percussion

from Bonham, and Page laying down a dense mesh of guitars. At the end the drummer can be heard coughing, symbolic no doubt, of the sicknesses and diseases that can so easily be picked up on the road.

40. ACHILLES LAST STAND
RECORDED NOVEMBER–DECEMBER
1975; AVAILABLE ON PRESENCE

In Homer's *Iliad*, Achilles was the mightiest of the Greek heroes who fought in the Trojan War. After being dipped in the sacred waters of the River Styx he was meant to be invincible, but his heel remained dry and therefore was his one vulnerable spot. This fatal chink eventually led to his death when an arrow wounded him in the heel. The story had an obvious attraction to Plant following his broken legs and damaged ankle following his car crash in Greece in 1975, hence the song's title. But work had begun on the piece prior to the accident, when Page and Plant visited Morocco together in the summer of 1975 immediately following the Earls Court shows, and the lyrics reflect upon that trip and their plight as tax exiles.

At more than 10 minutes long it's a magnificent epic with which to announce their return after so much adversity and, as a sonic journey, it invites inevitable comparisons with 'Kashmir' on the previous studio album. The opening riff is complex and urgent and, as the piece develops, you're struck by the thought that this is as near as Zeppelin ever got to the "prog-rock" of bands such as Yes and Emerson, Lake & Palmer. Yet there's nothing flabby or indulgent: everything is taut and intense, and the cauldron is kept close to the boil. The track also features some of Page's most inventive guitar playing, which he overdubbed in a single night.

10

"I wanted to give each section its own identity and I think it came off really good," he reported, and suggested that as a personal milestone the track's first guitar showcase was on a par with the solo in 'Stairway to Heaven'.

41. FOR YOUR LIFE

RECORDED NOVEMBER–DECEMBER 1975; AVAILABLE ON PRESENCE

Built around a grinding stop-start riff, Plant sings of his discontent with the rock-star lifestyle ("a cry for mercy in the city of the damned"), although he has also suggested that lines such as "wanna find myself a crystal, payin' through the nose" were inspired by the plight of a friend mired in the Los Angeles drug scene. The song was worked up by Page and Plant when they convened in Malibu following his accident, and offers eloquent evidence of the unease and disillusionment that would come to characterize his final years in Led Zeppelin. 'For Your Life' was surely one of the tracks he was thinking about when he said that *Presence* contained "some of the hottest moments Led Zeppelin ever had – agitated, uncomfortable, druggy, pained".

42. ROYAL ORLEANS

RECORDED NOVEMBER–DECEMBER 1975; AVAILABLE ON PRESENCE

One of the problems of rock stars is that they can become so cocooned from real life that all they are left to sing about is the artificial life that is a rock star's fate or reward, depending on which way you look at it. Bill Wyman has likened it to living in a fishbowl. Led Zeppelin never fell totally into the trap, but their epic, on-the-road adventures in America inspired several songs

and 'Royal Orleans' is one of them.

Named after the hotel in New Orleans where the band habitually stayed when playing in the city, the lyric recounts an incident in which John Paul Jones allegedly took a transvestite up to his room, thinking he was a she. The line "And when the sun peeked through, John Cameron with Suzanna, he kissed the whiskers, left and right" only conceals Jones' identity with the flimsiest of veils: John Cameron was an old studio friend and rival from his pre-Zeppelin days. The song further jokes about waking up with a "New Orleans queen" with a voice as deep as Barry White's.

The only song on *Presence* credited to all four members, Plant allegedly set out to poke fun at his colleague in jovial revenge for an interview in which Jones had suggested the vocals were the least important part of the band's music. Bolstered by a spirited funk rhythm reminiscent of 'The Crunge', it's one of the more light-hearted moments on an album that for the most part was inspired by the band's trials and tribulations.

43. NOBODY'S FAULT BUT MINE

RECORDED NOVEMBER–DECEMBER 1975; AVAILABLE ON PRESENCE

Like 'In My Time of Dying' on *Physical Graffiti*, Nobody's Fault but Mine' was written by Blind Willie Johnson. The original was a stark, gospel-influenced number which depicted a man confessing his sins and looking for deliverance, and it was obvious that Plant in his post-accident plight identified strongly with the song's sentiments. The singer embellished the lyrics with a few lines of his own about "got a monkey on my back" but that hardly

LED ZEPPELIN

10

excused leaving Johnson's name off the writing credit. Many years later, Page offered this explanation: "The arrangement I came up with had nothing to do with the original. Robert may have wanted to go for the original lyrics but everything else was a total different kettle of fish."

Up to a point. Certainly, Johnson would not have recognised the blistering, *blitzkrieg* of the band's sonic attack, but he would certainly have known the tune as his own. As they had credited Memphis Minnie for 'When the Levee Breaks', it made little sense to deny Johnson's authorship here, a fact Plant seemed to acknowledge when he sometimes credited the song to Johnson on stage. The controversial credits apart, it's another monumental Zeppelin blues performance, with some of Plant's best harmonica-playing ever heard on record.

44. IN THE EVENING

RECORDED NOVEMBER–DECEMBER 1978; AVAILABLE ON IN THROUGH THE OUT DOOR

After two years away and all the rumours that they were breaking up following the death of Plant's son, Zeppelin announced their return with an opening track of emphatic pedigree. The gentle opening swirl of Eastern sounds produced by Page's violin bow is mere camouflage. After Plant has sung the song's title a minute into the track, Page breaks into a swaggering, cascading riff that is his most impressive contribution on an album otherwise dominated by Jones and Plant – and which the guitarist later complained was too "soft" for his taste.

The lyrics are ostensibly addressed to a woman, but the girl who "don't come" and shows "no pity" could well be the fickle

mistress that is fortune, as Plant goes on to bemoan "bad luck and trouble" and notes that although it's lonely at the bottom, it's dizzy at the top – a reality that he had been forced to find out the hardest way of all.

45. FOOL IN THE RAIN

RECORDED NOVEMBER–DECEMBER 1978; AVAILABLE ON IN THROUGH THE OUT DOOR

One of the most unusual songs in the Zeppelin canon was inspired by a samba tune that caught the fancy of Jones and Plant when used as a TV theme during the 1978 football World Cup in Argentina. Jones contributes some convincing Latin keyboards and Bonham proves a surprisingly dab hand at some tricky and complex Afro-Cuban poly-rhythms. Page's untypically meandering guitar solo is the track's only weakness, but Plant sounds fresh and optimistic on a lyric that talks of the redemptive power of love, even if – as usual – its course doesn't quite run smoothly.

46. CAROUSELAMBRA

RECORDED NOVEMBER–DECEMBER 1978; AVAILABLE ON IN THROUGH THE OUT DOOR

Conceived as the album's "epic", 'Carouselambra' is an ambitious but less than totally satisfying piece. The main problem lies in Jones's over-dominant keyboards, which sound dangerously close to something Rick Wakeman might have come up with. Page unfurls the famous double-necked Gibson but the jabbing, high-pitched organ riff won't go away and gets increasingly irritating. The second section is far better as Page essays a slow, moody theme marked by heavy guitar effects, but the good work is undone when the third section finds Jones' keyboards back with a new but even more irritating motif. Plant's poetic lyrics are fascinating, telling an allegorical tale that mirrors his recent experience, although his vocals are recessed too far back in the mix.

"The whole story of Led Zeppelin in its later years is in that song and I can't hear the words," he later complained. Most agree that ultimately 'Carouselambra' is an opportunity missed: it could and should have been the album's high point but sadly punches considerably below its weight. Had the drug-ravaged Page been in full control he surely would have checked some of Jones' organ excesses and the track might easily have taken its place alongside the likes of 'Kashmir' and 'Achilles Last Stand' among Zeppelin's greatest achievements.

47. **WE'RE GONNA GROOVE**
RECORDED JUNE 1969;
AVAILABLE ON CODA

For a posthumous, contract-fulfilling miscellany of odds and sods, there was some remarkably potent material on *Coda* from different stages of the band's career that, far from sounding like inferior out-takes, were in several cases as strong as many of the tracks that were released at the time. Among them was 'We're Gonna Groove'.

Recorded in June 1969, it would in no way have lowered the quality of *Led Zeppelin II* and would surely have improved side two of the album had it been included at the expense of 'Living Loving Maid', 'Moby Dick' or 'Bring It on Home'. The quality of the track is underlined by the fact that the band used the song as a set opener throughout the first half of 1970. Quite why it failed to make the cut at

the time remains a mystery. The version that surfaced on *Coda* is the original 1969 recording with the addition of some sub-octivider guitar effects added by Page at his Sol studio in early 1982.

48. **POOR TOM**
RECORDED JUNE 1970;
AVAILABLE ON CODA

Another legacy of Page and Plant's productive stay at the cottage in Bron-Yr-Aur to write the material for *Led Zeppelin III*, the only reason 'Poor Tom' was not included on that album at the time was that it would have been an acoustic track too far. Cut from similar cloth as 'Bron-Y-Aur Stomp', 'Gallows Pole' and 'Hats off to (Roy) Harper', the song loses nothing in comparison, with some great Plant harmonica work and a slightly over-booming but insistent shuffle from Bonham. The lyric is based on the *crime passionnel* tradition of American folk ballads, along the lines of 'Delia's Gone' (recorded by Johnny Cash and Bob Dylan among others) or 'Frankie and Johnny'.

49. **WALTER'S WALK**
RECORDED MAY 1972;
AVAILABLE ON CODA

Had 'Walter's Walk' appeared on *Houses of the Holy*, for which it was originally recorded, it would arguably have been the best track on the album, and certainly the heaviest. There's none of the clever crispness here that characterised that album, just urgent and dense guitar riffs from Page, a classic Plant vocal (even if the lyric doesn't seem to go anywhere) and sheer, animal ferocity on the drums even by Bonham's violent standards. Who Walter was is unrecorded: perhaps the band simply liked the alliteration and 'Percy's Perambulation'

LED ZEPPELIN

10

didn't quite fit. Why it didn't make the album at the time is another mystery, for the band clearly had some affection for the song, using it as part of the 'Dazed and Confused' medley during the 1972 tour, in which form it can also be heard on the live album *How the West was Won.*

50. WEARING AND TEARING
RECORDED NOVEMBER 1978;
AVAILABLE ON CODA

In which Led Zeppelin play at being The Damned – or something similar, for Plant has often claimed that this track was Zeppelin's direct response to the punk revolution. "Listen to 'Wearing and Tearing' on *Coda,*" he claimed in 2005. "That was our contribution to the whole thing, saying 'yes, you've got it right'." Certainly the breakneck pace could have had them pogoing up and down at the 100 Club, although it's hard to imagine any three-chord punk guitar merchant keeping up with the manic speed and precision of Page's hell-for-leather licks. Plant effects a vibrant punk shout but never quite masters the crucial sneer.

The track was intended for release as a single or EP aimed at the Knebworth audience in 1979, and there was even talk of issuing it under the name of a fake band so it would not be judged as a Zeppelin track, but could then compete against the punk bands on a level playing field. In the end that never happened, but it's fascinating to wonder what the reaction might have been had 'Wearing and Tearing' been slipped out clandestinely on an indie label under the name of The Nobs, or some such. Frankly, it makes The Clash sound like Freddie and The Dreamers.

ZEPPOLOGY
ALL THE ZEP THAT'S FIT TO PRINT

11

"Led Zeppelin is probably the most aggressive, masculine rock group anywhere. They batter at the mind and ear, insisting they will penetrate."

JIMMY PAGE, PRESS RELEASE FOR *LED ZEPPELIN I*

ZEPPOLOGY

MUSICAL CO-CONSPIRATORS

11

TERRY REID

Originally Jimmy Page's first choice as Led Zeppelin's singer, Terry Reid has entered rock history as the man who recommended Robert Plant for the job instead. Yet if Reid has ever regretted his decision, he's never let it show. "People say I'm the unluckiest man in rock but it doesn't feel like that," he told this writer in 2004. "In fact, I think I've been extraordinarily lucky throughout my career."

Yet it's hard not to see Reid as one of rock 'n' roll's most cruelly ill-starred nearly men. Born in 1949, he was a teenage prodigy and at the age of 16 his band The Jaywalkers were supporting The Rolling Stones. His first two solo albums were produced by Mickie Most, and although they showcase his soulful voice well enough, the cheap pop production makes them today sound very dated. "I have to say that Mickie Most's conservatism held me back on those albums. He'd made these great records with The Animals and Donovan but then music started to evolve and he didn't move with it. I'd want to try new stuff and he wouldn't go to the next page," Reid recalls. "Then I got friendly with Jimmy Page, who Mickie wanted nothing to do with. Jimmy asked me to be the singer in Led Zeppelin but I'd just done a deal to support the Stones on their first US tour in three years." According to the singer's account, he told Page that he was prepared to join but that they would have to compensate him for what he would have lost by not doing the

Stones tour. Whether this was a serious offer is not clear, but in any case he also recommended his mate Robert Plant – and that was that. He was also approached by Deep Purple but turned them down, too.

After several years in The Jaywalkers, Terry Reid went solo, supporting several major acts including the Stones, Jethro Tull and Fleetwood Mac

While Led Zeppelin set about conquering the world, Reid's career stalled and he was silenced for two years by a legal dispute over contracts. By 1971 he had grown fed up

LED ZEPPELIN

with the UK and moved to Los Angeles. Two years later he made the album *River*, a semi-acoustic set on which he came across like a cross between a blue-eyed soul singer and the jazz-folk stylings of John Martyn. Today the album is regarded by the cognoscenti as a five-star classic but Warner Bros. hated it. "When I handed in *River* they said I'd made a jazz album and they wanted a rock 'n' roll record," Reid says. "So they paid me 20,000 dollars to go away and didn't get behind it. But I loved that record. It was the first time I got to do what I wanted to do."

A handful of further albums followed at sporadic intervals on different labels, the last studio release being 1991's *The Driver*. Today, Reid spends his time playing bars in L.A., his sets regularly enlivened by guest appearances from passing rock legends. "I play every Monday night at The Joint in Beverly Hills," he reported a couple of years ago. "When Robert Plant dropped by we did 'Season of The Witch', which he said he'd always wanted to sing with me. Keith Richards has been down a couple of times, and when Roger Daltrey turned up we did 'Stand By Me'."

ROY HARPER

Famously commemorated on *Led Zeppelin III* in 'Hats off to (Roy) Harper', the idiosyncratic English singer-songwriter became one of Led Zeppelin's closest friends during the 1970s, both making music with members of the band and raising hell with them, too.

Born in Manchester, England, in 1941, Harper led a colourful early life that included running away to join the Royal Air Force at 15 and then feigning insanity to earn a discharge, followed by spells in jail, in a mental institution and bumming around Europe as a busker. He released his debut

album *Sophisticated Beggar* in 1966 and followed with a series of albums full of uncompromising songs with titles such as 'I Hate the White Man'.

Famously curmudgeonly, Harper was a long-standing friend of the band

Jimmy Page says he was first drawn to Harper's work because he stood by his principles and refused to bow to commercial pressures. "As far as I'm concerned, hats off to anybody who does what they think is right and refuses to sell out," he noted – hence the Bukka White blues song 'Shake 'Em on Down' on *Led Zeppelin III* being given the otherwise unconnected title 'Hats off to (Roy) Harper'. "They showed me this album sleeve and I said 'very nice' and handed it back," Harper recalls. "'No, go on – look again' they said, and then I saw this song 'Hats off to (Roy) Harper'. To be honest, it's been more of a burden than anything. A hell of a thing to live up to."

Credited as "S. Flavius Mercurius", Page played on Harper's critically acclaimed 1971 album *Stormcock*. Harper frequently attended Zeppelin gigs and toured as part of the band's entourage in America in 1973, when he was granted favoured person status by Page and Plant – much to the annoyance of some of Zeppelin's road crew, who found him self-obsessed and too full of his own importance. "Fucked if I know why they loved him so. He was just a pain in the ass to me," road manager Richard Cole later observed. Harper was also a famous hellraiser in his time: Robert Plant recalls the two of them one night in the mid-1970s getting "banned for life" from the London club The Speakeasy, although he cannot remember the exact nature of the bad behaviour that resulted in such extreme punishment.

Surprisingly, Harper did not sign to Zeppelin's Swan Song label but he did contribute sleeve photography to *Physical Graffiti* and appeared uncredited in the 1976 film *The Song Remains the Same*. Zeppelin weren't his only admirers in the higher echelons of the rock world and Pink Floyd asked him to sing lead vocals on the song 'Have a Cigar' on their 1975 album *Wish You Were Here*. Floyd guitarist David Gilmour appeared on Harper's next album, *HQ*, which also featured John Paul Jones.

After Led Zeppelin broke up, Page toured with Harper in 1984, playing acoustic sets at folk festivals under various guises such as The MacGregors and Themselves. The following year they released the joint album *Whatever Happened to ... Jugula?* The live album, *In Between Every Line*, also contained recordings from their joint performance at the 1984 Cambridge Folk Festival. Harper has continued to record and enjoy a cult status

and Page and Plant, who remain close friends, both performed at his 60th birthday concert at London's Albert Hall in June 2001.

RICHARD COLE

A handful of rock managers such as Brian Epstein and Peter Grant become famous in their own right but it's almost unprecedented for a humble roadie to become a celebrity. Not that there was much that was humble about Richard Cole, whose notoriety as Led Zeppelin's road manager is due to his central role in organising the sex and drugs to accompany the rock 'n' roll on the band's infamously debauched tours of America and to the salacious book he wrote describing those experiences when he was short of cash in the early 1990s. Cole's eventual downfall was due to the fact that he not only organised the debauchery for his employers to enjoy, he was frequently its most enthusiastic participant and he ended up with an out-of-control heroin habit which forced Grant to sack him in 1980.

Cole was born in north London on January 2, 1946. After a spell as a teenage boxer, he got his first job in the music industry in 1965 road-managing the pop band Unit 4 Plus 2. He went on to run tours of America for The Who and The New Vaudeville Band (who were managed by Peter Grant) and in 1967 moved to America to work for Vanilla Fudge as a sound engineer. He continued his association with Grant when he road-managed The Yardbirds' tour of America in 1968, during which time he got to know Jimmy Page well. This put him in pole position when Led Zeppelin formed later that year and he remained the band's road manager almost until the end, working with them on every tour bar their final 1980 European jaunt.

LED ZEPPELIN

to heroin. Arguably, both would have happened anyway, but instead of seeking to curb such destructiveness, Cole was there egging them on.

After he was sacked from Zeppelin's 1980 tour, Grant sent him to a rehabilitation clinic in Italy. The day after he arrived, Cole was arrested as a terrorist on suspicion of blowing up Bologna railway station and spent long weeks in prison before the Italian police accepted his innocence. He was still in prison when he was given the news that John Bonham had died.

Cole stopped using drugs in the early 1980s and in his book, *Stairway to Heaven*, he wrote that he had given up alcohol in 1986, too. He continued to work in the music industry, serving as the tour manager for Eric Clapton, Black Sabbath, Lita Ford, Ozzy Osbourne, Three Dog Night, Gipsy Kings, Crazy Town and Fu Manchu.

The former members of Led Zeppelin undoubtedly felt betrayed when he sold his story to the author Stephen Davis in the sensationalist *Hammer of the Gods*, although Cole claimed he was paid just 1,250 dollars for his revelations and so rejects charges of 'cashing in'. But he then wrote his own book, *Stairway to Heaven: Led Zeppelin Uncensored*, ghosted by Richard Trubo. Today he is said to be a stable family man who divides his time between homes in California and London, grateful to have been there to witness the Led Zeppelin maelstrom up close and personal – but even more grateful to have survived it.

Zep felt betrayed by Cole's sensationalist book, but nobody could deny he knew where the bodies were buried

Cole's name is littered throughout this book for he was ubiquitous as the band's ultimate 'gofer' and there's no doubt that he was brilliant at his job – at least when he was (relatively) straight and sober. When Plant and his wife had their car crash in Greece it was Cole who organised their evacuation. When the singer received the news on tour in New Orleans that his five-year-old son Karac had died, Cole was the first person he told and who then took charge of all the arrangements. Such close bonds transcended a mere employer-staff relationship. On the other hand, his influence had its malign side for there are those who blame him for encouraging Bonham's alcohol-fuelled rampages and for introducing Jimmy Page

THE ZEP ROAD CREW

In addition to Richard Cole, Led Zeppelin were served by a loyal and tight-knit road crew over the years who tended to the band's every need – on stage and off. They were also often credited with having been the

ZEPPOLOGY: **MUSICAL CO-CONSPIRATORS**

instigators of much of the riotous behaviour associated with the band on tour.

Clive Coulson had sung in a band called Mecca in the 1960s and was part of Zeppelin's road crew from the outset. He was one of the roadies who went with Page and Plant to Bron-Yr-Aur when they wrote *Led Zeppelin III* in the Welsh cottage. He later road-managed Bad Company and died in January 2006.

Kenny Pickett was a member of cult 1960s band The Creation, whose Eddie Phillips played the guitar with a violin bow before Jimmy Page took up the trick. Pickett was a member of Zeppelin's road crew on their early American tours but left for a career in writing jingles and novelty pop songs, penning the 1971 children's favourite 'Grandad' for Clive Dunn. He died in 1997.

Other early road crew members included Joe Jammer, who was Page's guitar tech and went on to form his own band, Henry 'The Horse' Smith and Sandy MacGregor.

Into the 1970s, the crew included Raymond Thomas and Tim Marten, who both worked as guitar technicians for Page, Brian Condliffe, who looked after John Paul Jones's instrumental requirements, Benji LeFevre, who was Plant's assistant, and Mick Hinton, who was not so much Bonham's drum technician as his partner in all manner of crimes.

Other notable staff included Rex King, Bonham's assistant from 1977 to 1980 who later road-managed Page and Plant's reunion tour in the mid-1990s, and the notorious John Bindon, who controversially went on the road as the band's head of security in 1977. A former actor whose bit parts in various films including *Performance*, *Quadrophenia* and *Get Carter* usually found him playing violent gangsters, his on-screen casting was not too far removed from his other existence as a heavy in the London underworld and an associate of the Kray

brothers. He was responsible for much backstage violence during Zeppelin's tour and was one of those given a suspended prison sentence for the beating of a security man working for promoter Bill Graham during the band's final American appearance at the Oakland Coliseum in 1977. He was subsequently sacked by Peter Grant, who admitted that hiring him had been the biggest mistake he ever made as manager. This judgement was confirmed when Bindon stabbed someone to death during a knife fight in London in 1978. He fled to Ireland and was acquitted at the Old Bailey after pleading self-defence, claiming he was in fear of his life and was being blackmailed over a drug deal that had gone wrong. During the 1980s, he fell into heroin addiction and he died from AIDS in 1993. For reasons best known only to Morrissey, the former Smiths singer chose to commemorate him on the sleeve of his album *Maladjusted* with the dedication: "John Bindon 1943–1993".

JASON BONHAM

Jason Bonham's first public appearance can be seen in the Led Zeppelin movie *The Song Remains the Same*, playing a mini drum kit while his father, John Bonham, looks on proudly. Born on July 13, 1966, he later recalled how he would be asked as a boy to perform for famous house guests: "Sometimes I would be woken up at two o'clock in the morning to come down and play that scaled-down kit. Robert Plant, Jimmy Page, Jeff Beck, members of Yes, Bad Company and Emerson, Lake & Palmer would often drop by our house after shows in the area and a major party would follow. After being woken up for a few of these nocturnal performances, I was able to negotiate my first fee, a much needed

LED ZEPPELIN

His first solo album, *The Disregard of Timekeeping*, appeared in 1989 and included the minor hit single 'Wait for You'. A second solo album, *Mad Hatter*, followed in 1992, before he formed the band Motherland, releasing the 1994 album *Peace 4 Me*.

In 1995, he again played with Page, Plant and Jones when he represented his father at Led Zeppelin's induction into the Rock and Roll Hall of Fame. His next project was an album called *In the Name of My Father: The Zepset*, which found him playing Led Zeppelin songs such as 'Communication Breakdown', 'The Song Remains the Same', 'Ten Years Gone' and 'Since I've Been Loving You'. He later drummed with the band Healing Sixes and recorded and toured with Debbie Bonham, his father's younger sister.

TONY THOMPSON

After John Bonham's death Led Zeppelin have only ever once seriously contemplated reforming – and when they did the man they asked to replace their deceased drummer was Tony Thompson. Born in 1954 of Antiguan descent, Thompson began his career on the New York session scene before becoming a founder member of disco pioneers Chic and playing on hits such as 'Le Freak' and 'Good Times'. After Chic disbanded in 1983, Thompson became an in-demand session drummer, playing on records by Madonna, Rod Stewart, Mick Jagger and David Bowie.

He also became a member of Power Station, along with Robert Palmer and John and Andy Taylor from Duran Duran. Power Station played the American leg of *Live Aid* in 1985 and he was drafted in alongside Phil Collins to provide a double drum attack during Led Zeppelin's performance. The following year, Page, Plant and Jones invited Thompson to join them in a putative full-

Jason Bonham followed in his father's footsteps as an accomplished drummer and bon viveur – although that's only toothpaste

day off school."

He joined his first band when he was 17 and in 1985 joined Virginia Wolf, recording two albums with them and touring America supporting The Firm. In 1987, he joined Jimmy Page for his *Outrider* album and tour, and the following year drummed with the three surviving members of Led Zeppelin at the reunion for Atlantic Records' 40th anniversary concert in New York. The band were highly self-critical of their performance but all concurred that Bonham had acquitted himself with great credit. The next time Page, Plant and Jones played together was at Bonham's wedding reception in 1990.

11

The Who. When Track dissolved in 1974 he set up his own company, Trinifold, and took over The Who's management.

With Peter Grant having retired, in 1986 Curbishley took on Robert Plant's solo management. In 1994, he added Jimmy Page to his roster of clients and set about effecting their reunion. "I encouraged it because I really felt it was a tragedy that these two guys who had written one of the best catalogues of songs in rock 'n' roll history weren't together," he later said. "Robert wasn't unwilling to work with Page; he was unwilling to work with Led Zeppelin because he didn't want to take a backwards step. Every time he worked with a band or a unit, it became quite apparent to me that he was trying to turn the guitarist into another Jimmy Page. In the end I said to him: 'Look, you can work with Jimmy without being Led Zeppelin. Besides, you two write all the songs, so there's no reason why you can't play them.'"

His pride in bringing them back together was evident in an interview he gave in 1999. "On a personal level, I think they both walk with a lighter step now," he said. "The fact that they got back together and started playing again unloaded a lot of shit and that's been very important to them. I think they came out of it with a wealth that was way beyond materialistic. It has equally benefited them spiritually and they are both better people for it." However, Curbishley's professional relationship with Page did not survive when the singer and the guitarist fell out again after Plant pulled the plug on further joint touring at the end of 1998. He no longer manages Page or Plant but was instrumental in coaxing the latter back from his late-1990s pub rock anonymity with Priory of Brion and into the studio with The Strange Sensation. Trinifold's other clients at the

John Bonham's shoes could never be filled , but Thompson was the only drummer who ever came near to doing so

scale Led Zeppelin reunion. After the first rehearsal, he was seriously injured in a car accident and his unavailability effectively put an end to the reunion plan. He died of cancer in November 2003.

BILL CURBISHLEY

As the manager of both Robert Plant and Jimmy Page, Bill Curbishley played a key role in bringing the two former Led Zeppelin giants back together in the mid-1990s. Curbishley started his career in the music business at Track Records in the late 1960s, working with bands such as The Crazy World of Arthur Brown, Thunderclap Newman and

LED ZEPPELIN

If anybody could reunite the warring Page and Plant, it was Curbishley, whose music industry experience dated back to the halcyon days of the late-1960s time of writing included Judas Priest and UB40 and the company has also branched out into film production.

Curbishley's younger brother Alan is the fomer footballer and ex-manager of Charlton Athletic and West Ham United, and among all the photographs of Trinifold's famous rock star clients in his office in Camden, pride of place is given to a photograph of him at a football function with his brother and the now retired Manchester United manager Sir Alex Ferguson.

TEN TALES OF EXCESS

Young, rich, a long way from home and with time hanging heavy on their hands between gigs, in their early years Led Zeppelin created a new benchmark for boorish on-the-road behaviour. Many of the tales came from road manager Richard Cole, who spilled the beans to author Stephen Davis in his book *Hammer of The Gods* and then wrote his own 1993 book, *Stairway to Heaven.* "We didn't give a fuck," he recalled. "The doors had to open now. If they didn't we'd break them down. And that was it. We made our own laws. If you don't want to abide by them, don't get involved."

Some of the detail may have been exaggerated and some of the stories may be apocryphal, but the tales Cole told have entered rock'n'roll folklore, forcing even Robert Plant to admit: "I want to believe

Hammer of The Gods because it has done us huge favours in terms of aura."

1. THE SHARK EPISODE
SEATTLE, MAY 1969

When the British tabloid newspaper *The Sun* broke a story about "a young lady who is said to have been whipped by a live octopus", a matter-of-fact John Paul Jones remarked: "I don't think that's entirely true. As far as I can remember it was a dead shark." This was one of the most notorious tales of rock 'n' roll Babylon first revealed. The incident took place at the Edgewater Inn, where it was possible to catch fish from the hotel room balconies out of the ocean below. One night, road manager Richard Cole and John Bonham tied a 17-year-old redhead from Portland to the bed and proceeded to insert the shark-like fish they had caught earlier into her vagina and rectum. The proceedings were allegedly filmed by Mark Stein of Vanilla Fudge. Cole later claimed the fish were not sharks but red snappers.

2. OCTOPUSSY

PASADENA, MAY 1969

Despite Jones's protestations, there was some truth in the octopus story. After playing two dates at the Rose Palace in Pasadena, for some bizarre reason Zeppelin were given four live octopuses by promoter Barry Imhoff. Back at the hotel, Page persuaded two young groupies to take a bath, threw the creatures in with them and settled back to enjoy the show.

3. BONZO BARED

FLUSHING MEADOW, JULY 1969

Having already wrecked Ten Years After's set by dousing guitarist Alvin Lee mid-solo, an extremely drunk Bonham then hijacked Jeff Beck's set by running on stage and stripping completely naked. The police arrived on stage to arrest him but Bonham was rugby-tackled and dragged off by Grant, who locked him in a dressing room before an arrest could be made.

4. THE ART OF VANDALISM

COPENHAGEN, FEBRUARY 1970

Having had to play a gig as The Nobs after a descendant of the von Zeppelin family had threatened legal action over the use of the name, the band were taken to a Danish art gallery where the record company had organised a reception. Former art student Jimmy Page announced that the modernist abstractions hanging on the gallery walls were "bullshit" and took out his magic marker and added his own embellishments to three of the offending paintings. Allegedly, the gallery owner failed to notice the full extent of the vandalism and the band were only asked to pay for one redesigned masterpiece.

5. THE MEN GET THEIR MOUNTIE

VANCOUVER, MARCH 1970

Spotting someone holding a microphone in the audience, Peter Grant and a couple of Zeppelin roadies decided to teach the bootlegger a lesson. Dragging him backstage, Grant smashed his equipment and gave the miscreant a good kicking. Except that he wasn't a tape pirate at all, but a Canadian local government official checking decibel levels. Grant was charged with assault and was unable to return to Canada for several years. Naturally enough, Bonham's response to his manager's arrest was to smash up his hotel room in protest.

6. THE SAMURAI SLASHERS

TOKYO, SEPTEMBER 1971

After buying two Samurai swords from the gift shop in the Tokyo Hilton, Bonham and Cole then used them to chop down the door of John Paul Jones's room. The bass player was comatose and didn't even wake when they carried him out into the corridor and proceeded to chop everything in his room into splinters with their new blades. As a result the entire band was banned from the Hilton chain for life. Further mayhem followed when the band got into a fight on an overnight ride on the famous 'bullet train', the story of which was plastered all over the front pages of the Japanese papers.

LED ZEPPELIN

11

7. JAIL BAIT
LOS ANGELES, JUNE 1972

It was always said that Jimmy Page liked younger girls and they didn't come much younger than the 14-year-old child model Lori Maddox. Virtually kidnapped by Richard Cole one night from the Rainbow Bar in L.A., she was taken to Continental Hyatt House on Sunset Strip (affectionately known by Zeppelin and other touring rock bands as the Riot House) for a secret assignation with the guitarist. No question of sending her back-to-schoolin': Lori stayed with Page on and off on the band's US tours for the next 18 months. Grant insisted that she was kept locked in a hotel room with a security guard on the door, fearing that if Page was caught with an underage girl he would be deported and refused further work permits.

8. TVS A GO-GO (AND THE SNOOKER TABLE,TOO)
SEATTLE, JUNE 1972

By their eighth American tour, throwing colour TV sets out of hotel windows was routine, but when Zeppelin were around it became infectious. When Grant came to settle the bill for their usual mayhem at the long-suffering Edgewater, the hotel manager confessed to a secret desire to join in the TV-hurling. Grant promptly peeled off 500 dollars in crisp bank notes and told him: "Have one on us." The manager allegedly went upstairs and heaved one off the balcony. In L.A. the following year, Bonham was to go one better by somehow launching a snooker

table off the 11th floor after those below had the audacity to complain about glasses being thrown.

9. MOTORCYCLE MADNESS
LOS ANGELES, JUNE 1973

After the band had taken the entire ninth floor of the Continental Hyatt House hotel on Sunset Strip, Page decided he wanted to try out a new Japanese motorcycle. Tour manager Richard Cole went out to buy one and then rode it through the hotel lobby and into the elevator. Page and other members of the band's entourage then spent all night racing it up and down the corridors. By this time, Jones had had enough of such shenanigans and his hotel bookings wisely specified that his room had to be two floors away from the rest of the band.

10. BEATING UP THE PROMOTER
SAN FRANCISCO, JUNE 1977

Playing the first of two nights at the Oakland Stadium, Bonham attacked one of promoter Bill Graham's security men after seeing him push Peter Grant's son, Warren. Grant and John Bindon, head of Zeppelin's personal security, then took the guard to an empty trailer and beat him so badly that he required hospitalisation. An uneasy truce prevailed the following night but the next morning, Bonham, Bindon and Grant were arrested – Graham had delayed filing charges so as not to risk losing income from a cancelled second show. All three were found guilty of assault and given suspended sentences.

TEN KEY ZEPPELIN LOCATIONS

11

The four members of Led Zeppelin came from radically different backgrounds in greater London and the West Midlands and their formative years and the circumstances in which they grew up are dealt with in the first section of this book. The 10 sites listed here are all associated with the band after they came together as Led Zeppelin in 1968...

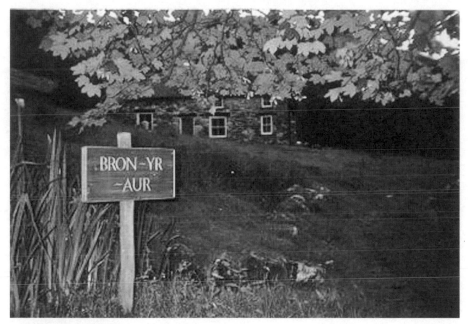

BRON-YR-AUR

Read the small print of the liner notes to *Led Zeppelin III* and you will find the following dedication: "Credit must be given to BRON-YR-AUR, a small derelict cottage in South Snowdonia for painting a somewhat forgotten picture of true completeness which acted as an incentive to some of these musical statements."

The cottage on a hilltop overlooking the Dyfi Valley near the town of Machynlleth in Powys, Wales, is the most visited site on any Zeppelin pilgrimage and hundreds of fans seek it out every year. Plant had known the place from his boyhood, when his family rented it for summer holidays, and it was here

that he and Page stayed in May 1970 to write material for Zeppelin's third album. At the time the cottage had no electricity, gas or running water and the Zep men had to trek to The Glyndwr Hotel in Machynlleth for a weekly bath.

Commemorated in the song 'Bron-Y-Aur Stomp' on *Led Zeppelin III* and 'Bron-Yr-

11

Aur' on *Physical Graffiti*, the cottage was renovated some years ago and subsequent owners have complained repeatedly about Zep fans from as far away as Japan turning up on their doorstep.

Plant regularly returns to the vicinity, although not the house, and has suggested the spirit of the place continues to exert an influence on his songwriting. He reported in September 2014 that the

current residents, driven to distraction by visiting fans, were urging him to buy the cottage from them.

The Welsh name Bron-Yr-Aur translates as 'breast of the gold' or 'golden hill'.

HEADLEY GRANGE

Headley Grange in the village of Headley, East Hampshire, is where Led Zeppelin recorded regularly during the early 1970s and, most famously, where one night sitting around a log fire, Robert Plant wrote the lyrics to 'Stairway to Heaven'.

The place has a fascinating history. Built as a workhouse in 1795 at an estimated cost of £1,500 to shelter the infirm, aged paupers, orphans and illegitimate

children of the parish, it was originally known as the 'House of Industry'. On November 23, 1830, a mob of rioters estimated at 1,000 strong sacked the place. Seven men were sentenced to transportation for their part in the riot. After the building had been repaired, it continued to be used as a workhouse until it was sold in 1870 for £420 to a builder, who converted it into a private house and renamed it

Headley Grange.

After the conversion, the house was sold in 1872 for £490 and was occupied by just three owners over the next 90 years. Theophilus Sigismund Hahn lived there from 1872 until his death in 1907, aged 83. The Grange was then transferred to Col Francis Frederic Perry, who lived there until his death in 1939, aged 85. After the Second World War, the house was bought by

Lieutenant-Col Michael Smith, whose family lived there until his death in 1961. His widow then let the house and it was used for a number of years as a hostel for students from Farnham School of Art.

During the 1970s, Led Zeppelin were not the only rock band to take up residence and Genesis and Bad Company also worked there using a mobile recording truck. The drawing room was used as the main recording room due to its perfect acoustics, although Bonham's drums on 'When the Levee Breaks' were famously recorded in the stairwell. The house is now a private residence but reportedly still contains the piano that was in the house when Zeppelin rented it.

11

THE BOATHOUSE, PANGBOURNE

The boathouse once owned by Jimmy Page on the River Thames at Pangbourne was put on the market in 2007. Listed by estate agents as The Thames Boathouse, it was here that Robert Plant was staying in the summer of 1968 when Page formally invited him to join The New Yardbirds – or Led Zeppelin, as they were soon to become known.

As its name suggests, the property was originally a boathouse with a wet dock. Owned since Victorian times by Hobbs of Henley, its sole purpose was the hiring and maintaining of river craft until 1959, when the property was converted into a private dwelling with a 40-foot river mooring. Page bought the boathouse in 1967 and sold the property in 1973. In 2000, the owners converted the basement, where the wet dock had once been, into a heated indoor swimming pool and undertook other substantial improvements.

11

BOLESKINE HOUSE

Once the home of Aleister Crowley, who infamously used the property to practise magical ceremonies, Jimmy Page bought Boleskine House in 1971. Set amid rugged scenery a mile north of the Scottish village of Foyers, close to the southern shores of Loch Ness, the house was built in the late 18th century by Archibald Fraser. According to local legend, a church once stood on the site but was burnt to the ground with the entire congregation trapped inside. Other macabre stories are also attached to the house, which was owned by Crowley in the early decades of the 20th century. It was Page's interest in the magician that led him to purchase the house, and the grounds of the house were the location for some of the fantasy scenes in the film *The Song Remains the Same*. Page seems to have revelled in the place's ill-repute, regaling visitors with ghoulish stories of its history. After he sold Boleskine in 1992, it was run for a while as a guest house offering bed and breakfast but is now a private residence.

PLUMPTON PLACE

For many years, Robert Plant has lived contentedly on his farm in the Midlands and maintains only a modest London town house in Camden. Jimmy Page, however, has enjoyed the rock-star country mansion trip to the hilt. He purchased the Elizabethan manor house Plumpton Place in Sussex in the early 1970s and immediately installed a recording studio there. *In Through the out Door* was mixed at Plumpton and the property can also be seen briefly in the film *The Song Remains the Same*, in the scene in which Page plays a hurdy gurdy.

The grounds contain a water mill built by the Earl of Chichester in 1802, and which remained operational until 1916. The Earl is also said to have placed the first carp introduced into England into Plumpton Place moat. The manor house and gardens were remodelled in 1927 by Sir Edwin Lutyens for the then owner Edward Hudson, the founder of the magazine *Country Life*. The Sussex Gardens Trust occasionally organises visits to the gardens.

LED ZEPPELIN

11

THE TOWER HOUSE

Jimmy Page's London home since 1974 has been The Tower House in Melbury Road, Kensington. The late-Victorian building was built in medieval style by the Victorian architect William Burges in the 1870s.

Burges completed the building by 1878 and then took charge of the interior design. Many of the original features are still preserved in the house but Burges himself had little time to enjoy his home and died in 1881. Page purchased the house from the actor Richard Harris. The property is now estimated to be worth around £10 million.

STARGROVES

Led Zeppelin recorded *Houses of the Holy* and parts of *Physical Graffiti* at Stargroves, renting the country house at East End, a few miles south-west of Newbury, Berkshire, from Mick Jagger. The Rolling Stones also recorded much of *Sticky Fingers* at the house and The Who cut the classic 'Won't Get Fooled Again' there. Jagger bought Stargroves complete with 37 acres of gardens and parkland for £25,000 in 1970, his interest allegedly piqued by an estate agent's claim that Oliver Cromwell had used the house as a Civil War field headquarters, although there is no historical evidence for this. The house was in need of improvement but Jagger never spent a great deal of time there, although Marianne Faithfull for a brief while took some interest in the gardens. Jagger subsequently sold the property and the current owners undertook a major programme of renovations, which won a conservation award for best restoration of an historic building in 2005. The house was also used for filming episodes of *Doctor Who*, featuring the actor Tom Baker.

JOHN BONHAM'S GRAVE, RUSHOCK

The resting place of Led Zeppelin's drummer lies in a small cemetery at Rushock church, Kidderminster. It is not easy to find, but driving south from Kidderminster towards Droitwich on the A442, you turn left into a narrow country lane that is marked with a sign saying "Rushock village". At the top of the lane turn right, then almost immediately left and follow the curving, single-track road for two-thirds of a mile until you see the church. The grave is easily located and the stone bears an inscription from his wife Pat which reads: "He will always be remembered in our hearts. Goodnight, my love. God bless." The stone is often scattered with drumsticks, left in tribute by Zeppelin fans.

LED ZEPPELIN

HYATT HOTEL, WEST HOLLYWOOD

On their first trip to Los Angeles over Christmas 1968, Led Zeppelin stayed at the Chateau Marmont, but on all their subsequent visits to the city they stayed at the Hyatt West Hollywood, half a mile further down Sunset Boulevard. It was here that many of the most legendary tales of Zep excess took place, with the management taking a lenient view of their behaviour since Peter Grant was always ready to pay up for any damage and destruction in cash.

When on tour, Zeppelin rented as many as six floors of the hotel in the mid-to-late 1970s for the band members and entourage. Scenes in Cameron Crowe's film *Almost Famous*, based loosely on the antics of Led Zeppelin, were filmed at the hotel, refurbished for the occasion with original 1970s decor. The end-of-tour party scene in the film *This is Spinal Tap* was filmed on the roof of the hotel, and in the film *Rock Star*, the character played by John Bonham's son Jason is seen throwing a TV out of one of the Hyatt's windows. In real life, in addition to Led Zeppelin, Keith Richards and Keith Moon are also reported at different times to have indulged in acts of TV-hurling.

Originally called the Gene Autry Hotel when it opened in 1958, it was renamed Continental Hyatt House in the mid-1960s. Its popularity with touring rock bands was based on its close proximity to popular clubs on Sunset Strip such as the Whisky a Go Go, and its *laissez-faire* attitude towards its clients' unconventional behaviour led to the hotel becoming known among the rock 'n' roll fraternity as the Riot House. It was here that Richard Cole once drove a motorcycle around the hotel corridors one night.

Despite advertising itself as "the rock 'n' roll hotel", today the Hyatt exudes a somewhat bland corporatism, although it does house a restaurant called "CHI", which is part-owned by the singer Justin Timberlake.

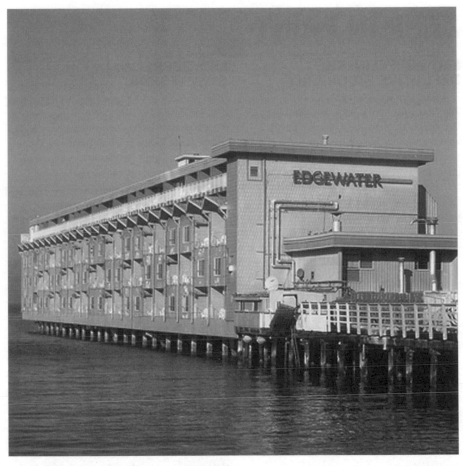

11

EDGEWATER HOTEL, SEATTLE

Second only to the Riot House on Sunset Strip in Zeppelin mythology as a scene of on-the-road debauchery is the Edgewater hotel, Seattle. Its reputation is largely due to being the location of the infamous shark/red snapper episode (see page 234) but it was used by the band on every tour of America. Situated on a pier at the north end of the waterfront, its attraction as the only hotel situated directly on the bay is obvious and it was designed to resemble a deluxe fishing lodge. On a clear day, the Olympic Mountains can be seen across Puget Sound, while the best rooms are done out as mountain lodges with rustic fireplaces and pine furniture. The hotel doesn't advertise a 'shark room' in commemoration of Zeppelin's most notoriously debauched on-the-road episode, but it does offer the chance to stay in the suites occupied by The Beatles in 1964.

11 ZEPP IN PRINT

LED ZEPPELIN: THE DEFINITIVE BIOGRAPHY

RITCHIE YORKE (1974, REVISED 1993)

The first into hard covers to chronicle the Zeppelin phenomenon was Canadian writer and broadcaster Ritchie Yorke. With the distinct advantage of knowing the band and enjoying their confidence (he introduced them on stage at every one of their five Toronto performances over the years), Yorke's book has

provided the platform for all subsequent Zep scholarship. There's rather too much of the buddy-to-the-stars school of journalism, but he was genuinely there and his judgements remain largely objective, although he's perhaps guilty of being a little too veiled over the excesses of the road, which are alluded to but not described. Nevertheless, when the book was substantially updated and revised in 1993, its common sense and sobriety seemed oddly welcome after the salaciousness of Stephen Davis and Richard Cole's books.

LED ZEPPELIN: IN THEIR OWN WORDS

PAUL KENDALL AND DAVE LEWIS (1981, UPDATED 1995)

For a band who were famously suspicious of the press, Zeppelin's four members were actually quite loquacious – and were certainly far more accessible to the press than bands of similar stature today. Through

direct quotes without any commentary, the story is told chronologically and subject by subject, with Plant by far the most eloquent of the four. The one drawback is that none of the quotes are dated, so it's not always clear if band members are speaking at the time or with the benefit of hindsight.

HAMMER OF THE GODS

STEPHEN DAVIS (1985, UPDATED 1995)

Most of Davis's biographies, which include books on The Rolling Stones and Jim Morrison, have deliberately courted controversy by concentrating on the sordid, sleazy side of rock 'n' roll. But with the band's former tour manager Richard Cole as his 'deep throat', in *Hammer of the*

11

of it is true, who knows: if those who were there with him at the time consumed even a fraction of the drink and drugs that he says they did, then none of them could have been in a fit condition to remember. Yet Cole himself claims perfect recall, recounting alleged conversations at two decades distance and reporting them in direct speech. Even if much of it is nonsense, it all makes for a great read.

Gods Davis hit an all-time high – or low, depending on how you look at it. Most of the more notorious stories of Zep's debauchery began here, and if band members can pick holes in the accuracy of some of the more salacious detail, nobody has denied the broad thrust, if you will forgive the phrase.

STAIRWAY TO HEAVEN
RICHARD COLE (1992)
Having spilled all his best stories to Stephen Davis in *Hammer of the Gods*, Richard Cole came back seven years later with a semi-ghostwritten account of much the same material under his own name. Nobody knows where the bodies are buried better than Cole and he tells his tale with relish. How much

IN THE HOUSES OF THE HOLY: LED ZEPPELIN AND THE POWER OF ROCK MUSIC
SUSAN FAST (2001)
Not a biography but a musicological dissertation in deconstructing rock 'n' roll riffs. Fast isn't interested in how many groupies Led Zeppelin laid; she's far keener in telling us how many diminished sevenths they laid down. At times the acuteness of her analysis disappears in impenetrable jargon ("Just under the surface of the melodic and rhythmic squareness is a harmonic and formal openness and irregularity that is

highly significant in terms of the semiotics of the piece."). Fortunately it's not all as dense as that, and although her approach is rigorously academic, many of her insights

LED ZEPPELIN

11

on subjects such as the creation of myth and the use of ritual in rock music and the band's appropriation of Eastern music and the blues are informative and rewarding.

WHEN THE LEVEE BREAKS: THE MAKING OF *LED ZEPPELIN IV*
ANDY FYFE (2003)

As the joint third biggest-selling album of all time in the USA it's unsurprising that authors have tended to concentrate on Led Zeppelin's fourth album. Former *NME* writer Andy Fyfe's book is a workmanlike affair that not only tells the story of the fourth album, but offers plenty of before and after context. There's a tendency to unsupportable over-wrought phrases ("with its fourth album Led Zeppelin helped to give rock music immortality") and you have to wonder about the judgement of a writer who reckons "the most obvious parallel acts to Led Zeppelin were Black Sabbath and Deep Purple", which is akin to comparing a *premier cru* from Bordeaux with a cheap merlot from Bulgaria. Even more bizarre is his claim that in the 1980s

Kiss "advanced heavy rock nearly as much as Led Zeppelin had before them". Such *faux pas* aside, however, the book marshals

the obvious sources well and presents them attractively.

LED ZEPPELIN: THE CONCERT FILE
DAVE LEWIS AND SIMON PALLETT (2005)

The estimable Dave Lewis strikes again with a splendid gig-by-gig account with set lists where available. Yet it's far more than just the concert file suggested in the title: in chronicling their tour and stage performances, Lewis in many ways gives a more comprehensive picture of the band and their development than an analysis of the snapshots that their 10 albums could do. He also takes the story on into 2005 with details

of the solo appearances of all three surviving members. Invaluable.

LED ZEPPELIN: DAZED AND CONFUSED: THE STORIES BEHIND EVERY SONG
CHRIS WELCH (2005)

Part of a successful series that now covers most of rock's major figures, when it came to turning the spotlight on the songs on Zeppelin's 10 albums, there was no better choice than Welch. Writing for *Melody Maker* in the late 1960s, he championed the knowledge gives this book a distinct advantage over many of its competitors. He tells the story of the band's 12-year existence in highly readable style, but the best aspect of this rather good coffee-table volume is his detailed analysis of the band's music. The approach is musically literate without becoming academic and fussy: the bridge section after the first two verses of 'Stairway to Heaven', he tells us, is made up of "luminescent A minor sevenths in banks of 12-string guitars and organ pedal tones". It's just enough information without becoming laboured. Sometimes his conclusions are surprising and perhaps far-fetched, such as his comparison between Plant's wail at the start of 'Immigrant Song' and 'Bali Hai' from the musical *South Pacific*. Yet whether he's right or wrong, such observations are never less than fascinating and his readiness to offer firm opinions that sometimes swim against the tide rather than simply repeat received Zep wisdom is refreshing.

band from the outset when Zeppelin were being derided or just plain ignored by the rest of the British music press. Welch reviewed most of the albums at the time of their release, and bringing to bear all of his long personal history with the band, his analysis is revealing and his judgement sound, although the format of the series of which the book is part has its limitations.

LED ZEPPELIN: THE STORY OF A BAND AND THEIR MUSIC 1968–1980

KEITH SHADWICK (2005)
Shadwick is a musician himself and writes widely about jazz and classical music as well as rock and his breadth of musical

IF WE ALL CALL THE TUNE: THE STORY OF *LED ZEPPELIN IV*, THE GREATEST HARD ROCK ALBUM OF ALL TIME

BARNEY HOSKYNS (2006)

LED ZEPPELIN

11

You can argue with the second half of this book's title (the album was surely so much *more* than that), but not with the quality of Hoskyns' lucid writing or the thoroughness of his research. Like Andy Fyfe's book on the same subject, Hoskyns does far more than tell the story of one album, setting it in the wider context of Zeppelin's career. All the key quotes are assembled and the facts are marshalled superbly, supported by the writer's own astute assessments. If you only want one of the two books about *Led Zeppelin IV* reviewed here, Hoskyns wins over Fyfe by some distance.

THE ORIGIN OF THE SPECIES: LED ZEPPELIN: HOW WHY AND WHERE IT ALL BEGAN

ALAN CLAYSON (2006)

The prolific Clayson recounts the pre-1968 tale of the four musicians who would become Led Zeppelin with great gusto, combining a prose style full of verve with an encyclopaedic knowledge of 1960s British pop, a subject on which he could probably win a round of *Mastermind*. Not only do we learn about the formative events and influences that made the band, Clayson gives us a terrific insight into the era and

how British pop music moved from Cliff Richard to Led Zeppelin in the space of one tumultuous decade. His style is a sheer joy, too: where else can you read a discussion of the influence of Bert Weedon on British rock guitar that quotes Baudelaire?

PETER GRANT: THE MAN WHO LED ZEPPELIN

CHRIS WELCH (2006)

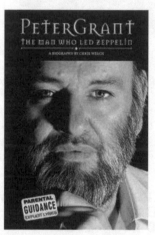

The back story of Peter Grant is a fascinating sub-text to the Zeppelin narrative, and as ever Welch tells it with great professionalism. There are plenty of stories about the band, of course. But the book offers far more than simply the same old Zep tales refracted through the experiences of their manager, with lots of little-known background to topics that tend to merit just a paragraph in the standard band biographies, such as the suspended prison sentence, Grant's retirement from the music industry and his heroin addiction. An insider who knew him well, Welch paints a compelling picture of an extraordinarily complex man, although by the end the enigma in many ways remains intact.

11

JOHN BONHAM: THE POWERHOUSE BEHIND LED ZEPPELIN
MICK BONHAM (2006)

'By the man who knew him best – his brother' is the boast of this soft-hearted portrait. That means there isn't much about 'the beast', the wild man whose behaviour on tour with Led Zeppelin grew increasingly out of control and frequently crossed the line from the merely loutish to the unacceptably abusive. Instead, his brother concentrates on a man who away from the band was by all accounts warm and generous, and there are plenty of appealing anecdotes from his childhood, told not only with obvious affection but with considerable wit and humour as well.

WHEN GIANTS WALKED THE EARTH
MICK WALL (2008)

If you can get beyond Wall's annoying conceit of writing long italicised passages in the second-person, as if he is in inside the head of band members and relaying their interior monologues, there is much to commend this heavyweight tome that runs to more than 500 pages. Wall chronicles all

of the wanton sex and drug consumption with steely attention to detail, but without the salaciousness of Cole or Davis. He's less comprehensive on the rock'n'roll, apparently having concluded that he's a biographer rather than a musicologist, but his account of how the band wrote and recorded the early albums on the run is a tour de force, and his examination of how Peter Grant's business practices transformed the template of rock management is instructive. He also makes a more serious effort to understand and explain Page's occult beliefs than perhaps any other biographer.

TRAMPLED UNDER FOOT: THE POWER AND EXCESS OF LED ZEPPELIN
BARNEY HOSKYNS (2012)

One of rock music's most skilled and painstaking biographers, Hoskyns interviewed 128 people including band members, intimates and close observers for his forensic and exhaustive but highly readable history. His appreciation of the power of the music is insightful and thought-provoking ("encoded within their metal blitzkrieg lies a deep funk that gives even James Brown a run for his money") but he doesn't skimp on the more unedifying elements of the back story, either.

11

It is evident that Hoskyns regards Plant as the hero of the story, a kind of white knight to Page's dark lord, but at the same time he's astute enough to acknowledge that such stereotypes are over-simplistic, making a cool-headed and rational effort to transcend "the hoary metaphors of light and dark, good and evil" that continue to surround the band.

FROM A WHISPER TO A SCREAM: THE COMPLETE GUIDE TO THE MUSIC OF LED ZEPPELIN
DAVE LEWIS (2012)
Editor of the Zeppelin fanzine *Tight But Loose*, Lewis has authored several books on the band, starting with 1991's *Led Zeppelin: A*

Celebration. This volume distils much of the material from earlier works into an attractive, one-stop compendium, with his album-by-album, song-by-song analysis combining intelligence and enthusiasm. And if his judgements are sometimes coloured by his role as the band's self-proclaimed ultimate fan, when so much of what is written about Led Zeppelin is cheap sensationalism, his assiduous, constructive and dedicated chronicling commands nothing but respect.

GET THE LED OUT: HOW LED ZEPPELIN BECAME THE BIGGEST BAND IN THE WORLD
DENNY SOMACH AND CAROL MILLER (2012)

Lavishly illustrated, this book begins with a useful day-by-day timeline and ends with a full discography. However, the meat comes mostly in the middle section, which is based on interviews with band members, hangers-on and various rock celebrities. If you want to know what the likes of Alice Cooper and members of Yes and Aerosmith think of Led Zeppelin, it's all here. The approach is workmanlike, sometimes mundane, and the blurb's claim that it is "the ultimate book for the ultimate fan of the ultimate band" is risible. But the coffee-table presentation is attractive and it's an accessible, undemanding place for the more casual fan to start.

LIGHT AND SHADE: CONVERSATIONS WITH JIMMY PAGE
BRAD TOLINSKI (2012)

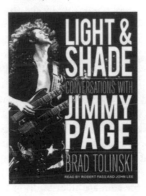

Tolinski has allegedly interviewed Page more than any other journalist in the world and in doing so has developed a relationship of considerable trust, as reflected in the 50-plus hours of conversation that were the raw material for this book. Stitched together, however, the interviews don't quite create the personalised "oral autobiography" for which one might have hoped, not least because they were conducted over a period of several years and for different purposes. Aspects of Page's off-stage persona inevitably creep in but, as befits his day job as editor-in-chief of *Guitar World* magazine, Tolinski's primary interest is in the music. It's no surprise that Page comes across as far more articulate and gracious when talking about guitar effects and recording techniques than when he's being asked about drugs and groupies, and he's pleasingly generous in his praise of other musicians.

ROBERT PLANT: A LIFE: THE BIOGRAPHY
PAUL REES (2013)

11

The first full-length 'solo' biography of Plant is a well organised, non-sensationalist account that reinforces the image of a fundamentally decent human being who went feral for a few years in his youth while basking in the adulation of being "the golden god of cock rock". Rees, a former editor of *Q* and *Kerrang!* magazines, has met and interviewed Plant several times over the years – and like almost all of those who have had the pleasure, he has clearly fallen under the spell of Plant's considerable charm and bonhomie. The singer's appealing mix of self-confidence and self-deprecation, his love-hate relationship with his own past, and his refusal to be defined by a phase of his life that ended when he was 32 years old are astutely conveyed as the book refreshingly grants equal attention to the well-known stories of 1970s excess and Plant's post-Zep achievements.

11 ZEPP ON SCREEN

THE SONG REMAINS THE SAME (1976)

Pretentious self-indulgence or one of the best concert films of the 1970s? Led Zeppelin fans still argue over the matter but it really requires a blinkered loyalty above and beyond the call of duty to find anything worthwhile to say about *The Song Remains The Same*. The initial idea to film Led Zeppelin in full tilt over three nights at Madison Square Garden in New York in July 1973 was a sound one, although insufficient planning went into the logistics and as a result, some of the on-stage scenes later had to be recreated at Shepperton studios. The band were exhausted at the end of a long and gruelling tour and by Jimmy Page's own admission, they did not play anything like their best. In particular, Plant's voice was in poor shape. But they were still good enough: they were Led Zeppelin, the greatest rock'n'roll band in the world, after all. But unfortunately, rather than a straight in-concert film, rock star narcissism then took over with the decision to add fantasy sequences, an idea based on the improbable role model of the T Rex film, *Born To Boogie*.

Each member was allowed to 'script' their own segment. Bonham had the good sense to be filmed more-or-less as he was - a down-to-earth working-class lad who is seen driving his Harley Davidson motor bike , drag racing at Santa Pod and beaming contentedly with his family and on his farm. The rest frankly made utter fools of themselves. John Paul Jones's scene involved him dressing as a masked highwaymen in a pantomine Phantom of the Opera costume. Plant indulged his Knights of the Roundtable fantasies as he stormed a castle single-handedly to rescue a witless damsel is distress and Page went in for some very un-magical wizardry and sorcery, rooted in his Aleister Crowley obsession. The scenes are lent even more of a silent moves/Keystone cops comicality by the absence of dialogue as the band woodenly act out these lame vignettes to music from the Madison Square Garden performances, Even manager Peter Grant insisted on getting in on the act, and the film's opening sequence portrays him and tour manager Richard Cole dressed as 1920s gangsters.

Flawed doesn't even begin to describe it. The non-musical sequences were slated by critics at the time and historical perspective has done nothing to redeem them. The best parts of the film are all at Madison Square Garden, but even the on-stage performances are marred by being mixed with some uncomfortable looking re-shoots from Shepperton. Best forgotten.

LED ZEPPELIN THE DVD (2003)

After the disappointments of *The Song Remains The Same*, a visual record that did justice to the power and the glory that was Led Zeppelin live finally appeared 23 years after the band had split. Over two discs with a total running time of five hours and twenty minutes, the Led Zeppelin DVD showcases the band across a ten year period and its quite fascinating to track their development from the Albert Hall in 1970 to Knebworth in 1979. In between we also get film of Earl's Court 1975, including the acoustic segment of the show, and four tracks from Madison Square Garden in 1973, originally filmed by for *The Song Remains The Same*. Intriguing extras include a New York press conference, Plant being interviewed by Bob Harris on *The Old Grey Whistle Test*, rare early television performances and grainy bootleg footage sent in by fans.

Culled from thousands of yards of previously unseen film and audio tape both sound and vision are excellent due to some painstaking restoration and remastering by Jimmy Page and co-producer Dick Carruthers working hand-in-glove with Jimmy Page. On its release, it broke all sales records for a music DVD – and deservedly so.

CELEBRATION DAY (2012)

Film director Dick Carruthers, who had helped Jimmy Page put together 2003's Led Zeppelin: The DVD was re-employed four years later to film Zeppelin's reunion for the Ahmet Ertegün Tribute Concert on 10 December 2007 at London's O2 Arena. He shot the concert with 16 cameras and the resulting film eventually hit selected cinemas in October 2012, with premieres in Berlin, Los Angeles, New York City, Tokyo and London, where the band attended a screening at the Odeon West End. A month later the film appeared on DVD and Blu-ray, featuring bonus footage from the concert rehearsals at Shepperton Studios.

The film opens with archive newsreel footage of Zeppelin's 5 May 1973 concert at Florida's Tampa Stadium and a TV reporter reeling off the impressive statistics, hailing "the biggest crowd ever assembled for a single performance in one place in the entire history of the world". Cut to the O2 Arena some 34 years later and the stats are even more impressive, with an alleged 20 million applying for tickets, although only 18,000 of them could be accommodated.

The contrast between then and now is dramatic, and not simply because Page, Plant and Jones have aged. That was only to be expected. But unlike, say, the Rolling Stones, we never saw Led Zeppelin grow old on stage. They quit in 1980 when Plant, the group's youngest member, was 32 years old, and so in our mind's eye they are forever freeze-framed in their prime. Despite the historic footage in the opening credits, the film makes little or no attempt to feed the Zeppelin myth or romanticise the past. Intimate rather than epic, the director's ambition is merely to put the viewer on stage with extended close-ups of the band in action and virtually no gimmicks, other than a handful of freeze-frames and a few cut-away audience shots. As Page said in the press conference to announce the film, "the concert was what it was". And that is how Celebration Day presents Led Zeppelin in ripe maturity – not gods descending from Valhalla for one last earthly rampage; just four men of a certain age with a storied history playing some of the greatest rock music ever made. For old times' sake.

LED ZEPPELIN

11

WEBSITES

OFFICIAL LED ZEPPELIN SITE
www.ledzeppelin.com
Good-looking official site, although the news feed is hopeless (just two items added in the course of 2013) and the 'merch' content is a little pushy. But behind the home page exhortations to buy Celebration Day videos and T-shirts lie plenty of good features, including a detailed concert file of every gig Zep ever played and a very active fan forum.

ACHILLES LAST STAND
www.led-zeppelin.org
Independent site launched in 1996. Regular news updates (far better than the official site), discographies, song tablatures and a nice 'this month in Zeppelin history' feature.

TIGHT BUT LOOSE
www.tightbutloose.co.uk
The website of Dave Lewis's Led Zep fanzine of the same name, updated with Zep sightings and citations on an almost daily basis. Obsessive but essential.

LED ZEPPELIN LIVE
www.stryder.de
News and all the usual features, but above all useful for the most comprehensive listing of bootlegs to be found anywhere.

ROBERT PLANT OFFICAL SITE
www.robertplant.com
Like the man himself, Plant's official site prefers to concentrate on the here and now rather than wallow in nostalgia. Photo and video galleries feature recent shows and guest appearances, while an impressive file of press reports dating back to 2008 is kept assiduously up to date.

JIMMY PAGE ONLINE
www.jimmypage.com
You have to register, obtain a password and log in to gain access, but once you have done so, it's a quality site with plenty of exclusives – for example, the site was the only place to purchase the now sold-out Lucifer Rising soundtrack. Other music is also made exclusively available from time to time, such as the mash-up 'Ramblize', which blended Zep's 'Ramble On' with the Notorious B.I.G.'s 'Hypnotize' and streamed on the site in November 2013.

JOHN PAUL JONES
www.johnpauljones.com
A low-key official site with news, bio and videos. At one time the site included a personal blog updated on an irregular basis by JPJ himself, but sadly this appears to have been discontinued.

11

LED ZEPPELIN

LED ZEPPELIN

ROCK ATLAS
UK AND IRELAND SECOND EDITION

*800 great music locations and the
fascinating stories behind them*

Rock Atlas is more than just a guide to over 800 music locations. You can visit many of the places or simply enjoy reading this extraordinary fact-packed book's fascinating stories. Some are iconic, others are just plain weird or unusual, such as Bob Dylan turning up unannounced on a public tour of John Lennon's childhood home or the musical park bench commemorating Ian Dury's life that plays recordings of his hits and his appearance on Desert Island Discs.

Providing insights into many performers' lives, Rock Atlas includes artists as diverse as The Beatles, Sex Pistols, Lady Gaga and Lonnie Donegan. Presented in an easy-to-read, region-by-region format, every entry provides detailed instructions on how to find each location together with extensive lists of the pop and rock stars born in each county.

Illustrated with hundreds of rare, unseen and iconic colour and black and white photographs, Rock Atlas is a must for anyone with an emotional tie to contemporary music and the important places associated with it.

On sale now

For information on Red Planet books visit www.redplanetzone.com

Heddon
Street,
London
David
Bowie
poses for
the iconic
Ziggy
Stardust
album
cover

ROCK ATLAS

800 great music locations
and the fascinating stories
behind them

Written and res_____ by David Roberts

PLACES TO VISIT

Album cover
& music
video
locations
**Statues,
graves
memorials &
plaques**
Venues,
festivals and
places that
influenced songs

Hundreds
of new
photos
and facts

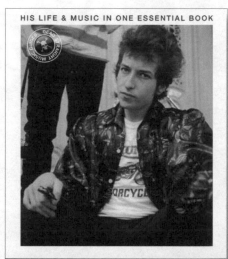